5 July 1948, Amman Valley, South Wales

Born one minute past midnight, hospital midwives told little Nye's mother to "Hold on, Edna!" – aware that if the birth happened before the clock hit the hour mark, she would have to pay one shilling and sixpence at the very least. A lot of money back then.

This is Nye's life story. The first baby delivered by a new National Health Service. It involves the stories of generations of her family who battled to survive before the NHS was there, through to some who dedicated their lives working for the NHS – and, ultimately, those who were saved by it.

It is easy to lose sight of the way our families, just one generation back, lived and died. It is not so long ago that your life literally depended on the weight of coins in your pocket.

This story is a touching human drama, but also a fierce defence of our nation's most important accomplishment – the NHS.

HOLD ON
EDNA!

HOLD ON EDNA!

ANEIRA THOMAS

MIRROR BOOKS

First published by Mirror Books in 2020

Mirror Books is part of Reach plc
10 Lower Thames Street
London EC3R 6EN

www.mirrorbooks.co.uk

ISBN 978-1-913406-31-8

Typeset by Danny Lyle

Printed and bound in Great Britain by
CPI Group (UK) Ltd, Croydon, CR0 4YY

A CIP catalogue record for this book is available from the British Library.

Every effort has been made to fulfil requirements with regard to
reproducing copyright material. The author and publisher will be
glad to rectify any omissions at the earliest opportunity.

1 3 5 7 9 10 8 6 4 2

Cover credits: mirrorpix

Dedicated to the memory of my mother and father,
Edna May and Willie Rees.
I feel they are still walking beside me...
See you on the Sunnyside.

*"Do not allow to slip away from you freedoms the people
who came before you won with such hard knocks"*
D. H. Lawrence

CONTENTS

FOREWORD

Healthcare based on need, rather than ability to pay.

This simple idea has been copied around the world since Britain's historic introduction of the NHS on 5 July 1948.

In the seven decades since its foundation, life for the average citizen has been transformed beyond recognition.

Before, life was precarious for all but a wealthy few. The true potential of the many, blighted by treatable illness and injury, often went unfulfilled.

After that day we could suddenly expect to live to a grand old age. Childbirth and work accidents stopped routinely claiming lives in every community.

Aneira 'Nye' Thomas was the first person born in to this brave new world and the story of her family is the story of our most treasured institution.

These heartbreaking and touching tales from the mining communities of South Wales are the story of how our society changed to one no longer gripped by fear of death and disability.

Nye puts it best when she says of universal healthcare: "We see it as a basic human right, but it wasn't always.

HOLD ON EDNA!

"If the stories of my ancestors show me anything it is this; human survival and a decent quality of life came at a premium."

Martin Bagot
Health Editor, *Daily Mirror*

PROLOGUE

Timing makes all the difference. Between contractions there is panting, breaths coming quick and fast. There is such a thing as too much pushing, between the pains propelling her forward. This baby is Edna's seventh. She lies on the bed in Amman Valley Hospital, exhausted. Funny how the mind forgets the pain after each birth, after the child lies safely in her arms. There is no way she could have done it again, after the first, if she remembered the agony of it all.

It is 1948. The war feels like a more distant memory day by day, and the country is starting to climb back onto its feet. Food is becoming more readily available after years of scrimping. Here, in south Wales, some men have returned; others will never come home.

Edna could be at home, right now. She could have called for a midwife, or "handywoman", as they were known then. But the house is small and full of children. It seems safer here, in the bustle of the local hospital. Women rush around, carrying towels, hot water, jars of pale white cream, trays of long metal instruments. Their hair is neatly pinned back, their uniforms starched and pristine. She feels a mess beside them, trying to steady her breathing, sweat running down her temples and into her ears. They've seen it a thousand times before, she tells herself. Nothing will surprise or disgust them. Just keep going.

Another contraction, now. It's a big one and it pulls a moan, deep and loud, from her chest. She didn't know she was capable of making such noises. Its intensity frightens her. A nurse, standing by her side, takes her hand. Behind her head there is a clock, large and perfectly circular. It's soothing, somehow. The time is ten minutes to midnight.

It's been a warm summer, so far. June seeped into July with no sign of rain. The fields that spread around Edna's home, a smallholding she and her husband struggle to maintain, are parched and turning brown. She wishes it were cooler, September perhaps or February even. Pregnancy during the summer can be a wretched thing, but it's not as though she had much choice.

When she was 14, desperately unhappy and homesick, Edna worked for a brief period for a family in Cardiff. Miss Millie and Master Jack were sweet children, as sweet as her own. But the man of the house, their father, was a different story. She doesn't want to think about it now. But there she is, a tiny dark-haired girl once again, boiling a pan of water in the scullery. She's determined, watching it boil. When it's ready she steels herself and grasps the handle, noticing the bubbles rising to the surface of the water. She pours it down her leg in one swift movement, before she can change her mind. The pain is blinding, mind-numbing in its force. Hours later, when they find her, she's scooped up and returned home to her mother, and she never sees Miss Millie, Master Jack... or their father again. She escaped, but at what cost? And why, at seven minutes to midnight, is she remembering this now?

Nurse Richards has stayed with Edna through the hours that have passed since she was admitted. There is a doctor, too, watching the clock. Edna knows why he is watching it, but the seconds seem to be ticking by so slowly. For a moment she allows her muscles to relax: they've been tensing under the strain of anticipation, waiting for the next wave of pain. Her brow is slick with sweat and Nurse Richards dabs at it with a damp cloth. Down the corridor, Edna can hear the shouts of another woman. "She's got a while to go, though," says Nurse Richards, nodding her head back towards the sound. "Won't be a few hours yet." She pauses, looks up at the clock again. "It's her first," she explains simply.

The pain is building again now – a knot growing in size deep in her belly. Everything feels like it's being pulled in, preparing, getting ready. It's like the split seconds before a wave breaks the shore. Her face contorts as it hits her, and she is shouting now. She just wants it to stop.

Nurse Richards stands at the foot of the bed, gripping one of Edna's feet, watching and nodding. She spots a head, and calls the doctor. The time is three minutes to midnight.

"Edna," says the doctor, coming to stand beside the bed. "You need to wait. It's not long now. Don't push. Just hold on, Edna."

She recalls, dimly, why they want her to wait. Just hold on, she thinks to herself. Three minutes. Soon, it will be 5 July. She furrows her brow, concentrating on the long arm of the clock above their heads. Three minutes. 180 seconds. It's a drop in the ocean compared to all the minutes that she's lived through, but it's the longest wait of her life. When the clock strikes twelve, everything will be different. She doesn't know it yet, but her baby will be born into a new world. I hope it's worth this pain, she thinks, and all the pain that's come before it. It has to be.

* * *

Edna, my mother, is the last in a long line of women for whom childbirth could mean disaster. As I prepare to make my entrance into the world, she hears the calls of the nurse and doctor, and remembers why she has been asked to wait. There is nothing so tortuous as resisting this urge to push: it's taking every fibre of her concentration, and she can't hold out much longer. What if her delay causes harm to the baby?

Decades later, when the time comes to deliver my own children, I am filled with awe at her tenacity, her refusal to give in. It takes an awful lot to refuse such an instinctive feeling, to resist the urge to perform something so natural, so necessary in that white-hot moment. Midwives working in our busiest London hospitals today tell me that even after incredibly high levels of sedation, the body knows what to do. Twilight births, where vast injections of morphine and scopolamine were administered, were thought to relieve not only the pain of childbirth, but also any psychological trauma associated with it. The baby would be delivered via forceps: in 1960 Queen Elizabeth gave birth to her third child, Prince Andrew, in this manner, but the practice had been largely abandoned by the time Prince Edward was born, due to health complications for the babies. Right now, it's like Edna's hand has accidentally brushed an open flame, but she's willed it to stay there, to feel the burn. There's no sedation here.

Outside, the weather is unsettled; it has been for weeks. This makes life so much harder for the growing young family on the smallholding. January was the wettest month since records began, February brought severe chills and flu spread like an unpleasant rumour. It was difficult to stay fit and healthy, to ensure that the young ones were thriving. They were so much more susceptible to everything, it seemed, so vulnerable. In the weeks before my birth, my mother prepared herself and the children for her stay in hospital.

"While I'm away," she'd say to my sisters, "You'll need to help your dad."

"Where are you going?" asked Beryl, nine years old and the most curious. "Are you coming back soon? Who's going to give us our tea?"

* * *

I was the only one of my mother's children to be born in a hospital. By this point she was 39, and the risks were greater. She fretted over the money my birth would cost the family – at least a week's groceries, and they could barely afford to keep everyone fed and clothed as it was. Now there'd be one more mouth to feed, a tiny child needing care and attention, and six more bustling around getting into mischief.

Every morning began in much the same way: my brother, Phil, and Dad carrying huge pails of water from the well to the farmhouse; the younger children sitting perched on the stone steps eating bara – sugary tea dunked with chunks of toast. Cast-iron pots were heaved onto open flames to begin the long process of boiling water. A stack of laundry awaited Edna, standing by the Belfast sink, surveying the scrubbing board, the floors soon to be washed, the daily grind required to make the house run smoothly. And soon she would have to leave it all for the hospital, and return with her hands – quite literally – full. There was always the prospect, pushed away to a dark corner at the back of her mind, that she might not come back at all. Just days earlier, she'd had a very strange experience. She walked into the kitchen and received the shock of her life: "He was *there*," she told my father, pointing at the window. "A man, a stranger, and his face was *covered* in blood." She took this as an omen; my father never found anyone lurking outside, despite a thorough search of the smallholding. No one could explain what it was that she'd seen. Perhaps it was some sort of sign.

* * *

The clock strikes 12 and suddenly everything changes. Now they want her to push; they want her to do it quickly, to respond to that next contraction. It's all happened so fast, from the long wait to here, when action is so suddenly required. "Now, push now, Edna!"

Their cries fill her ears and she does as they ask, giving in at last. There is a sound that surely she cannot be making – a shout that cannot be hers. The baby is crowning. For the past few hours she's heard measurements increase: five centimetres, six, seven, eight, and now 10. She has no idea what it means, but it doesn't seem to matter.

Nurse Richards is standing at the foot of the bed. Then, as now, her job is centred around observation. She intervenes when necessary, easing a tiny shoulder to prevent it jutting against the mother's pelvic bone, or – in extreme cases – using the forceps waiting on the tray table. But she knows that at this stage, it's a battle between the mother and the pain. Once the baby's torso is clear the rest follows more easily in the final push; Nurse Richards eases it out gently as Edna's effort finally pays off.

She feels a sense of great relief, a release, and the room is filled with a harsh cry, deep and loud, coupled with the high-pitched, tinny wailing of a newborn. The screams of the baby are added to the din, but there's no sound more welcome.

At first, Edna cannot comprehend this new noise. She's so tired; the air is thick with the smell of blood and sweat. She looks down and sees the nurse wrapping something in a long white shawl, watches her softly wipe bright redness from a face the size of Edna's palm.

It's me. I'm shouting. Hello, world!

Edna recognises dimly that Nurse Richards is crying. She holds the baby out to its mother, not trying to hide her tears.

"Well, Mrs Rees," she says, "You've done it." She smiles as Edna takes the child and cradles her in the crook of her arm. "A baby girl. Looks lovely. She's a good weight, I reckon."

The doctor is writing on a large pad of paper; he, too, seems overcome with emotion. "Congratulations," he says, noting the time of birth. "One minute past midnight." It's 5 July 1948.

Edna tries to smile but everything hurts, and she's grateful when Nurse Richards takes the baby and tells her to sleep. "We'll look after her, lovie."

* * *

At the end of July, the UK is plunged into the hottest spell ever recorded, with temperatures soaring to 34°. By the end of the month we are in the midst of summer storms, sweltering in the muggy damp heat. My father sets off for his shift down the mines every morning after bringing in the water; my siblings continue to munch buttered toast on the front porch and Edna, for a few months at least, is all mine.

I don't remember the heatwave, of course, but I know the toll it would have taken on the community, our small village not far from the Black Mountains. The pits were ghastly at the best of times – there was no "perfect season" to be going so deep underground, but hot summers were definitely the worst it could get.

If my father had been injured, just a year before my birth, we'd have starved. And if one of my siblings had fallen seriously, critically ill, they mostly likely would have succumbed to their sickness. Edna has lived with this knowledge all her life: hearing the stories of limbs withering away, cancers left untreated, hacking coughs slowly turning into something more sinister until, one day, they'd stop and there'd be silence. Edna knows the risks just being alive brings with it, every day. She sits by the Belfast sink, feeding me, fanning herself with one hand. She thinks about her mother, dead at 44. About Willie's mother, at 33. About all the generations gone before us, taken too young. On 5 July, all of this was set to change. Two years previously, in May 1946, a bill had been passed through the House of Commons that would change Edna's life, as well as my own. It would transform the fortunes of my children, and indeed those of the whole country, forever.

* * *

"Have you thought of a name yet?" asks the doctor, that day, his pen balanced over the sheaf of papers in his hand. It's a few hours since my birth, and Willie has arrived – my father.

Edna's face has regained some of its colour. "Because if not," says the doctor, "I have an idea."

Edna sits up, listening, eyes scanning for me. I'm there, in a cradle at the far end of the room, sleeping soundly.

"She should be named for the man who made this possible," says the doctor. "After the man who allowed her to be born here, for free. After Nye Bevan. Call her Aneira."

Edna thinks for a moment, the word filtering through the air. It has a lovely lilt to it – strong and playful all at once. She starts to nod, smiling. "My National Health Service baby," she says. "Yes. Aneira."

PART ONE

THE HODGES FAMILY 1835-1909

ONE
LITTLE TORY

WELLS UNION WORKHOUSE, SOMERSET, 1835

"What on earth are you doing here, child?"

Her voice cut through the air like a whip; Tory turned around just as quickly, dropping the vase she was holding. It shattered into tiny pieces on the ground, a mess of snapped porcelain and water, a smattering of half-dead daisies. Mrs Lowe was a fearsome woman, and anyone who angered her did so at their own risk. Tory quaked before her flashing eyes.

"Please, Mrs Lowe, I was taking these flowers to the san," she whispered, her eyes on the ground.

"You know you're not allowed in there, Tory." Mrs Lowe's voice was quiet and bitter. She was the sort of person who let out her resentment in dribs and drabs, great heaving sighs and sudden, unexpected outbursts, often when you least expected them.

"I'm sorry," said Tory. "I wasn't going to go inside, just leave them outside the door—"

Mrs Lowe glared at her. "And what if it were to swing open, Tory? What if somebody, one of the nurses, was coming out as you stood there?"

Mrs Lowe didn't have time for this. The warden had drunk two pints of brandy since 11am. She would be running the show today, and she was feeling a little groggy herself. She really ought to stop accepting Jacobson's moonshine, but it made for such a dreamless sleep…

Tory continued to look at the ground. She didn't like to think about the san, except to leave her flowers. She wished she could draw something to go with them, write a little note like she'd seen some of the other inmates do, but try as she might nobody had yet agreed to teach her. Plus, there were no colours here, no soft pencils to fill a sheet of paper with – she'd seen some once, in the stationer's window, and had dreamt of them solidly for a week. Blues, greens, reds and purples – all the colours of the rainbow, sharpened to points in deep brown boxes. She couldn't imagine owning something so decadent, something that didn't serve any practical purpose whatsoever.

"Tory?"

She started to attention, looking up into Mrs Lowe's face for the first time. She was still glowering down, waiting for an answer.

"I asked you what would have happened if you'd been outside when a nurse left, and the door swung open?"

"I don't know, Mrs Lowe." Tory had no idea, but she could guess it wasn't going to be good.

"The nurses try their best to contain illnesses inside the san," said the older woman. She leant down and stared into Tory's eyes. "They do what they can, but it's almost impossible

4

to keep everything in there. Things spread… Boils, pustules, coughs and sneezes." Mrs Lowe seemed to be relishing this slightly. "Things you can't see but which creep out and get you. It's not pretty in the san, my girl." She paused. "You don't want to get sick, too, do you Tory?"

"No, Mrs Lowe," whispered Tory.

Mrs Lowe straightened up, adjusting the blue, cross-shaped badge on her lapel. "Exactly. Now fetch the pan and a brush and clean this mess up at once. I want to see this floor spotless, or there'll be trouble."

Tory dashed off to the basements, where stacks of buckets, thick wooden brushes and broken-handled brooms jostled for space in the gloom.

At just nine years old, Tory is one of the older children living at the workhouse. She's been here ever since she could remember. Her father died just days after she was born. She, her mother and her sisters, having no money of their own and needing a place to live, came here in 1827. She is slight, dark-haired, pale. She looks a little healthier than some of the others, but the bar isn't high: everyone here looks as though life has somehow got the better of them. Everyone looks ill. Wherever she looks there is difficulty of some kind or another: a limping leg, missing teeth, slurred speech, hunched backs, arms inexpertly amputated at the elbow and sewed up again. It is gruesome, but perhaps it's made her tough. She's no stranger to these things.

The infirmary is a different story. At night, the sounds of screams fill the air. The hacking coughs and sneezes she hears from her own ward are nothing compared to the shouts of pain that issue from the workhouse hospital, where the invalids are kept, locked away. Tory cannot imagine anything worse than spending a night in there, listening to it all so closely, watching the horror unfold. Whenever she thinks of her sister, she imagines herself right beside her, and blocks all else from her mind. The flowers, picked quietly that morning on the way back from the milk collection, were wilted by the time she'd placed them inside the chipped vase found in the basement. You could find most things down there, if you looked hard enough.

The same is true of Tory's life. It is difficult to track people who didn't matter in the early 1800s. Few records were kept. It was on a trip to Glastonbury with Maris, my sister, that we first became aware of Tory. It seemed incredible to us once we started digging. But she was there, fretting about the smashed china and the wrath of Mrs Lowe, wondering what a pustule was and how on earth to escape, how best to help her family. Almost 100 before I was born, here she is – my great-great-grandmother, Tory Churchouse.

Her own mother, Ann, had been born into poverty in the late 1700s. Two years prior to Tory's birth, the Churchouses had welcomed Toriano, a bright-eyed little girl with a mischievous smile. But shortly after her first birthday, Toriano had suffered some sort of fit – nobody knew the cause – and passed away in her father's arms. Soon after, they welcomed another child: Tory Ann, the stand-in, the replica of her sister. And by the time Tory was born, her own father John was dying – he was a farmer based in Godney, Somerset.

The will he produced still exists; it was written just before Tory's birth. For a man who didn't have much, he made sure to itemise the little he had. The will runs to six feet of parchment – the scroll unrolls as long as a coffin.

"I, being sound of mind, but sick of body, bequeath the sum of one hundred pounds to my lawful wife Ann Churchouse and my unborn child, with condition that she will not marry another. This was the last Will and Testament of John Churchouse, 28 years old. Witnessed, Signed, Sealed and Delivered."

Under the Poor Law, the Wells Union was set up to provide relief – both to the destitute and, by proxy, to taxpayers. Parishes were split into unions, and each was required to build and maintain a workhouse. Prior to 1834, relief for poor families came mostly from wealthy patrons' charitable donations and local levies. Not long before Tory's birth the new system was rolled out across the country, and welfare could now be sought solely through the workhouses. If a breadwinner could no longer afford to feed his family, his wife and children would accompany him into the place.

The workhouse was every young mother's only option if they were widowed and any income slowly trickled away. These were places full of farm labourers unable to make ends meet, butchers, servants, glovers, washerwomen and seamstresses. John hadn't left Ann with a great deal of options by decreeing she couldn't remarry. "Jealous old lech," Tory had overheard her saying to Martha, one of the other women in her dormitory. "He'd rather I was in here than settling again with someone else. I've half a mind to take a lover, just to imagine the look on his face." She'd stared out into the yard, where the men were working, and grimaced. "Slim pickings, Martha, though, isn't it…"

Anna Maria, Tory's middle sister, had spent three days in bed the previous year with an unexplained sickness. They were convinced she would not recover, but their prayers were answered and she rallied. But now Susanna, Tory's darling eldest sister, was unwell. She was 22, more like a second mother than a sibling.

Tory herself had hardly ever fallen ill – something of a miracle. Infant mortality was high, and it seemed unbelievable that the children she played with, outside in the walled-in quadrangle, had survived at all. Childhood diseases struck hard and often: from whooping cough to pneumonia, measles, diphtheria, scarlet fever, narcotism and intestinal worms. Tapeworms were particularly dangerous, and could take between 8-10% of an already malnourished child's food intake. It wasn't until later that worm cakes, usually made of chocolate and containing a worm-killing vermifuge, were brought onto the market.

Among her friends Tory counted: Thomas and Eliza, the twins whose father was blind and couldn't find paid work; Henry and Martha, who were orphans; Bill, Susan and Arthur, whose mothers all lived at the workhouse too, and their fathers were dead – just like Tory's. Susan's father had died just two weeks before, but nobody had told her yet, and she was constantly chastised for lingering in the damp hallways, hoping to catch a glimpse of him through the dirty windows into the yard.

Thomas was Tory's favourite: a rising star in the world of petty theft, he could filch anything he put his mind to, helped along the way by a cherubic face and a mess of untidy blonde curls. "Butter wouldn't melt, eh Thomas?" Mrs Lowe would growl, searching under his mattress for the missing items – always to no avail. Only Tory knew where he kept his spoils – last summer they'd discovered a nook in the hollow of an ancient tree, an old oak with branches reaching up to the sky.

"Perfect," Thomas had whispered, and taken a wooden spinning top from his pocket. "The toy shop will never miss it," he'd said conspiratorially. "It's tiny. And it's not fair that everybody else should have something to play with, and we go without." Tory took the wooden top tentatively, holding it between thumb and forefinger. "Here," said Thomas, taking it back. "You've got to balance it on something flat, and then—"

He placed it on top of a pile of bricks stacked under the tree. They were old and broken, useless now. With one sharp flick of his wrist he sent the little top spinning across the surface, its colours blurring into one constant stream of oranges and whites. Tory gazed at it in fascination.

"If you want to look at it, I'll hide it in the hollow here, but make sure no one's looking," he said, watching her. "It's our secret. I won't even tell Eliza." His twin was shy and timid-looking, intimidated by the noise and bustle of the workhouse and forever being scolded for her clumsiness. She would never dare go poking into Thomas' things, but he was nonetheless wary of sharing. Perhaps he sensed, even then, that it was better not to get too close. By the time winter came that year and snow blanketed the ground in thick heaps, Eliza was in the san with what the nurses, grimly expectant, confirmed as tuberculosis. She died just before Christmas.

Days began and ended just the same here. At six o'clock the ward sister would arrive, ringing her bell and chivvying the girls awake. She was not an unkind woman, but five years at the workhouse had made her brusque, easily stressed. She had seen many children come and go, and resisted becoming too close to any of them, just like Thomas. That was the only way to survive: nothing could be taken for granted, especially not health. The children would scramble from their beds – thin, straw-filled sacks lain on hard wooden pallets – and pull on grey smocks or trousers that itched and were often several sizes too big. They queued in silence before the ward sister, pulling faces at one another, hopping on the spot to stay warm, shoving and whispering across the lines.

Outside, in the yard, the day's work had begun long ago for the older inmates: the men marching down from the east wing and the women from the west.

"Beth, is that you?" a man called out, catching sight of an older woman; she was having some trouble on the steps.

The woman called Beth spotted the man and cackled bitterly. "Ah, and didn't I know we'd both end up in here, Mr Jenkins."

She turned to the woman beside her and winked theatrically. "I used to know him, in our younger days on the Lawsons' farm. *Know* him, if you get my meaning."

They could hear the sounds of horse's hooves – deliveries coming and going, the arrival of post from outside, sacks of grain being deposited at the wrought-iron gates. Heavy thumps told them the stone-breakers were warming up: this was one of the most arduous tasks, only given to able-bodied men – or able-bodied enough. The hammers alone weighed half as much as Tory, and she marvelled as they'd swing them over their heads, relying on the momentum to scatter large pieces of rock into smaller and smaller pieces. Once there were enough, each around an inch and a half wide, the pieces would be shipped off around the country to rebuild England's roads. The scrape and turn of the corn-grinder could also be heard, millstones pushed along by four or more men in an endless circle until enough corn had been collected for the day.

Much of the daily labour carried out at Wells maintained the workhouse itself – growing vegetables, chopping wood, making repairs, tending to the boilers, carrying out odd-jobs. The rest, such as oakum-picking, when strands of hemp rope were separated and sold on to shipbuilders to line wooden vessels, was intended to create trading links between the outside world and the inmates, to earn some much-needed money.

The women's work may have been indoors, but it was no less easy. They must battle the additional stigma of having somehow fallen from grace: often their husbands had died or left, they were servants who couldn't find work or unmarried mothers. From scrubbers to sewers, knitters and nursery workers, there was no shortage of domestic roles. There were four kitchens, all the same size and a dull uniform grey, and all infested with rats. The children saw their mothers and fathers rarely: some had even been sent to different workhouses, but if they happened to live in the same building it was only ever minutes-long "interviews" that were permitted.

Every so often someone's mother would tell their children of encounters with rats the size of dogs scurrying beneath the copper pans, stealing scraps of bread. Most recently a fox had broken in somehow, causing mayhem as it panicked in the enclosed space, snarling at anyone who tried to come near. Steam billowed in great clouds from simmering pans full of broth. In the laundry rooms down the corridor it was even denser: bubbling cauldrons of sweat-soaked rags swirling inside shadowy depths. It was the children's mothers' dream to work in the kitchens – anything but the laundry, where barely a day passed without an accident. Clothes caught easily on open flames, hands became blistered and raw from constant scrubbing, and skin became sallow and dry from the moisture hanging in the air like smog.

For my great-great grandmother, Tory, days begin in the hall: a high-ceilinged, draughty room with hard tables and long thick benches. The children pad inside, barefoot as they always are, and shuffle along the rows. The older ones, the ones who will soon move up to the adults' jobs, hasten along the benches, depositing bread and butter onto chipped plates. The children are meant to wait until grace has been said, but some of them sneak a mouthful or two while the ward sister isn't looking. Breakfast is always the same. Lunch – then called dinner – is usually "hasty pudding" or frumenty: grains stirred into milk or water. Supper is identical to breakfast, with the occasional addition of a little soup.

They eat quickly: there is work to be done. They finish and bring their crockery to the metal container at the front of the hall. No one ever leaves anything, and if they did, their friends would eat it. The plates are licked clean; not a crumb ever remains.

The children are then ushered into their classrooms: girls under seven go one way, boys another. They have been learning basic arithmetic, practising their alphabets on slates and in copybooks. Some can even read passages from the Bible aloud. The girls learn needlework and household chores, too, and the boys help out with the gardening. They traipse to chapel each morning, a small building, barely noticeable, connected to the master's quarters at the back of the workhouse complex.

There is time set aside for playing, but not enough. It's a long day and Tory usually falls into bed – the bed she shares with three other girls in this grim, cold room – exhausted. One of them is potty trained: she reminds herself to be grateful for small mercies. The fires are extinguished at half-past eight, and silence descends. It's broken only by the occasional shouts, sometimes muffled, from the infirmary. When this happens, she scrunches her eyes up as tightly as she can and prays for Susanna. Perhaps, tomorrow, she will be allowed to see her. Perhaps tomorrow she will be cured of whatever is making her so sick.

* * *

I shudder to think of the worry that must have plagued her. So young and yet so worldly. There was no system in place to help, no social care, no support to assist the workers into paying jobs once they left – that came after, with the provision of teaching for skilled employment, like tailoring or shoemaking. For now, they were stuck. And for those born into the workhouses the stigma was great: it was only later that the location of a child's birth was changed, made up or otherwise altered on their birth certificate, to reduce the inevitable judgment they might otherwise receive.

It was meant to be hard, meant to be horrible in the workhouses. Nobody went voluntarily. They had appalling reputations and earned them justly. It was presumed that such a grim existence would galvanise them into changing their ways, and provide an incentive for poor people to work harder, for fear of suffering the same fate. Wells Union was tiny compared to other workhouses in larger towns and cities, and there were only ever around 150 inmates, though the space was built for double that number. Small mercies: perhaps Tory experienced less of the overcrowding, the terrible throng of too many bodies all locked up together, than some of her contemporaries in London.

She had heard dreadful things about what happened to those who stepped out of line. The punishments for rule-breaking were severe. Adults were frequently denied food for common misdemeanours, or confined in a room on their own for hours at a time. The "Pauper Offence" book, from nearby Beaminster Union Workhouse in Dorset, describes some of the privations endured by inmates: James Park, who attempted to escape on 4 September 1843, was whipped, while Isaac Hallett was sent to prison for two months after breaking a window in 1844. In 1863, Elizabeth Soaper was committed for 14 days' hard labour after a series of infractions including "making use of bad language in bedroom," "trying to incite other inmates into insubordination," and "refusing to work." I feel for Liz, she sounds like a hoot.

It paid to be a child, in some ways: young George Mintern, who got into a classroom fight one day in the summer of 1842, was simply denied cheese for a week. Others weren't so lucky. Years later, child inmates reported acts of horrific cruelty, from whipping with stinging nettles to being hung from the ceiling in cloth sacks.

Just four years before my great-great-grandmother was born, a young boy of 11 would start working at a blacking warehouse near Charing Cross, London, pasting labels onto tins of shoe polish. On weekends he went to visit his father, who'd recently been sent to Marshalsea debtors' prison in Southwark, along with the boy's mother and younger siblings. When that boy was grown he would immortalise the experience in a series of fictionalised instalments, a story published week by week between 1837 and 1839. Everybody was talking about the horrors of the workhouse after reading the adventures of the orphaned boy who was the hero of this young writer's book. That writer, of course, was Charles Dickens.

By the 1840s, years after Tory left Wells Union, the British press were gripped by the scandal of Andover workhouse, where inmates had been reportedly gnawing on scraps of putrid flesh from the bones they ground for fertiliser. It emerged that the master of the workhouse had been reducing ration sizes, channelling the savings into his own pocket, that he was often too drunk to stand, and that he'd been sexually abusing some of the female inmates.

Just two years later, Huddersfield's Union workhouse revealed similarly bleak stories when an enquiry into its conditions was published. Children often slept 10 to a bed; inmates received a quarter of an oatcake and three gills of soup for dinner, and there was such a shortage in clothing available that many people were left half-naked, even in winter.

It was the medical report, though, that left the public reeling and increased a much-needed discourse about the country's treatment of its poorest citizens: typhus raged through the population, and patients in a state of highly contagious fever were often lumped into the same bed – a meagre bag of straw and shavings full of lice – covered in their own excrement. Often, it was found, one patient would die but be left in the same bed as another, sometimes for hours or even days at a time.

In 1866, the chilly room that the girls slept in at Wells was converted – there'd been a huge outbreak of cholera, and the space was needed for a makeshift sanatorium. Finally nurses were instructed on how to treat infectious patients, and prevented from helping one before moving on to another without taking certain steps first. The idea of separating infectious or otherwise ill inmates into separate buildings entirely was born – a revolutionary concept which improved survival rates and reduced the risk of passing on disease. She was lucky, in some ways, my great-great-grandmother. Time was on her side.

This, then, was how Tory grew up, over 100 years before Edna brought me into the world. It seems incredible that she did in fact leave the workhouse, that despite the enormous toll placed on her and the likelihood of contracting a deadly sickness, she made it out alive. And she was right to be afraid of the infirmary. Once you went in, it was almost certain you'd never come out again.

TWO
THE HORSE DEALER

WELLS UNION WORKHOUSE, 1835 AND 1845

Three months have passed. Tory has not seen her sister in almost 13 weeks, though she knows she is lying just beyond the swinging doors, the ones she mustn't go near. She is too scared of Mrs Lowe to attempt any more deliveries of picked flowers, and not confident enough in her writing to slip a note underneath the door.

"Besides," she tells Thomas, as they whisper in the yard, "the infirmary's huge. There's no chance the matron would see it there on the dusty floor. She would never know who it was for."

She pines away in secret, hoping each day that she will spot Susanna, back at work through the laundry doors, or mopping the cracked tiles of the corridors. Her mother has always tried to make the best of things. Even when they first arrived, cold and shivering as the rain lashed the broken windows, even then she had tried to laugh, tickling Tory when the master wasn't looking. "It'll be fun, won't it, duck?" she said, her voice unnaturally high-pitched. "Loads of children for you to play with, and you'll learn your ABCs." She said this significantly, as she signed her name with a cross on the documents the master had placed before her. Ann was trying her best to smile, to keep up the pretence that everything would turn out just fine, but no one was convinced.

When Mrs Lowe approaches Tory one Thursday morning, her heart races. It's springtime, and soon the inmates will be rising an hour earlier each day; the sound of the men's calls filters in through the open window and a horse whinnies, though it's hard to tell whether it's within the gates or outside them. Tory hopes outside. Mrs Lowe's face gives nothing away – it's always set in such a grim line. She imagines that perhaps she has done something wrong, and will be denied her supper. She racks her brains to think what it could be. Has Mrs Lowe discovered the secret oak in the grounds, the one where she and Thomas hide their trinkets? Could it possibly be worse than that?

"Tory," says Mrs Lowe, placing a hand on her shoulder. The other girls look up, quizzically, before a flash of the older woman's eyes tells them to get a move on or there'll be trouble. Unusually, Mrs Lowe is lowering herself onto one of the thin dormitory beds. As she sits down Tory hears her knees crack. "I must tell you something, child. And you must be brave."

Tory had known, deep down, that it could only be a matter of time. She knew her sister would not return to her, but hearing it out loud, so cold and confirmed and clinical, feels like being doused in a bucket of freezing water. She lets out a howl and sinks to the ground.

I feel I'm watching her, kneeling there on the dirty floor, as she cries at the injustice of it all. Tory has no idea what the infirmary is like. She has no notion that her sister's illness – a bacterial infection caused by a burn she sustained in the laundry – could have been treated, were she anywhere else but here.

As it is, all Tory has ever known is illness spelling almost certain death, and yet hearing it out loud on this crisp morning feels unbelievable. Her world has changed. She cannot believe that everyone else is simply going about their daily business. She does not, for now, think of herself: she does not consider what might become of her, here in the workhouse, with nobody to help her and her mother, nobody to look out for them. She feels more alone than she has ever felt before, or ever will again.

When inmates died, their bodies were often sent to anatomists' tables. Workhouses received money for corpses delivered for medical research, and even children as young as Tory would have known this. "The killing of the poor," she has overheard older men and women say, "to cure the diseases of the rich." For many inmates, the wait was not long: they were barely alive when they entered the workhouse.

To make matters worse, local criminals had been known to rob the graves of recently deceased inmates – there was money to be gained in doing so. So not only is my great-great-grandmother contending with the loss of her sibling, she is also faced with the fear that her body will be snatched, desecrated, that someone else will line their pockets as a result of her death.

Mrs Lowe makes no move to comfort Tory, but neither does she scold her, for once. She feels guilt, still, for the length of time it took her to confess to Susan that her father had died. She has resolved to be better to the children, to be honest with them, but honesty seems to bring nothing but sorrow. She cannot think of anything to say to the crying girl, so they sit there, Tory on the floor and Mrs Lowe perched on the bed, for a quarter of an hour. Far off in the distance, a bell starts to ring. So conditioned is Tory to the sound that she leaps to attention, standing straight and looking around her wildly. When she realises what this means – that her morning lesson is about to begin, and that she must leave the dormitory – she seems to crumple slightly again. "Here," says Mrs Lowe, and hands the child a hunk of bread and piece of cheese from the lining of her apron. The cheese is sweltering though it is not warm outside, and the bread is hard as the stones chopped by men in the yard. "Hurry along now," she says, and Tory, straightening her back and wiping her eyes on the scratchy grey fabric of her smock, nods and leaves.

* * *

Walking north-east along the Glastonbury Road, it only takes around 20 minutes to reach the centre of Wells. The long, leafy road is flat and surrounded by fields; to the left the Keward Brook makes its way downstream to the River Sheppey. In many ways it should be an idyll, but Tory hates the weekly walk into town with the other girls, hates the stares of the townsfolk. These can be separated into two categories: pity or contempt, and there's not much in between.

Some people keep their heads down when the crocodile of boys and girls pass them, taking care to avoid touching them even with the hem of a cloak. To everyone else, the workhouse inmates are best kept in the workhouse – they serve as reminders of the constant what-if hanging over all but the very richest. The children are grubby and sickly, too, and nobody wants to imagine the sorts of lives they lead, back along the road behind the high walls of Wells Union.

"Well now, if it isn't the paupers come for their scraps!" shouts a boy in a straw boater, one morning. Susanna has been dead for six months now, and Tory has barely seen her mother and Anna Maria since. There's nobody to look out for her, nobody to tell about her day, what's happened and who she met. There's also nobody to tut at her, no wise older sibling or parent to scold her. She imagines punching the boy square in the mouth, reflects on how satisfying that would be. He's chubby, rosy-cheeked and dressed in a ludicrous outfit of puffed-up green velvet, giving him an unfortunate toad-like look. He has a small dog on a red leather leash; boy and dog have paused in the middle of the square facing the cathedral. His eyes have narrowed and the dog is panting; it looks as though they're both smirking.

"Come along," says Mrs Lowe, walking briskly past him. She's in a tetchy, volatile mood today, fractious since breakfast, when the workhouse warden pinched her cheek and called her "pet".

The boy reaches down to the ground and picks up a rock, more like a pebble, it's so small, throws and catches it once to himself, then lobs it at the passing inmates. It catches Susan on the ear; she immediately begins to cry.

"I say!" shouts Mrs Lowe. The children gather around their friend, some shake their fists at the boy, some swear, and Mrs Lowe leaves them to shoo him away. "I cannot credit it," they hear her saying, fury in her voice. "And a magistrate's son, at that!" The boy slopes off, chuckling darkly. He knows Mrs Lowe cannot do any more – his father will take his side, and he's much more powerful than a bunch of orphaned kids with broken shoes.

Tory wishes they didn't have to come into town, and not just because of the people and their stares. Everywhere she looks she spots things that make her heart ache. In the window of the bakery, shining brown buns sit studded with currants, fat layers of pearly icing support sticky-looking cherries, round as marbles. Across the square a lady emerges from a carriage: her dress is so long that her footman lifts the bottom to prevent it dragging on the floor. It's a pale pink and puffs out around her hips, pinching in at her waist. It looks like it weighs nothing at all, the seamless unwrinkled silk. The lady has thick, neat hair piled into two arches at the side of her head, and her cheeks bear the faintest trace of rouge.

She walks with her head held high, into a shop that sells books. It's the bookshop Tory cannot stand to walk past. Nobody else seems bothered, but the dark and dusty entrance has always fascinated her. If she lingers slightly as they walk along, she can see the long shelves, the heavy spines and the tottering piles around the floor. Sometimes the shop has donated books to the workhouse: old or tatty ones, ones that nobody else wants. Tory remembers one story of a pirate setting sail on the seven seas, a Jolly Roger flapping in the breeze, and the sharks he spotted lurking beneath the waves. The drawings were rough and sketch-like but they helped her to imagine what was happening, as her fingers slowly traced the words on the page. She longs to go inside and browse, but there's no way the man behind the old wooden counter would allow her so much as over the threshold. You can't go into places like that in the workhouse uniform. Everyone thinks they are diseased, and most suspect they are thieves. Well, Thomas sort of is, thinks Tory, but she's still too cross about what the boy did to Susan to smile to herself.

It seems impossible to Tory that a building as grand as Wells Cathedral could exist at all. The children gawk up at it, crossing the flagstones of the square and filing under the arches that surround it. It's like something from a fairy tale, a castle, but not as austere, its spires and turrets reaching upwards and its many narrow windows glinting in the sun. It dwarfs the shops and cottages scattered beneath it, almost like it's protecting them, sheltering them from some unknown storm.

Once or twice, they have walked beside it as the bells ring out on the hour or for daily matins. The deep, booming gongs are soothing in their rhythm and terrifyingly loud, so different to the tinny ringing of the workhouse bell, calling them to work or dinner! The children have been inside the cathedral just once, on a long-planned visit led by the Archbishop. He guided them round the pews and up to the altar, showed them the sacrament and blessed them as they stood in twos before him. Tory noticed that nobody else came into the cathedral while they were there. Perhaps the bishop had closed the doors for a time; perhaps the townsfolk had simply seen the snaking line of grey-clad figures and decided to stay away.

* * *

I like to think that if we'd met, Tory and I would have got along well. She sounds intelligent, plucky, determined. She took everything life threw at her and realised, from a young age, that there was no use complaining about things that couldn't be changed. And she would have every reason to at least attempt some perspective: she was healthy, wasn't she? She was able to work: she had survived.

Across the water, in Ireland, increasingly troubling reports told of a terrible blight creeping through the fields, poisoning the crops so heavily relied upon for food and trade. Tory may have heard about the queues at soup kitchens, the long treks along beaches looking for snails or seaweed to eat, the people unable to pay their rent and being cast from their houses, about the thousands dead each week, starved to skeletons. She may have heard, as the women prepared food in the kitchens, that their Queen has donated £5 to the relief effort, and on the same day bequeathed the same amount to Battersea Dogs Home, in south London.

10 years have passed since Susanna's death, and now eight since Anna Maria's. Experiencing the death of both her sisters has hardened Tory. Anna's stint in the san was shorter than Susanna's – something for which Tory is grateful. She felt more able to deal with this second bout of grief, just as she'd found a sort of peace following the first, but her heart has become stony. Something has calcified in her, and it's only since meeting Huw that things have started to change. I can picture her now: a grinning, shy 19-year-old, standing by the gates to Wells Union Workhouse. She has a small bag with her – more like a sack cloth. It contains every one of her possessions and weighs less than a bag of sugar. Somehow, the day has finally arrived. She's leaving at last.

For the past five years, Tory has worked on the cleaning roster. She can't imagine how many times she has dusted the same mantlepieces in the master's quarters, how often she has scrubbed at the same patch of hard stone, how much water she's collected and refilled and boiled. The master is often asleep in the chair behind his desk as she does this, his mouth hanging open. But soon Huw will be here and she can go. She fidgets with her hair as she waits: he's coming to fetch her at 11 o'clock, and it's not quite quarter to. It's a bitterly cold day and the thin shirt she's wearing – the one she's worn most days for the best part of two years – is doing nothing to keep the chills at bay. But it doesn't matter anymore. Things are going to be different.

I think about Tory a lot – what she must have endured, how she must have suffered, and the endless hours of thankless work she toiled away at during her early years. She had a roof over her head, which was something, but nothing to look forward to – no prospects worth carrying on for. And yet she persisted. She kept her head down and got on with it. For that and so much else I admire her, and part of me wonders if knowing about her youth helped me during my own struggles. Remembering what she went through helps to remind me that I can keep going, even when there doesn't seem to be any light. On a very deep level I feel connected to her, this woman I never had the chance to meet.

But I'm getting ahead of myself: we haven't got to me just yet.

Tory met Huw in Wells, at the city summer fair. The inmates were manning the stalls – some selling toffee apples, others bright dresses and shawls they'd sewn in the colourless walls of the workhouse.

The townsfolk greeted each other but treated the inmates with their usual contempt. It wasn't until late in the day when Tory, fanning herself with one of the rough woollen hats for sale at her stall, spotted a young man walking towards her. He was quite short, about her height, with a wide smile and dimpled cheeks. He wore heavy black boots, carried a round-brimmed hat in his hand, and his shirt was greasy and torn slightly over one shoulder. She wondered if he was a blacksmith and, if so, what he could want with one of the flimsy, shapeless hats sitting on her wooden table. He ambled along, one hand in his pocket, until he stood in front of her, still grinning.

"These are pretty things," he said, lifting one of the hats. It was the first time anyone had spoken to her all day, except Susan, who was serving too-pale lemonade in the stall beside Tory's. "Did you make them yourself?" said the man, still examining the hat in his hand. "Very nicely stitched."

Tory nods, but has no idea what to say to this. It was so patently untrue – the hats were sad-looking and unflattering – that she felt flustered, unsure what he wanted. Was he mocking her? "It's a fine day for it," she said, in the end, her cheeks scarlet.

He looked her full in the face, then, his broad smile like a lighthouse beam that's spotted a ship.

"It really is," he murmured.

* * *

Huw Hodges was 25, a horse dealer from Somerset. He was a catch, kind and compassionate. His family had never had much, but they'd never been so poor that they'd needed to enter the workhouse system. He had watched the men and women on their walks, the children in their snaking lines, from the paddock where he reared and trained his herd, and had always felt a pang of pity for their shuffling feet, their downcast eyes. He hadn't planned to attend the summer fair that day, but when his brother offered to exercise the horses he thought he'd take the opportunity for a wander. There was nothing especially interesting for sale, just knick-knacks and bric-a-brac, mostly broken, and he was about to head home when he caught side of Tory.

There was something about the way she carried herself: a certain pride, a refusal to submit to the indignity of this whole make-believe charade, when the haves and have-nots were seen to mingle happily for one day only. She was slender and her hair reached all the way down her back, tied into a long plait. He loved her the moment he laid eyes on her.

* * *

Tory and Huw are due to be married next week. She hums a little to herself as she watches the road, scanning for an approaching cart, the sound of hooves. She glances back at the workhouse, its dark windows hiding everything that happens inside. It feels anticlimactic, somehow, now that it's all agreed and the papers signed. As Huw's wife-to-be, she has no reason to stay here. He'll keep her safe. His job pays enough, more than enough, and they'd be happy together in his little cottage in Godney. She has never been to the village before, but Huw's told her all about it.

At 11 sharp, she hears the sound of a carriage approaching. Huw is driving fast, speeding along the quiet lane. His horses are sleek and glossy, covered in sweat. They are enjoying the run-around, the fast pace of the man urging them on. Huw does everything quickly – he is swift and efficient, but sensible when it matters. In true fashion, it hasn't taken him long to decide that Tory is who he wants beside him, Tory who made him gallop along the country roads at such a clip. He asked her to marry him at the exact spot she now stands, clutching her bag. She said yes before he even finished the question, and now here he is, her future husband.

"Hello, Miss," says Huw, leaping down from the carriage seat and kneeling before her. He kisses her hand, sweeps his dusty coat from his shoulders and places it around Tory's. She feels warmer immediately: a sensation that is, she knows, only partly thanks to the coat.

If the workhouse had been rural, it was nothing compared to these endless stretches of fields, green as far as the eye could see. Godney was heaven, surely, and despite being only three miles from the workhouse, Tory had never seen such uninterrupted, open skies. Low wooden barns and thatched roofs dotted the landscape, cows chewed lazily on thick clumps of grass, and the air was thick with the smell of honeysuckle. It was all so wild and free compared to what she was used to. She turned to Huw and smiled as they bounced along the lane, the horses slowing now as they turned into the paddock in front of the stone cottage. For the next week she would bunk with Huw's sister, who slept in the little attic room upstairs. Once they were married, the couple would move into the small annexe attached to the cottage. It would be Tory's home, now, for the next 24 years.

Meanwhile, in 1850s Vienna, a Hungarian obstetrician called Ignaz Semmelweis was making waves. "Wash your hands," he urged physicians, midwives, doctors and nurses. Semmelweis suggested that many of the sepsis-inducing puerperal or "childbed" fevers associated with childbirth, and the high rates of mortality for these women, were born as a result of cross-contamination. Many of his contemporaries found this advice hard to swallow. As if they, the ones treating their patients in the throes of their illness, were responsible for these all-too-natural – though of course regrettable – deaths! Slowly, this advice would come to be accepted. Slowly, midwives and nurses realised that cutting umbilical cords with a dirty knife, or tending to a patient with a dirty cloth, could have disastrous consequences.

THREE
POPPIES

GODNEY, SOMERSET, 1857 AND 1868

The autumn had been unusually wet, and the endless rounds of laundry for the children – always soaked to the bone when they came in from the paddock – had given Tory a nasty cold. She'd accidentally passed this on to James, who gave it to Robert, who sneezed on Thomas. Now they were all unwell, and Huw was sleeping in the parlour every night, away from the boys and his wife, to avoid getting sick himself. If he couldn't work there would be nothing on the table, and the larders were already running low. Many of the crops had drowned under the constant weight of water throwing itself from the skies. Tory had tried her best to help but it was becoming increasingly difficult.

She sighed as Robert, just two years old and the most sickly of her children, let out a cry up in his bedroom. Years had passed since she and Huw married, since she left Wells Union, but sometimes it felt like moments ago, like she's just stepped out into her new life. She bustled around the kitchen, preparing a cold compress for her son's sweaty brow. The baby kicked as she soaked the old rags kept beneath the sink, and she clutched at her belly, willing it to move again.

Tory had vowed that Robert, their youngest, would be her last child. And yet, try as they might to predict when to avoid sleeping together, it had happened again. She'd almost wept when she missed her period, and did weep during the first tell-tale, awful mornings of sickness. Huw was a perfect mixture of amusement and guilt: "Sorry, darling," he said, when she told him. "We'll make it work, though. We always do."

Tory wasn't so sure. With each pregnancy she felt her body grow weaker, more liable to breaking, like the hard rocks the men had used to hit with their hammers. She had her boys but she'd lost three babies – one very early on, one stillborn, and one, a girl this time, who'd lived for a week. She didn't like to think about this; it was still too raw. She'd longed for a daughter and Mary, born weighing less than the smallest sack of flour currently in the larder, was perfect. Tory remembers her hands curling over Huw's thumb, the miniscule crescents of her fingernails. She'd been hardy, despite coming three weeks early. Mrs Lloyd, who'd helped bring many a Godney baby into the world, had been amazed at the fierceness of her cries, the greedy suckling when Tory had offered her breast for the first time. But then, five days later, a fever. Mrs Lloyd came back.

She was flustered, the midwife, exhausted from a labour down in Wells that had taken much of the previous day and night to complete. She took Mary from Tory and Huw and inspected the baby's throat, eyes and ears. "There's no reason for it, or none that I can see," she said. "Such a high fever… I can't see why, though." She covered the baby in wet muslin, hoping to cool her. She blew softly on her head. Nothing worked and Mary continued to howl and grizzle until the sixth day.

"How're you feeling?" Huw had crept into the bedroom, whispering. It was so quiet, all of a sudden. Tory had tried to sit up but a weight – her own exhaustion – was pulling her back down. "I'm fine," she'd said. "She's sleeping at last." Huw looked down at Mary, curled into Tory's arms. "She's very pale," he said. "Well, Mrs Lloyd's coming back in an hour or so. We can ask her to take a look then. I think she's doing better, though. It's when they cry you've got to worry, Huw." When Mrs Lloyd arrived, she'd taken the sleeping child from Tory's arms. It was Huw who woke Tory some six hours later, standing by the bedside. "I'm sorry," he said quietly. "You'll have to get up, my love. Mrs Lloyd says there's something wrong with the baby." In a flash Tory was out of bed, her eyes searching. They were downstairs, Mary and Mrs Lloyd, sitting in the armchair by the fire. "She's been a real fighter, Tory," said the older woman. "But she can't resist it any more. If she was a little older, had a bit more weight on her, she might be ok. I don't know why, but she's become hot again overnight." She sighed. "It might be best to start saying your goodbyes."

Tory scrunches up her eyes, willing the images away, but they're stubborn.

The baby kicks her again and she hopes this is a sign of strength, a desire to live and to thrive. One of the reasons Tory cannot move on from Mary is the uncertainty. If she could know what it was that festered inside her child, that crept within her blood like poison and took her away from them all, she might then be able to make some peace with it.

But nobody could give her that knowledge: Mrs Lloyd had stayed to administer a sleeping draught to Tory and sat with her awhile. She shook her head sadly and said that it was "just one of those things, Mrs Hodges."

It was just one of those things.

* * *

Seasons change and 10 years pass and Tory's children are almost grown, some of them completely. William, the eldest, turned 21 just last week. Robert, her golden boy – the most sensitive and quiet, born at the start of May, like the best gift of spring – is just 12. He's the fifth son, the thoughtful one, silent where his brothers are loud. My great-grandfather – he's all chestnut curls and blazing green eyes. Huw and Tory's friends in the village say he'll break a few hearts, one day. Little Hugh, the baby who kicked for nine long months, is 10.

Tory has been blessed, she knows, with sons: six of them altogether. The frequency of her pregnancies has slowed down somewhat, and for that she is grateful.

It's a cool April morning but she wakes shivering, surprised by how long and how deeply she slept. Her dreams were tangled and confused: there was Thomas, hiding filched sweets in the old oak, and the little girl, her friend, running from the boy with the rock in the cathedral square. What was her name? Tory's mother was there, too, grinning at her from behind wafts of steam, and Susanna – whose image grows a little dimmer every year. How lucky we are, I often think, to have photographs now, snapshots that help us to remember. How lucky that all it takes is the snap of a camera's button, a quick-fire tap of the smartphone – and those we love are captured forever.

Tory hasn't dreamt of Susanna in some years, so she's surprised, and lies there for a little while, savouring the memories dredged through her sleep. Huw and the boys will be down at the paddock, by now. She really must get up, but the cough seems to be back and as she raises her head she is shaken by the violence of it. She places a hand over her mouth and it comes back streaked with blood. It's the third time this week, though she's sure it's not anything to be alarmed by. Just growing older, the body starting to slow down: she's 42, after all, not the young girl she once was.

There's a lot to do today and not much time, now she's overslept. The carrots and potatoes need tending to, and she'll have to spread fresh fertiliser across the patches. The cows need to be milked, and she may as well make a start on the sheep-shearing, while she's at it. Her mind is full of lists, constant and never-ending, and yet as she swings her legs from her and Huw's bed, she feels faint and everything seems to shimmer. She feels cross at herself. If it isn't pregnancy, she thinks, it's something else. And surely she is past the age at which women conceive: she must be. She pushes the thought away, it doesn't help to dwell and fret. She stands up, shakily, and makes her way outside to the privy, drawing on a thick woollen coat to keep the cold out. It's as she's coming back, watching the grass for thistles and the beetles that seem to love her lawn so much, that she feels the faintness again, the dizziness, and then everything is spinning wildly out of control.

* * *

The boys have had a good day with their father. Dancer, the new foal Huw purchased at last week's fair, was coming along nicely: clipping around the yard with more confidence, tossing her head and flicking her long black tail. She would make a fine horse, Huw had said, chewing on the end of his cigarette, watching her.

Robert has taken Felix out for a run – Felix who is generally bad-tempered, loath to follow instructions, and who loves nothing more than cantering through the fields, leaping over hedges. It was his temperament that prevented his sale, Huw pronounced, and had threatened on many occasions to stud Felix and put him out to pasture. But Robert refused. "He just needs more time," he said, stroking the long matted mane. "He's a good boy really – and he's fast."

When Rob comes back, William, Hugh and James are mucking out and the air is full of the smell of rich, fresh manure. The boys have grown up with the scent and aren't repulsed by it in the slightest. "John," calls Huw, "pack a couple of sacks there for your mother, she said she'd be doing the veg today."

"What a treat Mum's in for," sniggers William, "I bet she'll be thrilled." Nonetheless he helps his brother shovel the dung into burlap sacks. They're heavy but the boys are used to it – they're strong and capable, unafraid of hard work. It's about to stand them in very good stead.

"There's going to be a storm tonight," says Hugh, looking up at the overcast sky. "You can feel it, can't you?" Hugh loves bad weather. He is a child of comfort, their youngest, and enjoys the evenings spent by the fire, when everyone hunkers down and his mother makes potato soup.

As Huw loads the little cart, he thinks of his wife back home. He has been worried about her, this past week. "That cough doesn't sound right." He'd said it countless times, but she'd shrugged him off.

In the first years of their marriage, Tory had talked incessantly of Wells Union. "It's not…" as she would say, with a faraway expression, "that I miss it – more that it's such a part of me, so ingrained, that I can't help but think of it." She knew all its routines, all its habits, what everyone would be doing at any given time of day. It pained Huw to hear such horrors recounted so casually, but he never let on. He listened to her, helped her and comforted her when she became sad, or when she thought of her friends, her mother, her lost sisters.

One thing he'd come to notice about Tory was her refusal to discuss medical matters. "Leave it be, Huw," was her constant refrain. All those times she'd fallen pregnant, miscarried, even when she'd given birth, or when the boys were small and fevers raged across their temples – she'd not wanted to talk about the sickness, whatever it was. She'd never wanted details.

Tory had grown up so deeply in fear of illness that now, as an adult, she pretended it simply didn't exist. This, Huw thought privately to himself, was both a blessing and a curse. He just wished she'd let him bring her to a doctor; it wouldn't cost much. "And if it's something serious?" she'd retorted, finally losing patience with his questioning. "What then? How are we to pay for the treatment?" He didn't have an answer for that.

Before they set off back to Godney that evening, Huw picks a few straggling poppies from the field next door. They're half dead and the seeds are mostly gone, so he knows Mr Clarke won't mind. He hopes Tory likes them.

* * *

"Mother!" Robert's voice is just breaking, and his brothers scoff at him as he heaves a bag onto his shoulder and marches through the cottage's rusty gate. "We're home!"

William and Thomas help Huw to unload the remainder of the supplies picked up on the five-mile ride back to Godney. Huw carefully lifts the poppies from the front seat. He wants to surprise Tory tonight. He's got decent bread, some fresh butter and the special cheese she likes from the Friday markets. He crosses the front lawn, his arms full. It always feels like he's been away from his wife for months on end, come the weekend. He's going to make sure they have a wonderful Sunday. As he reaches the front door he hears a shout, high-pitched and terrified, and registers dimly that it's coming from the garden. Robert. What's happened to him?

William gets there first, and their voices – the voices of his elder sons, deeper, but somehow boyish again now in their fear – are ringing out, bouncing off the stone steps to the kitchen, ricocheting off the back walls of the house. Father, they're yelling, come quick. He does.

When he reaches the steps he drops everything in his arms and rushes forward. Tory is lying just feet away from the privy, splayed on her front, her arms outstretched like she was trying to break her fall. She has her woollen coat on and her night-dress underneath it. With a groan, he realises she must have been here since morning. He turns her over, onto her back, and John starts to howl. Hugh and James have run back into the house. Robert is backing away, his hands over his mouth, while William simply stands there, his hands shaking. Tory's lips are blue, and her face has become hard, the lips drawn back over her teeth and set in a sort of grimace.

When Huw leans down to listen at her nose and mouth, he can find no breath. Her perfect cheeks are ice cold. At the kitchen door, the poppies have already started to turn a mottled, conker brown.

* * *

For minutes, hours, days, months after her death, Huw cannot quite believe what has happened. He knew Tory was stubborn about her health, ignoring the aches and pains that came with each passing year. He knew she was often tired, sometimes irritable. But nothing could have prepared him or his sons for this. It's unthinkable. It has been six months now, and he still cannot shake the images that flutter unbidden into his head.

Tory Churchouse, the girl he saw across the market square all those years ago – gone, for no apparent reason and with no explanation. He pays the attending doctor and the undertakers who come to remove her body from the house they've been so happy in. It's expensive. Death and funerals are so much more costly than he could have imagined. What is he to do, and with six growing sons to feed?

In the evenings, he sits beside the fire, knowing that to place more logs upon the embers is wasteful and unnecessary, but feeling unable to stop himself. He is constantly cold, and it has nothing to do with the winds charging across the flat fields of Godney. He pictures Tory's face, her laughter, her refusal to be cowed, to be intimidated. He thinks of her early life, of her sisters – now long dead – and he wishes things could have been different. She was only 42.

Just three miles from here, the manor house sits like a fortress: its occupants the latest in a long line of aristocratic barons, lords and earls. He has seen the children of the present lord riding in the fields, their faces pale and their hands unblemished from manual labour. They are kind enough, the family, and only very occasionally raise the rent. They're descended from Lord Someone Or Other, a famous navigator and explorer at the court of Elizabeth I. Huw's always thought he sounded less like an aristocrat, more like a common pirate, a plunderer. The manor-house lords and ladies may just as well live on a different planet, in a different universe, to the Hodges. He tortures himself imagining his and Tory's life, had they been stationed at the manor instead. There'd have been servants, people who might have spotted Tory struggling down the stairs that morning, might have heard her rasping breaths from the garden.

In the depths of his despair, he has even considered asking Davey March for help. Davey is the local quack, a man so full of hot air and false promises it's a miracle he's not been carted off to prison. Davey lives outside Godney, alone, and spends his days advising desperate families to drink the urine of a badger, or eat their own toenails, as substitute for any real medicine. Sometimes, though, Davey's been right. Sometimes people have pulled through, unexpectedly.

The word "quack" comes from the Dutch *kwakzalver*: someone who hawks salves or remedies – in the Middle Ages, to quack meant to shout. It wasn't until 1858 that a medical register of qualified physicians was set up to separate the genuine article from the fraudsters. In 17th-century London, the most famous quack was one Lionel Lockyer, whose "miracle pills" purportedly contained *sunbeams*. He began work on a philosopher's stone, and sought out a medical licence, which was granted, but only on condition he worked at least eight miles outside the city.

Huw kicks the coal-scuttle and black, dusty lumps scatter across the stone floor. It isn't fair. The family in the manor have things the Hodges can never dream of. Yes, they get sick – they're human, after all – but the outcome of these sicknesses are often different. They would have, and he knows this as a fact, more time together, he and Tory, if they were able to afford the monthly checks, the health visits, the care available only to those with the deepest of pockets.

That's not the only thing he is worried about. There's Robert. His fifth boy, Tory's favourite. He has seen the glances Rob shoots him when Huw speaks to Rebecca. But why shouldn't he? She's helping him in his hour of need. Rebecca is already quite advanced in years herself. Pretty, still, but in a mature sort of way. She is 48, a local woman from Burtle. She is a widow herself, struggling and poor. She's known the family for years, everyone here does, and she's been attentive since Tory's death, leaving baskets of cabbage and runner beans on the stone porch, visiting to chat with Hugh and bring him toys – little wooden things her own grown sons have hewn from ancient oak trees.

For his part, Robert wishes his father well. He wants him to be happy. Rob never says very much, but he watches. He's an observer, and he can see which way the wind is blowing.

His father needs a mate – that much is clear. He is morose on his own. Their mother was young, too young, and a part of him feels that he cannot expect Huw to remain alone forever. And yet he misses his mother terribly. He lies awake in the night, listening to the sound of his brothers' snoring, wondering what to do.

It is summertime, now, and the fields are green and overcooked. The horses are hot and grumpy: sweat runs in great rivulets down their backs after even the slightest exercise. He doesn't know how much longer he can bear to watch his father sadly mucking out the stables, hunched over and quiet. Mother gave his father life, and now she is gone. But he notices how Huw straightens up slightly when he sees Rebecca walking down the lane. He has witnessed his father's smile, becoming broader again and less full of lines, of care. Perhaps it wouldn't be such a bad thing, after all. He is conflicted, full of painful, difficult feelings, a sense that his loyalties are being torn. Through the years, through the generations, I understand him – I can imagine how he must have wrestled with himself.

Robert knows that Thomas feels differently about Rebecca being around. His brother is headstrong, proud and loud. He sees his father as somewhat pathetic, moping about the cottage and sitting before the fire long into the night. Thomas doesn't like Rebecca, and makes no pretence of doing so. "Why was that woman here again?" he asks Huw, one night, and Huw looks embarrassed, confused and guilty all at once.

"Our mother has been dead not six months," says Thomas, "and already you are considering replacing her."

Huw says nothing to this, simply gets up and leaves the room. It's a warm night and Tom lets the fire burn down, frowning at the final spits and hisses of the dying flames. Robert watches him carefully.

Eventually Tom turns to his brother. "We must leave," he says. His words are hollow, exhausted. "I won't stay and watch our father be lured into a second marriage so soon. We've got to go, Rob. There's no future for us here."

Robert doesn't agree, not really, but Thomas is persuasive and James seems to like the idea, too. Leave Godney, their mother's grave, their father's business? "Well, not all of us," says Thomas. "Will must stay and take care of father and Hugh. He needs a mother, the little one." Robert accepts this fact grudgingly. Hugh is just 10, not old enough to fend for himself in the same way as the others. "This just doesn't feel like home anymore."

"Where will we go?" Robert asks.

He feels dubious but also, and he hates to admit it, excited.

My ancestors are about to embark on a journey that will have huge consequences for us all.

FOUR
ON THE ROAD

GODNEY AND GLAMORGAN, 1868-1887

Sun-kissed and tired, their knapsacks severely depleted after only three days on the road, they are walking. Thomas, James, John and Robert. William, knowing his duty as eldest son, stays behind with Hugh. It has been almost sixth months in the planning, and now they've finally set off.

Their father married Rebecca a fortnight ago at the parish registry. Thomas is furious. He imagines their mother, imagines her reaction to this betrayal. She has barely been laid to rest in the ground but here they all are, acting as though Huw's actions are noble, somehow, or necessary. "I won't stand for it," he fumes. He has envisaged leaving Godney for years, "but I never thought it would happen like this." He'd played the scene out hundreds of times in his head: telling his parents about his plans, their anxiety for him mingled with their pride, all coalescing into a shared look of wary happiness. He could see them, in this dim memory of an event that never actually took place, standing at the cottage gate and waving him off, an intrepid explorer with nothing but the clothes on his back and a loaf of bread to sustain him.

Now, here he is with his kid brothers, the whole lot of them, waving goodbye not to Tory and Huw but to Rebecca and Huw, Rebecca – a woman who sleeps in their father's bed and stands before the sink Tory used to stand at. She is even wearing some of his mother's old clothes. His rational mind knows these things can't be helped, knows that nobody round here has very much money and it's wasteful to throw Tory's possessions away. But still, the sight of her rankles him. It tears at a still-fresh wound, catching it and forcing him to look the other way. To his surprise, being on the road has helped calm his temper. He walks with purpose, deliberately not looking back over his shoulder as the brothers make their way north.

Wales. The destination itself was decided only last month. They sat down together and devised a plan. There were opportunities, over the estuary. More than there are here. They cannot stay and watch their father and Rebecca together, it's too much to bear. Even Robert, the round-eyed watchful boy that he is, feels a sense of betrayal whenever he smiles at Rebecca, whenever she is kind to him. They need to leave.

Huw thought, at first, that they were joking. "Wales?" he said, "you've never been, any of you. You don't know what it's like. You don't know anyone." He paused, looking around at them all, bewildered. He suddenly feels very old, looking at his boys. "What will you do for work?"

"There's pits, da," said Thomas. His jaw was clenched. "New ones opening up all the time. They need men. We'll be better off there than here."

Huw knew his second boy was the instigator of all this, but looking closely at the rest of his sons, he can see that their minds are made up.

"We'll walk. It shan't take long. A few days at most."

But this is where Tom is wrong. It has already become apparent that the journey, some 100 miles, will take them longer. Robert is only 12 and complains of his sore legs, his blistered feet. James, at 17, is somewhat hardier, but he eats everything, and yesterday he and Tom almost came to blows. Huw has given them some money – not much, but enough to get them over the border and into the country. It's all he has, and though it breaks his heart to watch them go, he knows he cannot stop them. He will remain here, at Godney, and Rebecca will become his wife. He needs the companionship. He needs something or someone to help him, to see him through this dark time. When life gives you lemons, make lemonade, I suppose.

* * *

It's Thomas who takes our family to Wales, and I wish I could thank him. It's a daring plan, a far-flung, far-fetched idea, one that might not come off. Huw is right: this band of brothers has nobody to help them once they leave the verdant, luscious fields of their youth and set off. And Robert so young – will they manage? Will they stay together, or branch out?

These thoughts plague them all as they trudge the country lanes. The light grows thinner as they enter the wooded canopy of the Mendip Hills. The path is clear but the trees are thick and heavy with the afternoon's rainfall.

"Three miles more," calls Thomas over his shoulder, "and then we'll stop awhile. There's a brook where we can collect water up ahead."

Robert nods, looking all around him at the forest. At 12 years old, he is nervous – Tory's fifth son, my great-grandfather. The story that began with his mother is continuing, now, and soon the boys will be in another country entirely.

He's never seen anything like this, and wonders if they're safe here, in the thick vegetation of this woodland. He can't believe they've lived so close to this place for so long and never been here. Up ahead, through a cluster of ancient oaks, he spots a strange, hulking series of shadows.

"Tom," he calls, "there's something through the clearing."

Thomas pauses and looks to where his brother is pointing. Up ahead, about 100 metres away, a cluster of rocks has appeared. They're jagged and tall, each seemingly falling over the other, a structure that seems all the more unexpected and random given the dense forest all around them. There's something about the rocks, as they draw nearer, that sends shivers down Robert's spine. As they stop in front of them, they notice a series of openings in the surface: caves. There are many of them, and the brook – flowing gently past them now – winds its way through the collection, sometimes cascading down onto lower streams to form mini waterfalls.

"What are they?" John asks, his voice fearful. "They're awful dark."

Robert and Thomas approach the nearest cave, not responding. It's true, though, what John says. The overhang of each opening is such that no light penetrates beyond a few feet into each cave. Robert crouches down and shuffles forward so he's almost inside, his head brushing the uneven ceiling.

A voice comes from behind them and they whip around, Robert crashing his head against the rock.

"Wookey Hole, lads," says a man standing on the path. He's about Huw's age, must be a farmer – his overalls are dirty and he wears a broad-rimmed hat to keep the sun off his face. It hasn't worked: he has clearly spent many hours in the fields, and his hands look like those of a man twice his age.

"Astonishing sight, aren't they?" He looks to where Robert has risen, shakily, to his feet. The brothers cannot think of anything to say, until Thomas' shock subsides somewhat and he steps forward.

"We weren't expecting them, that's all," he explains. "We were just looking for the brook."

The man chuckles. His teeth are chipped but he has a kind smile, and looks at John, standing closest to him, with fondness.

"Off on an adventure, are we?" he asks.

Thomas nods. "To Wales. We've come from Godney."

"Ah, you'll be the Hodges boys, then." The man nods at them. "I worked with your father for a bit, down at the paddocks. Before your time." He bows his head. "I was sorry to hear about your ma."

Robert is struck by the bizarre situation in which they have found themselves: standing here, before these ancient caves, their mother dead, and a man they've never met or heard of expressing his sympathy. It makes him think the world must be smaller than he thought, and he wonders if he's really ready to leave behind a community where people know, or knew, his father, his mother, their lives before him.

The man nods back toward the path. "I'll walk with you through the hills," he says. "I'm heading east afterwards, but we may as well travel this stretch together."

They fall into step behind him, John secretly relieved that this man will be accompanying them through the dark woods. Tom strides up ahead once more. Robert, John and the farmer walk together in companionable silence. The path thins out and widens again; the sun moves overhead, brightening between noon and tea-time. Occasionally Tom will pause to consult the worn map he carries, and the farmer will chuckle: "We've not gone wrong yet, lad. Straight ahead, north. We're following this till we reach the edge of the hills."

Thomas, offended for some reason, walks off, James struggling to catch up with him.

"You never heard of Wookey?" the man asks Robert, what seems like hours later, and the boy shakes his head.

"Strange place," says the man. "Ancient place. They've been there for thousands of years, them caves. Lots of fossils."

"You've been inside?"

"Oh aye," says the man, smiling at them. "You need to creep in a little, bend down like, but once you're in a little way you can stand up and walk right around."

"Isn't it terribly dark?" asks John, whose round, pale face is gazing up at the farmer. "How did you manage not to get lost?"

"There's maps, and things, if you know where to look," says the man. "The tunnels and caves stretch right back and under the ground. Some parts no one's ever been able to reach. Too much water, like."

He pauses, scratching his chin. Thomas thinks about the damp, close smell of the cave, the splashing he could hear from inside, the way his eyes hadn't yet adjusted to the gloom before they met the man. "And," he says now, twinkling at Robert and John, "There's the Wookey Witch, of course."

"The what?" asks Robert, and the man proceeds to tell them. He recounts the story of the powerful sorceress who lived in the caves, a witch who despised romance and love affairs, and cursed the relationship between a man from Glastonbury and a local woman.

"They went their separate ways, in the end," says the farmer, "and the man was devastated, right cut up. He became a monk, and decided to seek his revenge on the witch. One winter's night, he came to the opening – just where you were crouched down earlier." He nods at Robert. "The monk blessed the streams and pools of the caves, going from chamber to chamber, unafraid of the sorceress or her powers, not knowing where she was or how he would find her. Hours passed, and the night grew cold. A storm picked up outside, he could hear it, even through all that stone. The wind whistled through the caves' many openings, and still he waited, even falling asleep against one of the rock faces until he was awoken by movement. He raised his lantern, but the cave he was in was so deep, so dark, the light only stretched so far.

"The corner was flung into shadow, but he felt a terrible beating in his chest as he stared at it, the blackness invincible. So he stood, clutching his lamp, and moved backwards, towards the pool he'd blessed, and he scooped some of the water up into his hands and threw it, as hard and far as he could, into the corner. Legend says all the village was woken by the witch's terrible scream as, once the water hit her, she turned to stone. And she's still there, unable to move, trapped in the darkest corner of the largest cave."

Robert and John listen to the story with rapt attention. Once again, Robert is struck by the fact that they've been on the road less than two days, and already his mind feels opened, alert, a little afraid. It's a good thing, he decides. He would never have seen these caves, heard this story, however mad it is, if they hadn't left Godney, left Huw. Years later, I will feel a similar mixture of fear and excitement, a sense that my horizon is broadening, that things are being set in motion, and I can either resist it or go along for the ride.

* * *

The trip should last no more than four or five days. They're taking it slowly because they have to: their knapsacks contain clothes, water and meagre amounts of food. I can picture them heaving themselves up the hills surrounding Bristol, descending on the other side and scrambling over precipitous edges. They've never seen anything like it: these views, all this space, from vantage points they'd never imagined. They walk around 10 miles a day, stopping often to rub ointment on James' feet, to redistribute supplies, to stock up, to fight with each other and call Tom a bastard for dragging them out here.

In the evenings they head off the paths into the fields, onto quiet stretches of moor where – in the morning, after a fitful night's sleep brushing off insects and using their bags as makeshift pillows – the remains of a charred fire exists as the sole evidence that they were there. They smell awful and don't look much better.

After nine days on the road, they reach Aust, where they'll cross the old bridge into Chepstow. The estuary ripples below them and the air is fresh. It smells clean. Even Thomas is smiling, properly smiling, as they stand together on the last part of the bridge, the last link between the home they have known and the one they're about to build. Robert thinks of Tory, his poor mother, and hopes she would be proud of them.

They make the first step together, the band of brothers in sync, as they cross over. It's 1876, a new age is dawning, and they've entered Wales.

* * *

The brothers believe themselves ready for any kind of work, and their years of experience with Huw at the paddocks have prepared them well. Besides, they came here on foot, and this helps boost their confidence in these early days. They feel hardened by the journey, more like men than boys. The walk's put hair on their chests.

My great-grandfather finds work as a labourer. He's efficient and quick like his father, and it doesn't take long before he feels this community is his own, that he belongs here. Whenever he sees James and John – on one of their rare holidays from their own work, or out in town running errands – they seem happy, as happy as he feels.

The language is a problem, it's true: virtually everyone speaks Welsh. Thomas discovers this to his detriment at a local tavern one night, when a dispute over an unpaid tab leads the barman to insult him with words Thomas cannot understand. He flips the nearest table, sending coins and drinks flying, and storms out. Tom finds it the hardest to adjust to this new life. He would never admit it but he misses their father, he misses the horses and their old life. As they grow older, Robert tries to help his brother acclimatise, but there's only so much he can do.

11 years pass and seasons spin. Robert has married a local woman from Glamorgan named Jemima Richards. She's witty, sharp and chatty, and does the talking for both of them. Robert adores her. They welcome their daughter Elizabeth in 1878, son Thomas in 1880, Richard in 1885, Matilda in 1887, Amelia in 1889, May in 1891, Alice in 1893 and John in 1895. They were busy, my ancestors.

Robert is reminded, during all of Jemima's pregnancies, of his mother, Tory. The fear of something going wrong at the last moment, the incredulity when it didn't. He cannot believe that his children are healthy, that they continue to thrive, that – thankfully – he has to call the local doctor just twice during the course of their collective childhoods. He writes to his brothers, who have not been so lucky. John's wife died giving birth to their last child, a girl he named after the poor woman, and James' second son lived barely a week before something chilly and dreadful settled on his lungs and carried him off.

Robert returns home in 1892 to visit Godney – upon his father's death – this time taking the train. William has grown older more quickly than the others. He and his wife, Rose, moved to Melksham in Wiltshire not long after Huw's death, where he's since taken up work as a gardener.

Robert moves with Jemima and their children to Ystradvellte, deep in the Brecon Beacons. For a time, he works as a contractor, attending where he's needed and walking the miles of open country to reach the jobs he's been asked to do. But the land is changing, and soon Robert will find new work.

The South Wales Coalfield has been capitalised upon, with all the pride and fanfare expected for this enormous boost to the region's economy.

The mines have opened and local men are arriving in their droves, barely seeing daylight, knowing that each new morning could be their last. It's dangerous work, and Robert knows it. Nothing like the open skies and flat fields of his youth. But he loves Wales, and there's nothing so satisfying as finishing a day's work hewing and coming home to Jemima.

Thomas, his elder brother, finally settles down. He marries Hannah and has two daughters of his own. In his later years he will take a new job as a railway driver. The country, and the UK more generally, is transforming, becoming more accessible by the day. Sometimes Thomas reflects on the journey they took, the Hodges boys, so young and so inexperienced, to reach this great land. It seems so primitive, now, to him: the way they set out on foot, the obstacles they faced and the hardship they endured.

The Industrial Revolution blazes through the countryside, tracks are laid and smiths are working around the clock to construct the type of machinery many still regard as heathen, ungodly. In August 1868, such suspicions are confirmed when a travelling post office and passenger train, travelling from Euston to Holyhead, collides with a 43-wagon goods train outside Abergele in north Wales, spewing 50 wooden barrels of paraffin oil across the tracks and incinerating over 30 passengers and crew. Local men, forming a human chain right down to the sea and passing buckets of water along the line, report that they were unable to identify many of the victims, so badly were their bodies charred.

Thomas doesn't feel particular concern for the risks inherent to this new technology: he knows things are transforming, and that they're changing for the better. He loves the metal clanking of the driver's door as he swings it open, loves the hard wood of the seats he and his colleague perch upon as the trains rumble into life. Great billows of steam flood the platforms as the men direct these enormous tanks up and down the tracks. They learn all about how the coal Robert is soon to help mine powers these engines, how the men in the back rooms shovel and shout at one another in the blazing heat. As the seasons change, Thomas sees more and more of the country unfolding before him like a carpet in a fancy drawing room – towns and cities he has never heard of now become possibilities. He watches the passengers at tiny village stations lugging their trunks and baskets, cases and small children onto the locomotives. For many, these are their first train journeys, and they're excited. It feels good, now, to be able to see the impact of his work.

I think about Thomas, the angry brother, the volatile one, and I am glad to imagine him smiling through the steam, transporting people where they need to go. Maybe, though we'll never know, he took his own children, Annie and Hannah, on outings. Perhaps he took his brother, and Jemima, and all their many children, down south one weekend afternoon. Maybe they went to the Mendip Hills, to Wookey Hole, and he told them the legend of the witch petrified to stone.

FIVE
A NEW LIFE

GLAMORGAN, 1890-1909

We're getting closer now, closer to the woman who'd lie in the village hospital and be told, very kindly but firmly, to hold on. Thomas, my grandfather, Robert's son and Tory's grandson, was born in 1880. He was a kind child and adored by his parents. Robert, so calm and quiet, doted on his offspring: everything he did, he did to improve the family. When Huw had once come to visit, he had been pleasantly surprised at how well Tory's favourite had done, here in this strange new place.

Little Thomas doesn't have much education, but he has enough to get by. Jemima is illiterate, just like Robert: at their wedding, they sign the necessary papers with an X. Still, she spends hours sitting at the table with him, slowly encouraging him as he labours through arithmetic, reading and endless spelling tests. She can see the impact an education has had on him already, and only feels slight pangs of regret that her child is fast surpassing her own level of education. She feels it's important for her children to be prepared: that these skills might somehow help them to get ahead. Her own father ensured she was similarly versed in the basics of addition and subtraction, division and multiplication, and she has to admit that, although she hated the lessons at the time, they've stood her in good stead. She's grateful for his efforts now.

Thomas and Elizabeth, the eldest of the seven kids, are both fast learners. Sometimes, when Robert returns from the pits, tired and occasionally irritable, they laugh about him in Welsh, and he grumbles that it isn't fair when one member of the family is at a disadvantage, unable to defend himself. "If you're going to mock me, Tommy, at least do it in English," he calls good-naturedly.

Glamorgan is a wild place, in the late 19th century – or at least it is for a small boy with a rusty bicycle and an active imagination. Thomas spends hours pedalling through the hills, looping through farmers' fields and skidding off on stray rocks that fly up into the spokes. Sometimes Elizabeth comes with him, riding on the back of the bike or chasing behind with a ball and hoop. Elizabeth is brave and mischievous: she has the glint of her grandmother, the flash of Tory in her eyes. Her brother is the more reserved child, the reflective one. He likes to explore but he's always back on time, always home before Jemima has asked him to be. Elizabeth is a different story: she'd stay out, roaming the countryside, all night if she could. She's a terrible influence on the younger daughters, the band of sisters that is Matilda, Amelia, May and Alice. Mama, they call themselves.

Thomas, or Tommy as he's known, has a good life and he knows it. Some of his friends, the boys who he sees out on the streets or playing in the fields, are less lucky. Nearly all their fathers work in the mines, just like Tommy's does, but sometimes they don't come back. Samuel's father was lost in a slide two years ago, and Dylan's just last week. Each morning the streets follow a familiar pattern, as the first bells ring out from the county hall, summoning the men to work. They leave their front doors in soot-streaked clothes, clutching tin containers of lunch – bread and cheese, flasks of tea they'll drink on the way. Their wives accompany them to the door and there follows – usually – the briefest of exchanges, missed unless you were looking for them, when they glance at each other across the gates. Those quick stares speak volumes: come back, they are saying. Return to us.

Miners were required to pay into early health-welfare schemes that nominally protected them and their immediate families. Paltry sums, a penny a week, that were insufficient to cover some of the worst injuries seen at the mines, and also went into the upkeep of the hospitals. Each pit had its own medical room, and sometimes for smaller problems these were used to good effect – by both miners and local children getting into scrapes. For burns and amputations, there was little that could be done to rehabilitate a worker back into their employment, and many were forced into destitution.

In the collieries themselves, small cuts became infected quickly. Roof falls were common, as were explosions. This was new technology, new machinery, after all; there were few checks and balances, and few were fully trained to use the machines they operated. The noise was enough to render workers hard of hearing at best, and the use of dim oil lamps in the dark created eyesight problems too. Many men were run over by mine cart, kicked by horses. The concept of health and safety was laughable. By 1958, vaccinations for polio and diphtheria were introduced.

Recently the mood has been very tense, here in Glamorgan, ever since the slide that killed Dylan's father. It's normal to Tommy that each of their fathers' days should begin with the possibility of death, that these farewells may be their very last. It's only through stories – through telling it like it was, to younger generations – that perhaps in his later years he might appreciate just how bizarre, how heart-wrenching such an existence seems to anyone who has not experienced it.

A mine is a delicate thing. The drilling, splicing and construction alone can take years. In the early-to-mid 19th century, though, business was booming and the competition was fierce. Along with Wales, Yorkshire and Scotland were expanding their own empires. Iron, steel and coal brought men from across the country to settle in previously quiet towns and villages. The Rhondda Valley area, for example, exploded in size between 1851 and 1911, from fewer than 1,000 people to more than 150,000.

Glamorgan is scattered with them: Cilely and Fernhill and Fochriw – where at the end of a day's work five men were killed ascending the winding rope, which broke – and

Maritime, where bodies were recovered after a rock fall which suffocated them. Meiros, where a gas explosion killed two men and a boy in 1891, Rhondda Merthyr, where again, in 1891, two cages carrying workers collided, throwing two men 170 yards to the bottom of the shafts. William and Thomas, the miners, were just 17 and 18.

Cymmer, the Hodges' local, as it were, has an appalling history. Here, an explosion in the summer of 1856 killed 114 of the 160 men and boys working underground. Tommy has grown up surrounded by these stories, all told by survivors – miners who lived to tell the tale, or their wives and children. It is as though by recounting the horrors that happen down below they can somehow prevent them, or take them back. Tommy wishes he'd never heard of the accidents: it's worse to know what could happen, worse still to hear the details.

Pits were opening, at that time, faster than anyone could anticipate. There was work, but there was also great risk. At Bryndu Colliery, an explosion on the morning of 11 November 1852 occurred when four workers "rashly ventured to their workings in the pit before the fireman had examined there with a Safety Lamp, to ascertain if there was any firedamp accumulated during the night. As soon as the four unfortunate individuals ventured in with their candles, an awful explosion took place which deprived them of life." The men were listed as Thomas Jenkins, 35, David James, 25, Henry Jones, who was 17, and David Edmunds, who was just 12.

When Tommy is grown, he expects he too will work in the mine. It seems fated. The year of his birth saw the opening of Big Pit, in Torfaen, originally an iron mine that provided employment to over a thousand local workers. Disasters struck often – when Tommy is 11, he shudders at the stories that wend their way up from the pits. A little boy his own age is crushed by a roof. The Mines and Collieries Bill, passed in 1842, has attempted to prevent all women and girls, as well as boys under 10, from working in the mines, and in 1860 further regulation increases the boys' age limit to 12. But it's often overlooked – there are only so many inspectors, after all – and Tommy knows he is lucky not to be sent down into the pits before he's ready.

His young imagination runs wild with thoughts of ghouls and spectres lurking beneath the earth. Robert does his best to reassure his son that it's not all bad, that there's a great deal to be grateful for.

"At least," he says, one evening in September 1888, "we're here, and not in London."

Jemima gives a shudder, understanding his meaning at once, but Tommy is nonplussed. "Why? What's wrong with London?" he asks. "Terrible business," says Robert: "Last two months they've had four women murdered. Found them in the streets, they did, just lying there." "But people are killed all the time, in London," says Tommy, "aren't they?" "Aye," says Robert, darkly, "but these ones are different." A warning glance from Jemima and Robert falls silent, becoming suddenly very interested in his shoe-laces. The next day, Tommy and his friends will set off on a mission whose sole purpose is to discover the meaning of Robert's oblique story. Phillip Dyson's mother is all too happy to oblige: as one of the few women able to read and write in the village, she is seen as something of an oracle, and she takes the national newspapers every week. "Ooh, it's horrible," she says, with glee. "Throats slit from ear to ear, faces butchered utterly." She stares round at the wide-eyed boys before her, boys who are both desperate for her to go on and yet cannot bear to hear any more. "One of them," says Mrs Dyson, "was found with her heart ripped clean from her chest. Now, who would do such a thing?"

* * *

At age 21, Tommy finally goes off to work at the mines. His mother begins to cry, which sets Alice and Matilda off, as they wave him goodbye. Even Elizabeth, in her housemaid's uniform, tired and cross, looks less animated than usual as she hugs him. There was no question, really, of Tommy working anywhere else – he can see that now. This country needs coal like it needs water, and there's plenty to be found, once you know where to look for it. His younger brother Richard stares after him, knowing that soon it will be his turn...

My grandfather Tommy is a tall teenager, and it's a job stooping down as he enters the pit for the first time. The opening shaft is just under six feet high, and he curses the gangly body neither his father nor Jemima can account for. It would have stood him in good stead down in Godney, at his Grandfather Huw's paddocks. He is strong and able, and he knows how to work the land. Mining requires a different set of skills, though, a new set that he's not sure he's cut out for.

Cages take the men down: there's nothing to prepare them other than the stories they've heard, the accounts their fathers and grandfathers have described in hushed whispers round the fireside. The light dims as they climb into the cages, packed close as sardines, and the air changes into a wet, damp thing that sticks to the backs of their throats.

Tommy is not an easily frightened young man, but he wishes that his father could be by his side today. He cannot believe that this – the cold wet walls and the clanking of metal as they descend, the feeling of claustrophobia in this tight space – has been Robert's life for so long, and yet he has never complained. It's a lesson to Tommy, who tries to push the stories of horror, entrapment and death from his mind.

"New, are you?" says the man standing beside him. "I'd shake your hand, but, you know," he smiles ruefully, indicating his trapped arms with a nod downwards. The men are so tightly crammed together it feels almost indecent. Someone has clearly taken a little rum that morning, too. The heavy smell of alcohol wafts over from somebody's anxious pores, not an uncommon practice round here, and who – Tommy wonders – can blame them?

"Yes," he says to the man. "First time down today."

"You'll be alright," says his companion, chuckling. "I shook like a leaf at the beginning, but you get used to it. Just mind your head and keep your eyes peeled, and you'll be fine. Try not to breathe too deeply, either."

"Why not?"

Tommy's question is answered for him as they go deeper. It's a thick, cloying stench, one only found deep underground where the earth is packed close and tight.

"The smell of death," someone says helpfully.

"That's no way to speak about Davis' missus," someone else quips back. There's a brief, playful scuffle and the cart holding them all swings and sways.

There is so much that can go wrong in a mine. The cages are rickety and old – one body too many and they'll snap their ropes, sending them crashing to the pit floor. Gas explosions are common – has anybody checked the air today? Even when he emerges, though at this point it feels unlikely he ever will, there are still myriad dangers to contend with –falling piles of coal, carelessly brushed by another worker and sent tumbling, or collapsing roofs, or anxious pit-ponies running wild and trampling everyone in their path. And, even if nothing happens today, or tomorrow, or in a year's time, there are other dangers lurking underneath the bangs and crashes and snapping of ropes. Exposure to coal dust comes with its own risks, and a shortness of breath, a tightening of the chest and difficulty breathing means just one thing to anyone who'd worked in the pits, even if only briefly. Pneumoconiosis was so prevalent among workers that it became known as "coalminer's lung."

* * *

Tommy knows all this, and yet there aren't very many other options available to him. The one thing that keeps him going, as he lifts and carries, blasts and hews, is Esther. She's a local girl, just 19, and they've been married a year. Quiet and gentle, Esther adores Tommy. In the evenings, once he has returned from a day's shift at the mines, she takes his hand and they sit by the fire, murmuring in low voices. The villages may be growing in size but the nights are quiet – days begin early, here, and they don't want to wake their neighbours. It seems unfair that the largest part of their day is spent apart.

"How was today?" Tommy asks her, swigging from a bottle. Esther eyes it suspiciously, but he raises his hands in mock defence. "Ah, love, it's just a snifter. My back's playing up again. I'll never sleep otherwise."

Esther accepts this response silently – what does she know of the mines, after all? Her own father, John, worked at Caedefaid, and she remembers the long evenings he too would spend in silent drinking, trying to block out something he'd witnessed, or done, or heard from a friend. She turns to Tommy, deciding to tell him at last.

"There's a house," she says, "on the terrace at Sunnyside. It's up for rent next month. I saw the notices today in the village."

Tommy gives her a small, surprised smile. "A house, eh? What do we need with a house, there's just the two of us."

"Well," she says, and smiles. "Maybe not for much longer." She pats her belly shyly. Tommy throws the bottle down onto the stone floor, where it clatters and topples. Esther shouts at him but starts to giggle as he flings himself down on the hard arm of her chair, cupping her face in his hands. "Ah, sorry, sorry!" he says, as he realises he might be pressing on the bump, ever so slightly perceptible beneath her dress.

"And you, not even noticing!" she says, laughing, and swipes at him when Tommy says he thought she might have put on a little weight.

"My da will want to know," says Tommy. "I'll tell him tomorrow, we've the morning off."

It is Sunday the next day, and Esther accompanies Tommy to Robert and Jemima's house. Robert is thrilled at the news, congratulating his son and daughter-in-law. But his joy turns to worry as something dawns upon him.

"That space is too small, though," he says, "for the pair of you and a baby. And there'll be more: not just the one."

Tommy nods at him, knowing what he's getting at. Esther, normally so meek and quiet with Tommy's parents, leans across the table then. "There's a place that's just come up," she says. "It's on the main road, before you come to the forked part of Heol Y Glyn." She does not mention that she walked all the way there yesterday morning, once Tommy had left for work, and gazed at the three upstairs windows of the squat little house. It looked cosy, its front door set smartly in the middle, and flooded with light even in the weak afternoon sun. The road is set right down in the centre of the Afan Forest Park, and the Afon Corrwg river babbles contentedly just over the little fence that separates the wild, untamed valley from the row of houses.

"A house?" says Robert, looking just as nonplussed as his son, the night before. "How much do they want for it?"

Esther tells him and she hears, but does not see, Tommy suck in his breath. It's so important to him, she knows, to provide for her – and it'll only become more of a concern, now they're expecting. But the money he takes home, each week from the mine, would only just cover the rent. Robert knows how much his son will be making: he's young and inexperienced, is Tommy, and it won't be enough. He spares his son's having to admit this by closing his eyes for a moment and then saying, in one quick sentence, "I will give you whatever else you need, just take the house. Go and speak to the letting man today. You too, Tommy."

Tommy stares at his father. "Da," he says, "You can't. It's too much."

Robert waves his hand, a "don't start" gesture Tommy remembers from childhood. Robert and Jemima do not have a great deal of money, it's true, but as he watches his son and daughter-in-law, Robert remembers Huw. He thinks of the morning they left Godney, all those years ago, and the small bags of coins he'd handed to the boys, the band of brothers.

It was the only way Robert was able to make a start, a new life for himself once he arrived here in Wales. Perhaps, now, he can repay that debt to his own child.

He knows that Tommy's options are limited. And although Robert has never wavered in his conviction that the move here to Wales was the correct one, he sometimes wonders if he wouldn't have thought again if he knew just how heavily all his children's lives would entwine in the coalmining industry. There is so much danger in their everyday existence, and so much grief just waiting to happen. If the Hodges were still living in Godney, there'd be hardship still, of course there would. But there might not be quite so much fear, each and every morning, of disaster.

He remembers the days spent at the paddocks with Will and Tom, James and John and little Hugh. The sun shone on their backs and their faces were ruddy with heat and dust. Their clothes smelled of hay and manure and grass. Now, as he regards his son, he reflects that such a life is unthinkable for Tommy, that Tommy will spend his own days in a dark, wet cave, away from his own brothers, his wife, and praying that he'll make it out alive. It's not so dissimilar, Robert thinks, from the life his mother would have known at the workhouse. Grey, drab and colourless. Drenched in the fear of illness, of being unable to work, of not returning from an overcrowded sickbed.

"We can manage it," he tells Tommy gruffly, and Jemima – who trusts him – nods at Esther. They can manage it.

"I'll take up more work with Sarah-Jane, at the seamstresses' parlour," says Esther. "In a few months we won't need any extra. That'll be enough, both of us bringing in money. And when the baby's born, I can do repairs from home. It'll just take some time."

Robert nods, and later that day Tommy and Esther approach the lettings outlet in the village square and pay a deposit on 16 Sunnyside Terrace, Cymmer. They'll be moving next month.

* * *

Esther and Tommy build a life together, there at the house on Sunnyside. Theirs was a mining valley and a community, a series of villages clustered together by the common drive for survival. Doors were left unlocked and neighbours chatted, helped one another and took on extra responsibilities if wives were left widowed, or children orphaned. Like Tory, so many years before, Esther had no way of controlling the number of children she had. Education was scant, especially on the subject of sex, and few women had access to support should they feel unable to bear another baby. Tommy and Esther do the best they can with what they have, but it's a hard life.

In 1909, Esther is 27 and Tommy is 29. Their three sons are growing healthily, thank the Lord, and there's always just enough food on the table. Esther worries about the prospect of more mouths to feed: all the local women do. But it's impossible to resist that first flush of knowledge that someone new is on the way – Esther loves children, and babies especially. They make it work. On 10 January, as the cold winds flush their way through the valley, the couple welcome their eldest daughter, and name her after the American music-hall star Edna May Pettie. My mother – whose story would come to have such a dramatic impact on the country, and whose legacy spans generations, right up to the present day – has arrived.

PART TWO

THE REES FAMILY 1898-1908

SIX
THE MIDWIFE

GLAMORGAN, 1898

"I'm getting too old for this," Hannah mutters, as she draws her cloak tighter across her chest. A tiny woman with a loud laugh and a crinkly, older-than-her-years smile, she's an eternal optimist, exactly the sort of woman you'd want to help you in those long hours of the night, as a baby prepares to arrive, as you wait and wait and hope that everything will be fine. Hannah's delivered over 300 of them. As she trudges up the hill she shakes her head and watches the ground carefully. She can't afford to turn her ankle here, on this deserted road, before the sun has even risen.

"Too bloody old," she says again.

Hannah turned 57 last week.

The birth of Edna May will fuse the Hodges and Rees families, who in the year 1900 have never heard of each other, and won't for many years to come. While the Hodges descend from Huw, from Somerset, from Tory's days in the workhouse and hours spent in the pits, the Rees family begins, in my mind, with Hannah. Born in 1843, she married my great-grandfather William in Glamorgan, and went on to have 11 children, the eldest of whom was my grandfather.

The Rees family, therefore, were Welsh natives long before the Hodges. It's through my father's side that we can trace a long history back through the ages: the Reeses were not newcomers. They didn't arrive as a result of the Industrial Revolution and had been here since time began, it seems. This is probably why so many local women trusted Hannah so implicitly when their time came.

On a wet November morning in 1898 we can find her trudging up the side of the valley, a heavy bag in her arms. The mud is slick and coats the bottom of her dress. She pants as she walks – the hill is steep and the bag seems to weigh much more than it should. Hannah's bag has become a sort of sidekick. These days, she's never without it. She's been married to Will for the best part of 30 years, and yet he still appears to be getting used to the sheer volume of requests that come in for Hannah, at all times of the day and night. "Again?" he'll moan, rolling over in bed when he hears the tapping at their bedroom window. "How many bleeding babies does one village need?"

Inside the bag there is cotton – lots of it – some lard, scissors, Brown Windsor soap – a favourite of Queen Victoria, with its distinctive cinnamon smell – a litre-flask of water and some cheap brandy. Spirits and beer keep some of the pain at bay. In the early days she'd bring rolling tobacco, too: it helped to calm the breathing, to encourage deep inhalation.

When the summons came, at 2.30 this morning, Hannah was in a deep sleep. William answered the door, still rubbing sleep from his eyes, and fumbled to light a candle with a taper from the fire. It was Mrs Gold, the mother of Gwen Gold, whom Hannah is trudging up the hill to help. Mrs Gold asked Hannah to see Gwen through her first birth some weeks ago. Gwen's just 16, a thin, pale girl whose belly had caused her housemaid's dress to rip.

"It's only going to get bigger," Hannah told her. "You'll need to find other things to wear."

"Bigger?" said Gwen, her eyes flashing. "It can't get bigger, Mrs Rees. It already feels as though I'm carrying too much. Bigger indeed!" Gwen is like many of the women and girls that Hannah meets during her rounds. She has no idea what is in store, because Mrs Gold refuses to talk to her about it. Mrs Gold is furious enough with Gwen as it is. Nobody discusses such things: they're seen as unbecoming. As a result, Gwen is about as mystified by the whole process of her pregnancy as her as-yet-unborn child.

When Hannah arrives at the tiny cottage, she sees that all the windows are lit. From the yard outside, she can hear shouts and cursing. The voices are a mixture of young and old: Gwen and her mother. Mr Gold has made good time, back to the cottage after rousing Hannah, and it sounds as though a terrible row has developed in the meantime.

Inside, Mr Gold greets Hannah with a tired-looking smile and gestures upstairs helplessly. "They've been like this for days," he says. "I don't even know whose voice is whose any more."

"Get the water boiled, John," says Hannah, and points to the large cast-iron pot sitting by the fire. "We'll need more than you think. Just keep filling that pot up, and bring the warmed pans as soon as they're ready. You can leave them outside the bedroom."

Mr Gold nods, rising immediately to do as he's told. She noticed the flash of relief on his face when she instructed him where to deposit the water. Men, she has come to understand, become rather like little boys again when childbirth enters the conversation, enters the home. Suddenly girls are something to be avoided, all over again.

Hannah can understand this in part. It's a terrible thing to hear if you're not used to it – more terrible and agonising to see. She does not pull any punches when speaking to the pregnant women in the weeks before they are due. There's no use – it must be laid out on the table for them, plain as day.

Hannah doesn't know where this forwardness comes from. Her mother and father never discussed such things with her, and she can remember no specific instance at which she realised that subjects like this do not appal her, as they seem to do everyone else.

She needs to be especially careful with Gwen, because she's young and, from the sounds of it, extremely volatile today. Gwen's one of the many women Hannah helps who either do not know, or will not tell, who the baby's father is.

Hannah knows the options are fairly limited, and she has her suspicions, but now is not the time to voice them. All that matters is getting Gwen through it as smoothly as possible, and ensuring the baby is warm. That's it, she intones to herself as she climbs the stairs. Smooth and warm, smooth and warm, smooth and warm. Gwen's age will likely stand her in good stead, though. It's easier for the younger ones – they tend to recover quicker physically. Too young, though, and the hips aren't wide enough. A child giving birth to a child – Hannah's delivered a few like that.

Inside the bedroom there is a scene of devastation. The sparse furniture has been upended, the sheets torn from the bed. Mrs Gold is standing in the window-frame, shouting at her daughter, who is bent double over the bed, bellowing back equally loudly. This won't do.

"Right," Hannah says clearly, marching into the room. "Mrs Gold, please leave us. I will call you." Mrs Gold splutters once, casts her daughter a filthy look and sweeps from the room.

"Gwen, get into bed. Immediately." Gwen, presumably exhausted from the labour pains she's experiencing as well as the adrenaline of the argument, complies. Immediately. Her small, wide-eyed face is sheened in sweat, and her hair is plastered to her forehead. Hannah moves to the window and shakes her head when she realises it is shut tight. The girl needs fresh air. It's ludicrous how little common sense appears to prevail sometimes.

She moves back toward the girl, who's gripping the top of the wooden bedframe and howling as a contraction takes hold. Hannah places the bag on the bed and takes out a piece of towel, smoothly slipping it under Gwen's buttocks as she raises her back with the pain.

In 1813, a child named John Snow was born in York to a labourer, later turned farmer. He was the first of his parents' nine children, a bright boy with a talent for Maths and a growing sense of unease about the conditions in which he and his family lived. At the age of 14, he received a medical apprenticeship, and was later admitted as a member of the Royal College of Surgeons in 1838. Initially focusing on the cholera outbreaks he'd witnessed as a child growing up, and later on arsenic as a means of preserving corpses, John became increasingly interested in the news brought from America, where ether was being administered to patients as a form of pain relief. Over time, this developed into the possibility of giving chloroform for the same purpose.

There were widespread objections to the practice. For centuries, the idea of attempting to reduce a woman's pain during the act of childbirth was seen as sinful – God decreed that she should suffer the pangs of labour, after all. In addition, it was thought that administering something to take the pain away would reduce the necessary bonding of mother and baby, that it too closely resembled intoxication and that it was, on the whole, better to simply ride it out. In addition, given its novelty, there was much concern about the safety of an anaesthetic such as ether or chloroform — how much was too much? What if a woman in labour was rendered unconscious by the stuff and therefore unable to push, when the moment came?

Such fears were partly put to rest on the birth of Queen Victoria's eighth child, Leopold, in 1853. By this point Snow's reputation had grown exponentially, and it was rumoured that Prince Albert, the Queen's husband, had specifically sought him out for the delivery of the couple's next royal child. Snow obliged, and administered the queen with chloroform during her labour via a paper cone and a handkerchief placed over the nose and mouth, through which the droplets could be inhaled as vapour. He was called in again for the birth of Beatrice, the Queen's ninth child and fifth daughter. Charles Dickens' wife, Kate, was also one of the early adopters.

This development had enormous consequences on the provisions available to expectant mothers, the level of pain they were expected to navigate during childbirth, and the public trust of this new-fangled thing called anaesthetic. The age-old practice of rendering a patient unconscious during an operation or serious illness had competed with alcohol or herbal potions: henbane, cocaine, mandrake, bryony, opium, strychnine, foxglove, mercury and carbolic acid. Many of these caused more problems than they were worth, and even the slightest amount too much or little could produce hideous results. Now, it was realised, these could all be replaced with something altogether less harmful.

Hannah has brought a small amount of chloroform with her today. She doesn't think Gwen will need too much – she's young, and the labour hopefully won't last long. She needs just enough to make her forget the intensity of the pain, but not so much that she's away with the fairies, not so much that she won't be inclined to push when the time comes. Outside the door, she can hear Gwen's father place the first pan of water gently onto the floor before scuttling back downstairs to fill another. He needs to be quick. When the contractions increase it's likely that Gwen will tear, that there'll be blood. One of the merciful things about child-birth, Hannah has come to realise, is the relatively long distance between the woman's line of vision and the site of the action, so to speak. The expectant mother can rarely see the intensity of what is happening to her body, and only very occasionally becomes aware of the sheer amount of blood loss. This, thinks Hannah, is a godsend.

Over on the bed Gwen is growing restless. She glances at Hannah as though only truly noticing her for the first time. "Why is it taking so long?" she growls now, turning her sweating face towards the window. "I felt the waters come hours ago, hours and hours. You said it'd be quick once the waters came."

"It will be," says Hannah, taking the opportunity to feel Gwen's forehead and check her pulse. "It feels longer because of the pain. Try and move with it – try and expect it. Don't resist it."

Gwen's skin is warm but not so hot that Hannah's concerned. She begins to remove the other tools from her bag: the clamp and the forceps, the lard and the razor. She moves to the end of the bed and slowly raises Gwen's smock. Such an action, practised and assured as it is, would ordinarily provoke cries of outrage in the women Hannah tends to, but in these situations there's no time or thought for propriety. Nobody ever objects when they're in labour – Hannah may need to move Gwen later, ask her to squat or to go onto all fours. Anything to help gravity along the way. Gwen barely winces as Hannah slips two fingers inside her and feels for the level of dilation. So far, so good.

She covers Gwen up again and heads to the door, opening it only a crack to check for Mr and Mrs Gold. Despite what is happening in this room, she knows that the couple will remain out of the way until the baby is born – they won't dawdle or wait outside the door, but it's still a good idea to check. She lifts the pail of water outside and returns to Gwen's bedside, lifting the smock again and beginning to shave her. It's done in under a minute, and again Gwen has barely registered her presence: her face is taut with concentration. Hannah washes the blade clean and presses Gwen's shoulder. "Really," she says, "You musn't try and fight it. When they come, the pains, let them. You've got to let your body do the work. It can't if you don't let it."

Gwen gives Hannah a furious look. Hannah understands, but still, Gwen really needs to try. When she can see the contraction coming on – the girl's fingers clench and unclench, and her toes curl inwards – she presses her shoulder again, firmly. "Let it wash over you. Every time it comes on, let it. We're nearly there now."

Gwen's pregnancy hasn't been difficult or unusual, but Hannah knows there are things worse than morning sickness, a sore back and aching limbs. The village hasn't been kind to Gwen Gold since she started to show. It always strikes Hannah as odd, the attitude of these people she has known and lived amongst for so many years. Yes, Gwen is young. Yes, she's unmarried. But these things don't happen on their own. As she has tried to explain to Mrs Gold (as if such an explanation is necessary), it takes two to tango. But the young lad, whoever he is, is long gone.

Hannah cannot count the number of births she's presided over in almost identical circumstances – a young woman left breathless and scared, a secret growing bigger and more unmanageable by the day, and never a thought for the person who played just as large a part as the girl in question. And Gwen is still just a girl, Hannah thinks as she watches her try to ride the contraction. Hannah remembers Gwen as a child, just three or four years ago. She sat between her parents in the second row of Cefneithin parish church, one of the few who really opened their mouths to sing. There's nothing between the kid she was then and the woman she's about to become. Gwen likely had no idea of what could happen when she lay down with the lad, whoever he was. Now things are happening to her that are strange and upsetting and wonderful all at once. It's a hard way to learn a lesson.

"And why shouldn't they have a little fun, after all?" Hannah once asked her neighbour, a dour-looking woman whose nostrils had flared. They were talking about another case of accidental pregnancy. The neighbour seemed to be enjoying the grim pronouncements she made on the offending young woman, and Hannah had had enough. "There's bugger all else to do here. Might as well try and enjoy themselves a bit... I just wish they'd try and make sure it didn't always end like this."

Hannah looks around the room as Gwen's contraction subsides. She notes the peeling wallpaper, the damp stains on the walls. Mrs Gold has done her best with the place, but it's run-down, tired-looking and creaky. The curtains hang half off their poles and it's clear the moths have had a feast on the hems. In the corner, a cracked washbasin is coated with grime, small puddles at its base glisten in the moonlight filtering through the open window. Hannah wonders about bringing a child into this house. The dust and soot and dirt of it all will not help the baby, whoever he or she is.

Hannah doesn't know a great deal about illnesses and how they're contracted, but she knows enough to understand that children born into cleaner houses than this tend to thrive. Just last week, at the Jones', she observed the freshly starched sheets, the linens hanging ready on the line for Mrs Jones' fourth baby. The bedside cabinet had been scrubbed with soapy water, the little tub shone in the candlelight. It was a good baby, that one, heavy and strong. Hannah has hope for it.

It could be different, here at Gwen's house. Mr Gold is a handy sort of man but he's never home. These snatched hours of the night are the only times he'll be here. He wasn't able to get a job at any of the local mines – they'd filled their vacancies so fast – so he's been forced to look further afield, and the walk to his current pit takes a good 45 minutes each way. He's a strong, able man but Hannah knows his knees aren't doing so well. The ground is soft and gives way easily across these fields, and Mr Gold is often navigating them in the dark. He leaves at half past four and returns long after eight o'clock in the evening, just time enough for dinner, a wash and then straight to bed. There's no spare moment to re-align the window-frame, replace the curtains or scour the basin, and they'd never have the money to ask anyone else. Hannah hears Gwen's father depositing more water gently outside. She wonders where Mrs Gold has got to.

"I think it's coming," says Gwen, her eyes suddenly wild. Hannah knows this look all too well: they all get it at a certain stage. It's a mixture of mad relief and terrible fright. Their bodies have gone to another place entirely, a place of speed and urgency and more adrenaline than they've ever felt or will ever feel again.

"Good," says Hannah. "That's good, Gwen. Just keep breathin' for me now."

Gwen does as Hannah asks, looking at her with scared, imploring eyes. "I can't breathe," she says. "It's too hard, I can't."

Hannah sits beside her and places a hand on Gwen's chest. She exerts a little pressure, pressing down and then releasing. "Like this, in time with my hand. In and out now, in and out."

Gwen pulls her legs up to her chest and holds her knees. She sucks in the air greedily, holding it as Hannah presses down, feeling Gwen's ribs through the nightgown. "Keep your legs like that if it's comfortable," says Hannah. "But don't tire yourself. Put them down again if you need to." Gwen lowers one leg, slowly, and then makes to sit up completely, her face creasing once more. This is a bad one, Hannah can tell. Gwen begins to shout now – a long, low wail that fills the room and will travel all the way downstairs to Mr Gold, filling pans of water. She kicks at the bottom of the bed and looks at Hannah with fury in her eyes. "I need to get it out!" she says. "How do I get it out?"

"When you feel that happen again, Gwen, I want you to start pushing – not hard, but slowly and firmly. Can you do that for me?"

Gwen nods and Hannah moves to the bottom of the bed. She can see that Gwen has transitioned – she's fully dilated now, and this will be the phase of pure panic. The pain will be at its worst now, for however long it takes for the baby to make its way out. Hannah gently moves Gwen's legs slightly further apart, and feels her start to bear down. Her legs tense and she arches her back again. "Slowly, slowly," says Hannah. She doesn't want Gwen to tear. She has the fine sewing material needed for stitches, but hopes it won't come to that – she'd need to give her chloroform, and wants to avoid that if possible.

Gwen starts to swear. Hannah has heard all of it and worse many times before. She has developed a habit of cursing along with the women she helps – echoing their words and trying to help them giggle a little in the midst of their frenzies. Laughing produces a natural sort of push, a pressure in the abdomen, and so Hannah reels off the litany of profanities Gwen is now uttering, shouting it as loud, if not louder, than the labouring woman herself.

"Why," screams Gwen again, "is it taking so long? I can't do it anymore, I just can't."

Hannah darts to her bag and returns to Gwen's side with a half-litre of brandy. She uncorks the bottle and holds it beneath her nose for a moment, helping her tip her head back a little. Gwen gulps the liquor thirstily and relaxes almost instantly. She isn't used to anything stronger than beer, and the alcohol does what it's there to do. Suddenly Gwen seems a little braver, a little less frightened. Hannah slips a piece of tough wood between her front teeth and tells her to bite on it. Gwen fixes her gaze determinedly on the ceiling. She pushes. Hannah stands at her feet, shouting words of encouragement. "Just three more now, Gwen. Three more big pushes for me. That's it."

Three more pushes come and go. There is still no baby. Hannah slips a finger inside Gwen and feels. There is a head, but it's still some inches off. "Three more, Gwen," she says, and the head slides a little closer. She begins to coax the shoulder down, ever so gently. Gwen is moaning with the added pressure of Hannah's hand, which she's now pressing hard against the perineum. She does this at every birth she attends, applying pressure to prevent tearing. Gwen starts to cry, covering her face with her hands. "Oh, Mrs Rees," she sobs, "I could murder that man, I could wring his useless neck! I'm going to die, I know it."

"You want no such thing and there'll be no dying tonight," says Hannah. She finds brusqueness the best course of action when the women start to talk of death. It often happens near the end, just before the baby comes. The pain is too intense. They just want it to be over. "I can feel him now, Gwen. He's here. You need to concentrate. Two more big pushes."

Gwen cries harder than ever but pushes all the same, letting out a high, keening sound as the baby begins to crown. No matter how many times she's done this, Hannah can never quite grow used to that sound. It's so animalistic, so inhuman – a shriek of mingled fury, incomprehension and victory. Here is life, it seems to be saying, and no amount of crinoline, lace or cover-up can hide it. There is no polite society when it comes to childbirth.

The head has emerged. A smattering of dark hair sits on the bright-red scalp. Gwen gives another mighty shove down the bed and the baby's shoulders come out fast. Hannah places her fingers gently underneath them and in one motion

– careful and measured but deliberate – she lifts backward. The child slips from her mother. Her mother? His mother!

"It's a boy," says Hannah, and as she says it she swings the baby sideways, its mouth pointed down, until she hears a cry. Mammals are much the same when it comes to delivering their young: watch a horse licking its newborn foal, sometimes even kicking it. Anything to stimulate the heart, keep it vital. Hannah takes the towel she reserved especially for this some hours earlier, placed well away from everything else and in the cleanest spot she could find, and begins to rub the infant vigorously. The focus shifts quickly from mother to baby but, as soon as the child wails, Hannah is back to Gwen. She places the mewling infant into his mother's arms. Gwen looks utterly bewildered, but her face swims as she looks down. "A boy," she says, and simply stares at the baby as Hannah begins to clean her up.

SEVEN
THE BABIES

CARMARTHENSHIRE, 1898

"Beautiful, isn't he?"

Gwen is sitting up in bed, crooning to the baby. Hannah pauses for a moment, taking in the sight of them. It never fails to amaze her, the transition from chaos to order, and all in a matter of minutes. There is so much noise in a delivery room. Across the valley, my Hodges ancestors were thinking the same thing about the mines – the noise of the place, the drama. Perhaps there wasn't so much of a distance between them – the local midwife and the miners? Both jobs demanded an almost maniacal level of attention to detail: one slip-up, one wrong move and everything has the potential to go spectacularly wrong.

Hannah can add this birth to the list of the many that haven't gone wrong. She will say prayers of thanks for this tonight, as she always does. It wouldn't do to grow complacent in the face of success.

When she first accompanied old Mrs Leith on her rounds, she was almost put off the idea of work such as this for life. Mrs Leith was a fearsome woman with a reputation for extreme efficiency. She never suffered fools and was often to be heard barking at the parents, husbands and siblings of her charges whenever she felt they weren't pulling their weight. "You think this bairn will birth itself? Get on with those towels, Mary, we haven't got all night!"

Hannah has adopted a little of this attitude. It doesn't do to stand on ceremony, when a woman goes into labour. "All hands on deck," she used to say, smiling grimly as the contractions started. She was not afraid of bustle and drama, and it was famously difficult to intimidate her, though many had tried. Mr Jones, just last year, had set up a terrible row when Hannah had torn one of his bath sheets to shreds. He'd seen her marching into the bathroom and just as quickly come marching out of it, holding the flannelled blankets. They were new, Mr Jones explained. What on earth was she doing? Hannah ignored him and, outside the bedroom, began ripping the towels to shreds. It wasn't easy – the material was tough and burned her hands as she tore it. "Now listen here, Mrs Rees!" shouted Jones, striding toward her and trying to stop her. "Ellen has already washed all the linens she needs! What in God's name do you want with our brand new and, I might add, extremely costly bathroom mats!"

"Mr Jones," said Hannah, continuing to tear even as she spoke. Sweat was dripping from her brow. "If you would like your wife to bleed out on your marital bed at this very moment, go ahead and stop me. If you'd like me to save her, either help me with these or stand aside."

Mr Jones paled, ducked his head inside the bedroom and started back out of it as though he'd been kicked by one of his own horses. "What's happened to her?" he breathed. He ran his hands over his face, then turned back to stare into the room. Ellen Jones' arm was hanging over the side of the bed, her face the colour of sour milk. The baby, born some 10 minutes before, was gurgling away happily in the crib already placed beside the bed.

"It's a bleed, sir," said Hannah, trying to be kind now. "A bad one. I need to try and stop it. This material should help, but I may need some assistance."

"A bleed?" he asked weakly. "I can't see any blood, though. Where is she bleeding from?"

"For heaven's sake, Mr Jones!" They didn't have much time, but a part of her just wanted to sit down and laugh. "Where on earth do you *think* she's bleeding from?"

My great-grandmother Hannah was not to be trifled with. Her work made her resilient in the face of extreme pressure. She was known for her cool-headedness, her calm and, let's face it, her track record. Hannah delivered babies with a fixed determination to see life thrive. She didn't care who the parents were, how wealthy the grandparents were, or whether the family she was helping knew her own family or not. Nothing mattered but preserving the heartbeat that started tapping its rhythm out months before, in the womb, and that would either continue under her care or be extinguished before life even began. She was not, in short, a snob. She didn't go in for rumour or hearsay. She didn't care if her charge was the local charwoman's daughter or the lady of the manor.

It wasn't easy, at first. When Mrs Leith retired from local service Hannah was left on her own. She inherited the pinard – a horn-like an ear trumpet that's used to listen to foetal heartbeats. It was invented in 1895 by a French obstetrician, and is still used today. Despite all our technological advances, sometimes the most simple of tools does the trick. Hannah would never grow tired of the fingernail-like tapping sound of a fledgling heartbeat, the pitter-patter quickstep of it, and the overwhelming sadness when a child stopped kicking and the belly grew still.

She was only 20 when Mrs Leith put her feet up, with three babies of her own and William to look after. She quickly came to realise that no pregnancy was ever the same, no birth, either. What Hannah lacked, and what we – my own children and I – were able to benefit from, was the ability to see exactly what was going on inside the body before the birth itself. There was no way of knowing, then, if the baby was growing healthily, if it was male or female, no tests to determine its susceptibility to syndromes or lifelong illness.

There were some truly awful memories that threatened, if Hannah let them, to overwhelm her – even now, often years later. The little boy born with so much fluid in his lungs that he choked to death in her arms. Hannah didn't know what the problem was – his mouth was empty, his throat seemed clear. The girl who was born without eyes: blank sockets where bright pupils ought to have been. The girl who took one breath, wailed, and then fell silent. There was no reason for it, no logical explanation. The twins – one so much larger than the other, who cried and screamed as they took him away while his brother shuddered and fitted and passed on two days later, too weak to take the breast or the bottle. The girl who slid out of her mother already gone, her tiny eyes closed before they'd even opened on the room of expectant aunties and sisters. They were hideous moments, made so much worse by the fact it was she, Hannah, who was forced each time to break the news, to try and make sense of the inexplicable.

With all the pregnancies Hannah has attended, all she can go on is a visual inspection, the woman and the bump itself. When the child is born, there's no saying whether it'll live or die, thrive or perish. Obstructed pregnancies are the biggest problem. Hannah cannot see their cause – she can only do what she can see. When waters break too early, the risk of infection is enormous. The amniotic fluid protecting the baby in a sterile environment is gone. But Hannah has no idea what an infection is. No one does.

At this stage there are never any answers, and it is understandable that so many people believe so fervently in the whims of a god they cannot see, but who works in mysterious ways. When Mrs Leith stopped no longer taking calls, many families in Carmarthenshire remembered her assistant and started calling for Hannah when a baby was on the way. And there is no shortage of them. Within a mile of Hannah's house alone there are the Williams, who have seven kids, the Cartwrights with nine, the Jones with five, and the Davies with 12. It was one of the Davies girls, Stella, who became Hannah's first solo delivery. Stella now has children of her own, all brought into the world by the same worldly midwife.

Gwen is chirruping to the baby, cooing and stroking his cheeks. These are the moments Hannah works so hard to achieve. She wishes they could all be like this.

"Here, Mrs Rees, would you like to hold him?" asks Gwen. All traces of wildness have vanished from her face. She looks almost drugged, though Hannah – mercifully – has not had to administer any anaesthetic to the young woman. Hannah moves forward, taking the baby from Gwen and smiling down at him. His wisps of hair curl upwards and there's a cheeky, upturned look to his mouth, a little smile that will take some weeks to show itself – but no doubt about it, it's there. He opens his eyes and gazes up at Hannah. He looks surprised, suddenly, to be here. And no wonder! Where has he been, all this time? Hannah wishes she knew what went on, inside these women's bellies. She wishes there were some way of understanding how a tiny human like this one can be inside his mother one moment and here, distinct and blinking up at her the next. There's something strangely familiar about the way the baby's eyebrows form an almost straight line across his forehead that gives her pause, just for a moment, before—

"Hey, Mrs Rees, I'm starving." Gwen interrupts the silence. "How about some scran? Can you call for my mam?"

Hannah does as she's asked, leaving Gwen and the baby and heading back down to the kitchen. Mr Gold has left for work, by now. The light is just brushing the tops of the hills outside, bathing the fields in a tepid orange glow. It'll be a beautiful day.

Mrs Gold is standing by the table, slicing bread. "I heard her," she says, grimly, to Hannah. "I'll bring up some toasted bread. How was she?"

"As expected," Hannah grins. She likes Mrs Gold – they've known each other years, ever since Hannah first met Will.

"And the child?"

"Eyes wide open and almost smiling."

Mrs Gold lets out a sigh, and with it, she seems to deflate like a balloon.

"There's a terrible part of me, Hannah," she says, "that almost wished the child wouldn't make it. It's a terrible thought, isn't it. I just…" She stares down at the loaf in her hands, shaking her head. "It doesn't do for Gwen, you know, so young. She'll not have an easy ride of it. Most of her friends have already stopped speaking to her."

Hannah understands what Mrs Gold is saying; she appreciates the woman's honesty. It won't be easy for Gwen or her child.

"Look," says Hannah, "It might not be as bad as you think. People have short memories, you know? It'll blow over after a time. And we've just heard what a pair of lungs your girl's got on her. You think she'll let anyone mess with her boy?"

Mrs Gold nods and starts to brown the bread over the fire, turning the fork occasionally.

"Still, though," says Hannah darkly, "It's an outrage, her up there, crying and shouting away, and whoever he is not even aware his own child's being born."

"Well, that's the biggest problem, isn't it?" says Mrs Gold, "she won't tell me, or her da."

"Probably for the best, though," says Hannah, remembering Gwen's youth, her confusion at her own pregnancy, her fear during the birth. "I'd kill him if I knew."

* * *

There's not a great deal left for Hannah to do. Mrs Gold takes the toast upstairs to her daughter, and Hannah leaves them for a few moments, taking the opportunity for a few moments' peace. She'll just need to check Gwen for any small tears, administer a sleeping draught and weigh the baby. Mrs Gold knows what she's doing, even if Gwen doesn't, so Hannah doesn't have any fears for him.

Upstairs, Gwen is starting to drift off already. She'll wake soon enough with the cramps, though. Hannah pours a small amount of liquid onto a spoon and holds it out to her. "Here," she says. "This'll help you rest.""What is it?" Gwen eyes the spoon suspiciously. "Everything's all right, isn't it? Why do I need medicine?""Everything's fine. But you'll have cramps for a few hours, perhaps on and off for a day or two. It'll happen when you nurse, too, so you need to be rested.""Cramps?" Gwen stares at Hannah. "Where?""Not as bad as you've had today, don't worry, but smaller ones, like you get during your monthlies. In your womb.""My what?"

* * *

Gwen names the baby Percy. He's cooing away in the crib and Hannah is just preparing to leave, fastening her bag, when she hears a commotion outside.

Mrs Gold, standing in the yard, sounds shocked, even a little frightened. "Just go!" she shouts. "You've no place being here. Leave!"

A muffled response follows. A man's voice, but it isn't Mr Gold, and at any rate his wife would never address him like this. There's the sound of a door opening and heavy footsteps on the stairs. "Come back! You've no right, come back—"

"I've every right!" the man shouts back, and Hannah starts, the bag falling from her hands onto the floor. "I've every right, Mrs Gold, to visit my child whenever I damn well please."

Hannah knows this voice, and feels like she might faint with the shock of it. But in the few seconds before the door is flung open, until he strides into the room, tousle-haired and wild-eyed, she'd almost managed to convince herself it couldn't be true. Yet here he is. Johnny, her Johnny, her son and, apparently, Percy's father.

"Mam," he stutters, as he crosses the room. He looks cowed, shocked, caught red-handed, like a little boy again. He has the decency, at least, to look apologetic. "I didn't…" he begins, "I didn't know you'd still be here."

Hannah cannot speak; she stares at her son and then over at the baby. Of course, he looked familiar, he looked like Johnny, like Hannah and William and the Rees lot. Those eyebrows, that smile. It makes sense, a terrible sense.

Gwen is dozing, having taken the draught, but she stirs a little when she hears Johnny's voice. Her eyes are tired but alive, happy. Johnny moves over to her bedside and takes her hand. "How's it going then, cariad?"

* * *

She marches Johnny home, despite his protestations – "That's my boy, ma! My son!" – and it all comes tumbling out.

It's not just Gwen. Johnny has children all over the valley, and Hannah – though she still cannot quite fathom it – has delivered most of them herself! Her own grandchildren, their mothers led astray by her boy. It's too much to bear. And now Mrs Gold knows. She and Gwen's mother go back a long way, but she doubts Mrs Gold will be able to keep this to herself. And why should she? Her daughter has been left with a baby she has no knowledge of how to care for, and though Johnny arrived, he has no plans to play a role in the rearing of the child, and no money to offer Gwen for Percy's upkeep.

"It's an outrage," William roars, slamming his fist down onto the table. He has raided the small cupboard beside the fire, the one they usually keep locked, where the brandy's stored, and he's in full flow. "An absolute scandal, John – what were you thinking?"

"He wasn't thinking," says Hannah, drily. "At least not with his head."

"Ah, ma, don't," says Johnny, and throws himself down beside the fire. "I didn't know, did I? I didn't know that's how it went, with the girls – you never told me!"

"And you didn't guess, after the first time, or the second, or perhaps the 10th, John? Lord help us for raising such a contemptible fool, William!"

William is nodding. Hannah's rarely seen him so angry but there's a sadness, too, in her husband's face. He speaks quietly for the first time, now, since Hannah explained what had happened.

"Lad, you can't stay y'ere. You'll have to go." Johnny looks at his father quickly, confusion spreading across his face. "Go?" he says slowly, as though testing out the word. "Go where?"

"Away. Anywhere. You can't stay y'ere, not after this. People talk. You know how it is."

"Your father'll be denied work if we're seen condoning this sort of carry-on," says Hannah. And she's right. William is a respected farmer, one of the best and most efficient in the area. But the markets and trade arrangements are all organised by local men, men who have the right to refuse

William's produce and cattle if they believe the Rees family to be soiled, debauched, sinful. Everyone will know about what Johnny's been up to by tomorrow, and the easiest way out of this mess is exile. Hannah and William need to be seen putting their feet down.

"This is madness," says Johnny, rising to his feet. He swipes the glass of brandy off the table and paces back and forth between the fireplace and his parents. "You can't just send me away. I haven't done anything wrong."

"You have single-handedly fathered more children here than all the families in the valley put together, by the sounds of it!" Hannah barks back at him. "You think anyone will ask me to deliver their babies if they know you put them there in the first place? An unmarried, jobless lad who's left these women high and dry – and me, their own grandmother, delivering them! The bloody midwife!"

"Please, ma," says Johnny, kneeling down before her. He looks desperate, frightened. Furious though she is, Hannah wishes there were something she could say that would reassure him, if only for a moment. But what she and William have said is true. There's no future for Johnny in Carmarthenshire, not any more.

On 29 March that year, 1906, Johnny is driven to Liverpool in his father's horse-and-cart. The great ship *Canada* will take him, and many others, over to Portland, Oregon. From there he travels to New York, and later settles in Kentucky, before moving to Manitoba. He runs a shop there, and soon the wild hills and wilder ways of his youth begin to fade from memory. He will never see any of his family again.

Despite already having eight children of their own, Hannah and William discuss the matter with Gwen, and agree that Percy, their grandson, can come and live with them.

EIGHT
BLOOD AND BONE

Hannah and William are better off than most. They work for themselves, and provide services nobody can do without. For William, the toil and labour carried out on his land, his own small corner of Cefneithin, has lined his pockets nicely. There's something deeply satisfying about loading up the carts during harvest, knowing none of this would be here if it weren't for him. Hannah is similarly indispensable. It took some time for the dust to settle after Johnny left, but the villagers quickly came to realise that nobody else had the skill of Hannah Rees when it came to childbirth. Though they may have despised her son, they weren't about to let that get in the way – not when the stakes were so high. There's nobody so experienced as Hannah, and everybody knows it.

Philip Rees, my grandfather, was the eldest of Hannah and William's children. Born in 1868, he married Mary, my grandmother, and together they had six children: Sarah, Hannah, Katie, Maggie, Daniel and Willie, my father, the man who'd go on to marry Edna May Hodges.

Hannah helps to deliver all of Mary's babies. With each new daughter, Philip sighs and runs his hands through his hair. He loves his girls, of course he does, but he's worried about the future. William and he work together, for now, but at some stage it'll become too much for the older man and Philip will need somebody to help him. There was never the slightest notion, back then, of employing one of his daughters to help. The very thought!

Hannah is growing older now, too. Sometimes, at night especially, she lies awake and remembers the babies, Mary's babies, who she wasn't able to save. There are already three of them by the time my father is born, and now Mary – like Tory, all those years before – is pregnant again, and scared.

After Johnny, Hannah has tried her best to speak to her children honestly.

"Philip," she said, when he announced his plans to marry Mary. "You won't want to speak of it, but I feel I should tell you about the facts."

Philip, quiet and serious as he chopped logs for the fire, straightened up.

"The facts about what, mother?" he asked.

"You're soon to marry. You need to be aware of what's likely to happen, on the night of your wedding and afterwards."

Philip's face reddened. "I know about that, ma," he muttered. "Of course I know about all that."

"Obviously," Hannah said, trying to keep the sarcasm from her voice. "But there are things you probably don't know. It's better for the woman not to face pregnancy so often as they do. There are ways of stopping that."

Philip turned away, clearly mortified. "I know," he said again. He was squirming."When you go to bed together," Hannah began, as her son groaned, "it's better to do it in the fortnight after her monthly. Immediately before it, or during, carries a higher risk of her falling with child."

Philip looked taken aback: he always knew about the type of work his mother did, but she rarely spoke of it, and never in such graphic terms.

"Do you hear me, Philip?" she asked. "You will want babies, of course you will. But if you do not, there are safe ways to ensure Mary doesn't conceive. It will save you both a great deal of grief and hardship, just to know this."

Hannah was doing her best, bless her. In the 19th century, menstruation was still taboo – an untouchable subject, even by physicians. Licensed doctors risked having their names struck from the register if they ventured opinions, anecdotes or ideas pertaining to women's bodies and the process of conception. When a female member of the household started bleeding, she was described as being "unwell." The idea of an internal examination was abhorrent to most – men, women, rich and poor – so it was rare for anyone, even midwives like Hannah, to have a sense of what was really happening internally. Gynaecology remained a mystery to most until the 1930s.

For now, all Hannah can go on is what she has witnessed. She has tried, with all her might, to give advice to the local women, those who cannot afford more children or whose health would be threatened by bearing another.

For months now she has been watching William's dogs. There are two bitches in particular she has tried to focus on. Every few months the dogs will bleed, and it is during this time that William keeps them inside. Two years ago, Sandy – the more adventurous – broke free from the field during this time. Over the coming months they noticed she grew bigger, her belly stretched: she was expecting pups. "It'll be the ruddy Davies' dogs," William had fumed, rounding on Philip, "and you forgot to shut the gate properly. We need a litter here about as much as a hole in the head, boy!"

This had given Hannah an idea, and ever since she'd been observing the two bitches closely. When their bleeding began she'd set off past the Davies' farm, carefully watching. As they drew closer, the dogs tethered to Mr Davies' porch door grew wild, straining at the leash, barking at Sandy. Whatever was happening here had to do with the blood, Hannah realised. When they weren't bleeding, the Davies' dogs ignored them. You can't blame Hannah for assuming, then, that the same must be true of humans.

The result of this advice, of course, was children. Lots of them, many hundreds more, all delivered by Hannah. "You followed what I told you, did you?" she'd growl as the women came knocking, their bellies round and stretched. "I said – very clearly, avoid lying together when you're unwell. Any other time is fine, but when there's blood it's best not to take the chance."

God must be laughing down at her, Hannah thinks. There have been awful times over the past years. Women coming to her, begging her silently and emotionally to help them end their pregnancy. It cannot be done, and Hannah will never do it. She imagines there are ways, but she doesn't want to think about what they could be. So she just keeps delivering the babies, and now Mary's sixth is on the way.

It's a cold afternoon when she spots Philip running across the field towards the house. It's time. She gathers her bag as quickly as she can. It starts to rain as they cross back to Philip's smallholding together. The wind begins to howl. A storm is coming.

Immediately, Hannah can see that Mary is not doing well. Her face is slick with sweat and she is breathing rapidly, too quickly and too loudly. "Help me, ma," she croaks.

Hannah darts to the bottom of the bed and examines Mary. She is dilating, but there's a problem. She can see the cervix, although she has no idea this is what it's called, and something appears to be stuck above it. Hannah knows, right then, in that moment. She knows what will happen.

Inside her bag she reaches for the chloroform, so much easier to procure since the days of Percy's birth, and so much more widely understood, now. Mary will need a decent amount, if she's to push through this blockage. And there will be blood. A lot of it.

Twenty-four hours later, they are in exactly the same position. Mary is exhausted, drifting in and out of consciousness as her body contracts and she wails, not understanding why it's taking so long. Her other babies were born quickly – some too quickly, even. She's never known it to last this length of time, and can feel this thing, whatever it is, pushing back on her – it's like something's stuck, refusing to budge to allow her baby into the birth canal.

After another 24 hours Hannah is so tired she can barely see, but when she feels Mary's pulse slow, she knows she must act. She chloroforms the woman, knowing she is dying. She gives her too much, deliberately, to spare her the brutal pain she is about to inflict, and takes a scalpel, slicing into her belly, deep through layers of tissue and fat, to where she knows the baby must be. Inside she finds her, a tiny thing – another girl. The sac holding the baby has moved over the top of Mary's cervix, preventing birth entirely, blocking the way. She holds the child up, weeping. There are no cries, and she massages the tiny chest, trying to quickstart the heart. Nothing happens, and the baby – just like her poor mother – has no pulse.

Years later, my sister Maris and I will find Mary's gravestone. She was buried alongside all four of the children who did not survive. On her death certificate, the cause of her passing is listed as "placenta previa." What medical words, foreign-sounding words these would have been to my great-grandmother, to the woman who tried her hardest to give advice and nurture these expectant mothers through their childbearing. All she could see, as she looked down at Mary's wasted body, was blood. My father Willie, at the time of his mother's death, was just two years old.

PART THREE

EDNA AND WILLIE 1909-1938

NINE
EDNA MAY

In 1907, the great explorer Ernest Shackleton placed an advertisement in English newspapers. "Men wanted for hazardous journey. Low wages, bitter cold, long hours of complete darkness. Safe return doubtful. Honour and recognition in event of success." On 9 January 1909, the day of my mother's birth, Ernest Shackleton arrived at the southernmost point of Antarctica – a new record, and one achieved with exactly the difficulty described by the advert.

Shackleton's march was not an easy one. Supplies were heavily diminished, and the loss of the four-man team's final pony, Socks, meant the men were hauling what little they had behind them across treacherous ground, ice liable to break and throw them off crevasses at any moment. Realising that there simply wouldn't be enough to feed the team should they press on to the South Pole, Shackleton contented himself with the knowledge they'd reached within 100 miles of it – an exercise in endurance and tenacity that I cannot help but smile at, when I think of Edna.

This same year saw the introduction of the Russian ballet to Western audiences – the seats at the Theatre du Chatelet in Paris were packed, and introduced many thousands of spectators to stories, folklore and music from a remote-seeming and little-understood country. In July, Louis Bleriot became the first man to fly across the English Channel in a craft heavier than the air that carried him.

Twelve months later, in 1910, Florence Nightingale died, a woman whose contribution to the history of nursing and good medical practice in the UK and beyond cannot be overestimated. After completing her training at a religious community in Germany, Florence nursed victims of a cholera outbreak in London. This experience was to prove instrumental.

It was the Crimean War, fought from 1853-1856, which marked a turning point in the public understanding of disease and infection: of the almost 20,000 troops who died, 90% succumbed to cold and illnesses like cholera, typhoid and dysentery, rather than from enemy action. Florence spurned the upper-class women travelling to the Crimea as tourists, collecting wildflowers and illustrating their experiences. Instead, she was a leading light for the notion of equality of treatment: whatever a soldier's rank, she would help. She wrote to the relatives of those who died, sent money to their widows and thousands of letters back to those clamouring for news of their missing or ill loved ones.

It was Florence who led the charge for hospital redesign: the new pavilion-style of architecture was directly inspired by her study of cross-ventilation, and wings connected by the long corridors are still used today. Four years after her death, many thousands of women followed in Florence's footsteps and volunteered for military service as trained nurses.

It was a seminal year, 1909: a time of change and novelty, and there was a sense that progress was being made, advances achieved. The birth of my mother, on that cold mid-winter morning, was no exception. Tommy and Esther Hodges cannot have known just how important their child would prove to be, or what her own baby – born many years later – would come to represent.

Edna was born at Sunnyside, the house in Cymmer that Tommy and Esther had worked so hard to buy. There was one road leading in to the village and one leading out – a street of twitching curtains and whispers, but a friendly place nonetheless and one where secrets were a foreign concept. Some years later, just a few miles away, the velvet-voiced Richard Burton would be born to another coal miner, Richard Jenkins, and his wife Edith, who worked as a barmaid at the Miner's Arms.

"Edna May… or she may not," was my mam's constant refrain. She was a cheeky child, blonde-haired and blue-eyed, the apple of her parents' eye, and their eldest daughter. Soon, Jemima and Amelia would follow – bringing the total number of Hodges children to seven: four boys and three girls. It was a wild, unkempt place to grow up, devoid of ceremony or airs and graces. Doors were left unlocked on Sunnyside – there was little to steal anyway, and children were raised communally. It takes a village, after all, and the mothers and fathers knew that if the children were out roaming together they had a collective responsibility for them.

Tommy and Esther did not spoil them. Frugality was everything, especially in the early years: with each new mouth to feed came further small sacrifices, then bigger ones. The one item my mother's family prided above all others, though, was the mahogany piano.

Tommy had found it in Swansea just after he and Esther had moved to a row of terraced houses. Esther had always loved to play and he was determined to provide something that could bring the children pleasure, too. Years later, my mother would tell me the story.

"He told his friends, the other miners, what he wanted," she said, "and they advised him to go to the city. There was a shop on Dillwyn Street that took in second-hand instruments, repaired them if necessary and sold them on. They gave him the address and off he went." It was a Sunday in autumn, and fine enough to walk at least part of the way. When Tommy arrived he was struck by the commerce of the place: men and women in bright clothes and tall hats wandering between the stalls, carrying laden baskets and smiling. As he so often felt when outside the village, he noticed the cleanliness of the air, the lack of soot and smog, and reflected on how vastly different his life must be from those men and women milling around the market. Some would be factory owners or groomsmen, blacksmiths or dressmakers. He hoped, in that moment, that his own children would aspire to something other than the life he'd been forced into, deep down in the pits.

Outside the shop, Tommy hesitated for a moment before pushing the door open. In the window, shiny brass instruments were laid out on soft cushions, sheets of music were strung across guitar strings, clipped on with pegs like beautiful laundry. He could see immediately that many of these items would be far beyond his and Esther's means. But he was heartened when the shopkeeper, a small man with large round spectacles, approached him with a smile.

"Looking for anything particular today, sir?" he asked, gesturing around the room. "As you can see, we've quite the collection."

Tommy relaxed. Despite his shabby clothes and unkempt hair (the wind was strong on the final ride down into the city), the shopkeeper was respectful, kind and patient. It helped, as the intimidating mass of instruments winked at him in the dim October sunlight.

Music, Tommy knew, served no practical purpose. It would not feed or clothe or educate his children, it wouldn't enable them to make different choices later in their lives, or cure them if they fell ill. And yet there was a feeling, lodged in Tommy's chest, that a piano would help them. It was a necessity, he decided, as much as food or water or oxygen.

"I'm looking for a piano," he says. "My wife plays. We don't mind what sort, not really, but we haven't much money, so…"

The shopkeeper nods. He's the sort of man who likes problem-solving: pianos never come cheap, but there are solutions to be found, if only people will take the time to find them.

"We've many pianos, sir – at a variety of different price levels," he tells Tommy. "There are Challens in the back, a couple of Brinsmeads here" – he points to two at the back, standing side by side – "very old, mind, but they've been tuned and we produce a good sound from them."

The man continues to walk with Tommy around the shop, pointing things out and every so often moving one item to another area of the shop. Tommy notices he talks to the instruments as he does this, chastising a battered-looking saxophone when he finds it hanging among the clarinets. Tommy has never been inside a music shop before and it's a strange experience. Part of him wants to laugh at the waste of it all – the wood and brass and metal twisted into impossible shapes, the delicate-looking keys and reeds, the polish of ancient-looking violins. This place is very far removed from what he knows, from the grunt and labour of his everyday life. Another part, growing stronger by the minute, is enticed by the rich, earthy smell of the place, the quiet and calm amidst all these instruments that were once played and enjoyed – and will be again.

"And a lovely Danemann – solid, reliable, beautiful tone." The shopkeeper has led Tommy right to the shop's rear, where the deep-brown wood of the piano looks almost black in the gloom. Unlike some of the others he has seen, there is something hard and strong about this one, a lack of vulnerability that Tommy notices immediately. He marvels at himself slightly for having such a thought.

"It dates to 1900," says the man beside him. "Only a few thousand made that year. It arrived just last week." The shopkeeper has noticed Tommy's eyes lingering on the Danemann, and opens the lid. Its keys are a little dusty, and the legs bear scratches and scuffs. Tommy notices these minor defects but they don't bother him; he likes the idea that somebody else has already used the piano, that's it's been a part of someone's routine, their everyday.

"I'll need a few days to smarten her up," says the shop-keeper. He knows he has found a buyer when a customer stares at something like Tommy is staring at the Danemann.

"And we can come to an agreement about the payment."

Only now does Tommy look up at the man, wondering what he'll say next.

"I'll accept a small deposit today, Mr...?"

"Hodges. Tommy Hodges."

"Good, well, we can come up with a sum that suits us both for now, then. And I can offer a monthly instalment fee that should pay the bill in total within the next three years."

Tommy swallows. Three years is a long time. He bites his lip, thinks of Esther and the boys. He loathes the idea of debt – but then, what's one more? Work is plentiful right now.

Esther's haberdashery is progressing, and she's seeing more and more clients. When the shopkeeper names the monthly repayment, Tommy nods. They can manage that. It'll be a squeeze, but not nearly as much as he'd expected. And this piano – it's more than wood, more than the ebony and ivory flanking its middle. He shakes the shopkeeper's hand, signs the loan form and pays the small deposit. The shopkeeper hums as he moves to close the lid, ever so gently.

"Do you have children, Mr Hodges?"

"I do," says Tommy. "Three boys, and my wife's expecting."

"And do they play?"

"They will now." For the first time since he's entered the shop, Tommy laughs. "Yes, indeed, they will now."

* * *

Esther teaches the children, who are immediately entranced by the giant wooden structure being heaved into the tiny living area at Sunnyside. They begin to fight and bicker about whose turn it is. They practise scales and arpeggios and compose little songs to well-known tunes. Every evening when he returns from the mines, Tommy can hear them at it – in the first weeks the clanking, grinding bash of keys made him laugh, but since then their technique has grown more refined, more patient. They adore the piano – all of them, but especially Esther.

Many years later, my mother tells me about the long hours she spent sitting beside Esther on the battered old stool they used as a piano seat. With her long dark hair piled on her head using a tortoiseshell comb, Esther introduces little Edna to the Danemann just as she taught her boys. Esther knows that life will be tough for the children: Brinley and Robert are soon to leave school and join Tommy in the pits. They're clever children, and music – brought into their lives at an early age – has made them gentle, prepared to work at the things that matter. But none of this is of any consequence – not the arithmetic or the literacy or the fact that Brinley (on a good day) can whizz through a requiem with all the power and manic energy of a professional. These will be things to sustain them through their lives, perhaps, but they'll never be anything more than hobbies. Making a living out of hobbies is for rich people. And what will life bring, Esther wonders, for her daughters, for Millie and Mima and Edna May, perched on the hard stool staring at the keys?

She doesn't know, but she wants to give them this: the gift of music, the chance to pour their frustration into something besides fighting or gambling or drinking.

Recently, Tommy has taken to the pub much more often than before. It worries Esther and yet, as before, she contemplates the difference between her and her husband's daily lives: the sights he sees, the clenching fear, the loss of friends. It's small wonder he stays away long after his shift is finished, but she wishes he would turn elsewhere for comfort – to her, perhaps, or the children. The bottle is a dependable friend but not a faithful one, not one to be relied upon.

Edna loves these moments sat beside her mother. They always begin with *Gwahoddiad* and finish with *The Ash Grove*. When the music is too tricky, Edna turns to the lyric book Esther bought from the same shop that sold Tommy the piano, and sings. Her voice is clear and confident, but when Mima joins in the cat scarpers from the room.

* * *

Trouble was brewing across Europe as Edna May grew older, and she was just six years old when war was declared. Her life, and that of her father and brothers, however, was mercifully unaffected. Miners were exempt from conscription – the country needed coal now more than ever – but less fortunate classmates reported terrible stories of their daddies, elder brothers, cousins, uncles and grandfathers.

Around 40,000 Welshmen were lost in those four hideous years of violence and disaster, but Edna's everyday life changed very little. When you have nothing very much to begin with, a world war means you have only a little less. When Edna's friend Martha arrived at school months after the fighting had finished, they all crowded around to see the memorial medallion her mother had been sent. It was tiny, smaller than a penny piece, and cast in bronze. "He died for freedom and honour," they intoned in hushed voices, reading Martha's father's name engraved beside a picture of a knight and a lion.

Closer to home, there were atrocities that prompted more lasting impressions. In 1918, some weeks before

Martha brought the little medallion in to class, Edna noted down the following entry in her diary: "It is with extreme respect that I record the death of Doris Hawton... who in travelling home by workmen's train R&SBR yesterday fell out of the compartment and was killed. She was one of the most ladylike pupils of her class." Doris may well have survived this fall, it later transpired: she was alive when her classmates raised the alarm, and a local farmer lifted her onto the broad back of his pony. But the local physician was nowhere to be found, and the midwife was away in Swansea. "I didn't know where to take her," the farmer sobbed, as he arrived at the child's parents' house. "And I don't think she's breathing any more, poor little mite."

We lose children today: we hear about it through friends, or on the news, or via crowd-funding campaigns. Vicious illnesses threaten weakened immune systems, a winter flu can ravage an otherwise healthy set of lungs, a dash across a busy road can signal the end. But for Edna, growing up, the risks were that much greater. Technology was advancing, trains gathering speed and machines growing more intelligent, more capable. But the level of safety and security in place to handle such advancements had not yet caught up. There were no ambulances to call. Edna had heard the stories about her relative, Tory, a woman so far in the distant past as to seem unreal, and understood that she ought to count herself lucky. She lived in a spacious cottage with both her parents, healthy siblings – and a piano. They weren't sent off to workhouses, or up chimneys, or down the mines – at least, not yet. But despite all this, the provisions for action when somebody was taken ill seemed distinctly lacking.

By 1918, the world was gripped by a fresh wave of slaughter in the form of Spanish flu. Named after King Alfonso XIII, who became extremely unwell with the virus, it was enabled in part by the movement of people around the globe during and after the first world war. At its apex, 25 million people were infected in 25 weeks: only American Samoa, St Helena and various islands in the South Atlantic were spared.

At Marylebone Infirmary, where sick patients were arriving in their droves, nine nurses succumbed to the flu. It was a horrible death, usually characterised by secondary pneumonia, which caused the lungs to fill with bloody fluid, and the sufferer to choke.

* * *

Closer to home, Edna is aware of the deaths of three children at her school, Doris, Sarah and Bobby. Sarah's face had been covered in a thick, scaly rash the last time Edna saw her. She lay in bed for a week, refusing food and coughing up great handkerchiefs full of blood: scarlet fever. Bobby, who slept beside his faithful dog each night in his family's smallholding, contracted typhus and died months after Doris.

In the town square, after school, Edna watches the carts full of men returning from the battlefields. She is on the steps with Brinley and Mima.

"What's happened to them?" asks Mima, in a small voice. She is watching one man being helped from a cart by two young officers. He is missing a leg and an eye, both on his right side.

"Rifles," says Brinley. "They've been shot at."

Edna spots an older man walking towards his family, who have arrived to welcome him. The mother is weeping openly. He tries to smile at her, but his face is pockmarked with blisters. He bends down to stroke the head of his son – no more than three – but the boy shies away from him and hides behind his mother's legs.

"Probably hit by the mustard gas," says Brinley. "It burns you from the inside out when you breathe it in. That's why his face has all those sores on it."

What strikes Edna, as she watches the blistered man and the younger corporal missing a limb, is that they all seem to be turning for home, going back to their lives. But how will they manage to work, with injuries like this? Who will help them?

On 23 May that year, as the war drew to a close, Edna notes that "W. Jenkins Hirwaun gave lesson in alcohol" and, in April 1921, states simply that "The weather was inclement." She is growing aware of the sheer number of risks involved in simply living each day – a cold snap can mean sickness for her parents or siblings; too much time at the pub can render Tommy irascible, short-tempered. Once, he even missed a shift at the mine, complaining all day in bed of a headache, and drinking gallons of water from the well.

At night, and just like Tory all those years before, Edna prays for what seems like a miracle. She hopes, with every fibre of her being, that their house will be spared the endless rounds of risk that await them every day. She prays that Brinley and Robert can find work elsewhere, that her father will leave the mines and enter the fields as a labourer or herdsman. But then again, if there is to be another war, they will all three be required to join the front. What will she, Esther, Mima and Millie do when all they have, it seems, is the battered and ageing piano in the parlour?

TEN
BROKEN

"Edna, run and help Mima, will you?"

Edna is busy. She doesn't want to run and help Mima, who is continually getting into scrapes. Last week it was a bad fall from the top of the garden steps, yesterday she ran off during a game of hide and seek and wasn't found for two hours. She does it deliberately, Edna thinks, just for attention. As if Mima doesn't get enough of it. She's by far the most rambunctious of the Hodges children – this generation's Hodges children, at least…

She waits a few more moments before hearing Esther calling out to her again. "Coming!" she yells back, and finishes that day's diary entry. It's 30 September 1922, and Edna is 13 years old. The little green copybook is old and frayed, Tommy checks each page thoroughly before agreeing to buy her a new one, and she has to work for it. All the Hodges children muck in but, as the eldest girl and easily the most practical of the seven, Edna is lumped with the hardest and most boring tasks – scrubbing pans hard-crusted with porridge, walking into town for vegetables and fruit that's gone almost as soon as she walks in the door, sweeping the steps that lead to their bedrooms, not just once but twice a day. She is in a bad temper as she goes to find Mima. If we zoom in a little on the entry from today, this much is obvious:

Millie wet the bed at three thirty this morning. Chaos. Mima woke up and started shrieking with laughter. Of course, Mother asked me to sort it out and by the time I'd returned with fresh sheets and dumped the old ones in the bucket under the basin, they were both fast asleep again so was forced to make the bed around them. It is surely ridiculous to be sharing a bed with the girls at my age. They wake at five o'clock in the morning and seem hell-bent on using my stomach as some sort of springboard for acrobatics that continue until Mother and Father wake up. Next door I could hear the boys snoring – it isn't fair. Once I'd got them dressed and sent them off downstairs for their breakfast I started on my homework for Mrs Smith. She is a real dragon but I like her all the same. Nobody ever has a cross word to say within earshot of her but it means everybody does as they're told. I am determined not to spend next year working outside school – it is such an important time for my studies and I simply cannot—

At this, Edna trails off to help resolve whatever problem Mima is currently facing. It transpires, when she heads down into the parlour, that a fight has broken out between Eddie, Tom, Millie and Mima – being Mima – has assigned herself the task of sorting it out, but been boxed on the ear ("accidentally") by Brinley, who has the day off and is sick to death of their squabbling, and now Robert is standing in the midst of them all kicking his legs out at Brinley and shouting.

"For heaven's sake!" Edna cries, and rushes forward to grab Mima and Millie out of the way. "If you're going to knock each other's heads off, at least do it in the garden."

"He took my wooden train!" Millie wrestles out of Edna's arms. "He took it and wouldn't give it back and then he broke it and now look!"

She holds the splintered piece of wood up for Edna to see, her eyes brimming with fury. "Edna, help me find Eddie's tin soldiers. I'm going to throw them in the well, Eddie, just watch—"

"I'll throw you down the well," says Eddie, turning a triumphant face towards his sister. "I'll tip you in and no one will find you, so there!"

"Nobody's throwing anything down the well," says Edna shortly. "Mima, Millie, come with me. Eddie, go to your room. You'll give me the thruppence Millie spent on that train and I'll go to town tomorrow and buy her a new one."

Eddie looks as though he might have something to say about this, but the expression on Edna's face quietens him and he stomps off up the stairs, taking care to dislodge as much of the mud as possible from his little boots on the steps Edna swept just an hour before.

Brinley and Robert are still glowering at one another but when Brinley turns to Mima and apologises for knocking her ear, Robert calms down. They head off into the kitchen and Edna hears the boiling of water, the slicing of bread. Good, she thinks grimly, they're making lunch. Might as well make themselves useful.

Mima and Millie sit on the floor by the window and carry on with their drawing.

Mima is humming to herself, occasionally rubbing her tired eyes, and Millie is sketching a picture of the exact make and model of train that Edna is to buy tomorrow. Edna hadn't planned to go into town tomorrow. There's a lot of schoolwork still to be done, but it'll be so much worse if the toy isn't replaced. She lets out a long sigh and pushes her hair back off her forehead. She starts to practise her times tables in her head, trying to see how quickly she can get through to 16, 17, 18 and 19. 20 is easy. Edna's good at Maths – Mrs Smith says she "has the mind for it – the knack." Not everyone does, apparently. Brinley and Robert certainly don't. They were delighted when compulsory education finished, and spent their last days burning notes and primers in the parlour's grate. Edna hated watching them do it.

As she reaches 17 times 8, her eye is caught by something outside. From their house at Sunnyside the colliery is visible – or the opening shaft, at least. Three steel girders hold a winch high above the ground, and wheelbarrows stand grouped around the opening, which Edna cannot see, but she knows it's there. During the daytime there is barely anyone standing outside the shaft, perhaps a foreman or manager taking a quick smoke and catching the breeze.

But there's movement, quick flashes coming from the pit's entrance. She frowns and presses her nose against the glass. Across the field that separates 16 Sunnyside from the mine, she can hear moaning – a deep, animal-like sound that sets her teeth on edge. She doesn't know what the sound reminds her of, but it's nothing good. She continues to calculate in her head, and throws in some piano tunes for good measure. She hums slightly as she reaches 11 multiplied by 17, staring straight ahead at where the noise is coming from.

The figures become more distinct as they inch closer. There are three people, three men. Two of them are supporting the third. They're walking ever so slowly, hobbling along. The man in the middle has his head down – his friends are almost dragging him, and his limp feet are pulling across the parched late-summer grass.

Millie spots Edna staring and stands up, leaving the artist's impression of a new toy train scattered on the ground. She isn't quite tall enough to reach the sash and hops on one leg to get a better look.

"What're you doing?" says Mima, "You're nudging me, you made my hand slip—"

"Be quiet," says Edna sharply, and both the girls fall silent. The air is filled with the sound of the man's cries now. The group are about 200 metres from the house, but it's still difficult to distinguish them – the dark, sooty smocks worn by the men in the pits render them almost identical. Edna thinks, as she squints, that the man on the right is Mr

Williams, one of their neighbours. His ruddy face is strained with the effort of supporting the man in the middle, whose head continues to hang down, bumping against his chest with every shuffling step.

Mima lifts her arms up to Edna, begging to be picked up, and Edna does so mindlessly. The child is heavy on her hip – she smells a little sour and Edna thinks, vaguely, that she'll bathe the girls and Eddie tonight. Millie is furious at the special treatment being shown to Mima and starts to cry. Her sobs almost drown out the crash that comes, all too suddenly, from upstairs. Esther has been cleaning she and Tommy's bedroom, and it sounds as though a bucket has fallen to the floor. Edna, Millie and Mima turn around to see their mother scrambling down the stairs, grabbing a frayed, thin winter coat from the hook in the hallway and dashing outside.

"Mother, I—" Edna begins, but Esther cuts her off.

"Stay here!" she shouts over her shoulder.

Mima, her head nestled on Edna's shoulder, has spotted the trio making their way towards Sunnyside Terrace. "Daddy?" she says. Her voice sounds smaller than usual, and something in her tone seems to spook Millie, who clambers silently onto a chair and stares from the window, her face just below Edna's. All chatter from the kitchen ceases and now the boys are here, too – Brinley and Robert and, in a moment, hearing the silence from all the way upstairs, Eddie.

It's Tommy. Tommy's the man in the middle, the one with the head hanging low and a face as pale as milk. Millie starts to scream, which sets Mima off, and all of a sudden Edna feels more trapped, more hopeless, than she's ever felt before.

"He's dead!" screams Mima, bellowing straight into Edna's ear. "Daddy's dead, he's died, he's dead!"

"Shush now Mima, he's not dead," says Edna, but she knows she doesn't sound very convincing. The man on the left of their father looks exhausted. His feet are slapping the ground as he heaves Tommy's weight further onto his shoulder, and he looks up with relief as Esther comes barrelling towards them, throws the woollen coat over her husband's shoulders and tries to lift his legs. Edna watches, as though in some terrible dream, as Mr Williams stops her. He's told her something, and Esther backs away, leaving their father's legs hanging uselessly. They're almost at the house now.

Brinley and Robert leave the window and go outside, down the garden steps, and march back through the corridor holding a tin sheet. When the men finally arrive outside Sunnyside, they lower it to the ground and Mr Williams helps manoeuvre Tommy onto it.

Instinctively, Edna knows she must get the girls and Eddie away now. Mima is still howling; Millie has gone uncannily quiet. She does the only thing she can think of, and takes them through to the kitchen, out the back door and through into Mrs Williams' house.

"Hello?" she calls, and Mrs Williams comes hurrying out to meet them.

"Edna love, leave the children with me – I've just seen them, your father. I'll take them."

Mima and Millie love Mrs Williams, and by the time Edna leaves them five minutes later, they are sat at the Williams' scrubbed wooden table with hot sugary tea and a plate of Welsh cakes before them.

Back through the garden, back through the door, into the house. The terrible moaning has reached a pitch she had never imagined possible, and certainly not from her father.

"Edna!" Esther cries, as Edna walks into the parlour. "Where are the young ones? Where's Eddie?"

"They're next door," says Edna, looking around for a sight of Tommy. "They're fine. Where's Father?"

Esther collapses into sobs. Edna feels, at 13, that she is suddenly being admitted into a much more adult realm that she's ever been before. "Is he dead?" she asks, and feels her own voice cracking. "Where is he? What happened?" Esther sobs harder than ever but manages to shake her head. He is not dead, then. Her father is still here, but where? "He's in the kitchen. The doctor has been sent for. There's been an accident." "The *doctor*?" Of all the information she will process today, this is the part that surprises Edna the most. They've never sent for a doctor. Mrs Williams is a dab hand at patching up cuts and scrapes, and there's a lady in town who has given them tonics before – potions and draughts she brews herself. When Eddie coughed so hard they thought he'd never breathe properly again, a week's bed rest proved the final solution, and whatever it was passed – mercifully. Mima's fall just last week required a good few bandages and a stern instruction by Mrs Williams to keep Mima awake as long as possible (why? Neither Edna nor her mother knew, but followed the instruction). Yet a doctor – a real-life medical man, one who's been to school past 14 and then more school and then training and poking around in cadavers – such a person has never set foot in this house. The idea of sending for one makes Edna's head swim, and she feels that familiar swoosh of lightheaded imbalance again. This must be bad: worse than bad. But what has happened?

* * *

The Physicians of Myddfai are well known to the Welsh – whether they ever existed or not is up for debate, but with the level of folklore surrounding them perhaps it doesn't really matter either way. Rhiwallon, a doctor working in 12th-century Carmarthenshire alongside his three sons, is credited with passing on a variety of herbal remedies, prescription advice and healing methods. Here we see the mixtures of plantain, egg whites, clarified honey and barley meal mixed together to form a plaster designed to reduce swelling; there a remedy for deafness which includes a branch of ash, a newly caught eel, black wool and stale urine. To destroy fleas, we are told, one must take a hedgehog and roast it before taking the resultant oil and applying it to the affected area. On virtually every page there are solutions to the problem of piles, clearly a preoccupation for the physicians.

From crab apples to dock root, turpentine and goat's gall, nothing was wasted when it came to potential cures for both everyday and unusual maladies. And these practices continued long into the 19th and 20th centuries: before the advent of widespread antibiotics, or painkillers, or standardised medical training.

"Something fell on him," Esther is saying. "A crate, a barrow – we don't know. His leg is mangled. They managed to get him out, but – oh, Edna – he won't survive if we don't get him some help."

Edna doesn't know what to say or what to think. Her mind has gone utterly blank, and for some reason latches on once more to the multiplication tables she was rehearsing before anyone had noticed there was something wrong. If she can just get to 17 times 12, maybe everything will be ok. Maybe her father will be able to work again tomorrow – maybe whatever happened down in that mine looked worse than it was.

"Edna," her mother says, and she falls back to Earth. "Boil some water. Take the spare sheets from the crate in my bedroom, and ask Brinley to chop extra wood. We'll need to keep the parlour warm." Esther is crying as she says this but her face is set, determined, and Edna follows her directions to the letter. As she sets the copper cauldron on the fire, there's a knock at the door. A tall, thin man with a large satchel under one arm stands in the frame, panting. He has clearly been running, and pushes past Robert in the hallway, turning just once to ask, "Where is he?"

Robert points silently to the kitchen.

Edna brings the pan slowly inside, where the doctor – greeting no one, but laying out various tools and bottles beside the basin – has instructed Brinley and Esther to move Tommy onto the pine table in the middle of the room. He moves forward and in one quick movement slices Tommy's work trousers up to his thigh, then bends over his leg. Edna places the water beside the doctor's tools and stares at the lump of flesh that was once Tommy's right leg. It looks mangled, impossibly bent. There is a long, pearly white shard of something sticking out from the middle of his calf.

"I can set it," says the doctor, turning to Esther. "It's broken. You can see where whatever it was fell on him. It's been badly splintered in two places. I need to try, first, to place this" – he indicates the white shard – "back into position. It will hurt."

All this time Edna has avoided looking at her father's face but, at the doctor's words, she steals a glance at him. He is ashen, so pale in marked contrast to the soft brown wood of the table. His eyes have rolled back into his head and he is still moaning, but more quietly now. His mouth is slack.

"I'll need help," says the doctor, rolling up his sleeves. "All of you. I will give him what I can to ease the pain, but it won't be enough. You will need to hold him down as I work on the leg."

Brinley, his face almost as pale as their father's, steps forward. He takes Tommy's good leg in both his strong hands and applies a little pressure, nodding at Robert to do the same. Edna and Esther hold Tommy's arms.

The doctor covers a small flannel with liquid from one of the bottles on the side, then places this over Tommy's nose and mouth. Tommy's eyes close, momentarily, but snap open – wide awake and blazing – when the doctor takes hold of his withered leg and begins to manipulate it. His screams fill the room: high, curdling shouts of agony. Edna cannot bear it, and covers her ears with both hands – releasing her father's arm, which begins trying to swat the doctor away. "Miss, please, hold him!" the doctor cries. The room is suddenly filled with the scent of fresh blood as the man begins to move the shattered bone back into its original wound. Tommy shudders and hollers and strains against the arms pinning him to the table.

At the doorway to the back garden, Edna spots Mima – wandering through the green lawn, staring at the house, making a beeline for them. She too is crying. "Mima, get back," Edna shouts at her sister, and is relieved when she spots Mrs Williams hurry forward, scoop the little girl up and disappear once more.

It seems to take hours, but is over in no more than 15 minutes. When the doctor pushes the second break back into position, Tommy passes out. This should make things easier – the only sounds, now, are the grunts of the medical man as he works, and the sniffles from Esther as she stares down at her husband. But somehow the relative silence and the lack of movement are worse. It's like they're manhandling a corpse, now – like they're desecrating his body.

Finally, the doctor stands back and takes one of the sheets Edna brought downstairs. He cuts careful squares from the thin, cheap cotton and begins to wrap Tommy's leg, binding it tightly over the two breaks. The first bandages are quickly soaked in blood, but the doctor continues, laying one over the other, and after what seems an age the topmost layer of the cast is clean. The blood has stopped.

"Mix some brandy, water and sugar into a glass, please," says the doctor, as he finishes. Esther hurries to the cupboard. Then the doctor pauses, staring down at his blood-smeared hands, and looks around at them all: the Hodges family standing in the weak afternoon sunlight. "In fact, make up a good few." Once Esther has mixed the drinks, the doctor raises the first glass to Tommy's lips and tips it back slowly. Tommy splutters and his eyes flutter in half-open disbelief.

"What the bloody hell have you done to me?" he growls, and the doctor takes the second glass and watches while Tommy sips it. He shudders again and lays his head back down. The doctor nods, as if satisfied, and motions to Esther. "We'll all take one of these, I think," he says, and downs his own in one.

ELEVEN
HOT WATER

There are so many what-ifs racing through Edna's mind that she finds it difficult to lay her anger, her blame, on one of them in particular. The thoughts tend to begin with the day of Tommy's accident: what if he'd been taken unwell, had a cold, and been unable to work? What if he'd been sent to a different section of the mines, a less crowded one, a better-lit pit? What if he'd worn his shorter overalls, the one without the rip in the side – would whatever had caused him to stumble and fall have been unable to sink its teeth into him?

After ruminating on these thoughts her mind switches course, takes a longer view. What if Tommy hadn't worked down the mines at all? What if he were a farmer, a labourer, a soldier, a doctor like the man who treated him, a lawyer? Well, if he wanted to be either of the last two they'd need money – lots of it. And so her thoughts grow more rapid, more angry. What if they were better off? What if she'd been born to wealthy parents, parents who could afford to hire cleaning ladies, kitchen staff, gardeners and butlers? If that were the case, there is no way she'd be sat here, now, missing school. She wouldn't be leaving Sunnyside next month to go into the employ of a couple she has never met and their two brat children.

Tommy hasn't been able to work for four months, and though Esther tries to rally the children's spirits, Edna can see through the forced jollity. Brinley and Robert are working double shifts down at the mines, trying desperately to make ends meet. Esther has taken in three times as much dressmaking work. She sits by the light of the one candle they burn in the parlour long into the night, working. There's still not enough money, and Mima, Millie, Eddie and Tom seem to require more food per meal by the day.

That isn't the worst of it. Edna shudders as she mops her father's brow, wincing at the memory. A week after Tommy's accident the doctor returned, looking grave. He greeted the little ones and then, without fuss or preamble, asked Esther to sit down. Edna, waiting in the kitchen, went unnoticed.

"Mrs Hodges," he began, "I know this is delicate. Of course, I can understand your distress. But without your husband's weekly wages I cannot be expected to work on assurances."

Edna doesn't understand what he's talking about, and continues wiping down the cutlery. She keeps polishing the same fork for what seems like hours.

"Doctor," Esther is saying, "I know this is irregular. We'll have the money owed to you within four months. No more than six. I can give you a small amount now, as we discussed, but we won't be able to pay in full for some time." Edna hears the exhaustion in her mother's voice and is sorely tempted to dash next door and plunge the fork into the doctor's arm.

"I'm so sorry, Mrs Hodges. I need the money myself, to replace the medicine I administered to your husband." He pauses. The doctor is not an unkind man. He does his best in a village where nobody has very much and he knows the shame of an unpaid bill to an upstanding, hard-working woman like Esther Hodges. So he leans forward slightly. "Is there anything of value in the house that could serve as payment in kind?" asks the doctor. "I sometimes work on that basis. Anything at all."

Esther says nothing but Edna can imagine her shaking her head, sadly. Suddenly, something occurs to Edna. She walks swiftly out of the kitchen and straight into the parlour, no longer trying to disguise the fact she's been listening to their conversation.

"We have a piano," she says breathlessly. "An old one. A good one. Take that."

He stares at her, the doctor. He looks far less pale, less hurried and harassed, than the last time she'd seen him, when he'd asked them all to hold Tommy down.

Esther gives a little cry and her hand flies to her mouth. Edna ignores her. What else are they to do?

Growing up, my mother told me of this event many times, and it never failed to make her cry. The doctor had looked across to Esther, who seemed already defeated – she knew, as well as Edna did, that there was no other way to pay. There was nothing else of even the slightest value in the house. Edna's mother nodded at the doctor, just the once, and he shook her hand slowly and sadly before leaving.

Edna's troubled mind thought about the Diploma she had acquired from the London School of Music for pianoforte when she was 13. Would she ever play again? Could she have a last tinkle on the keys? Her diploma was found in a drawer after her death, tatty but treasured − she had kept it all of her years. Would her life have been different if the piano had stayed in the hearth of her home? Maybe, maybe not, but those melodies were forever in her heart.

Two days later, there was another knock at the door. One of the boys standing outside was Mrs Williams' son, Henry. "Doctor asked us to come," he said. "We're to take it away now."

Together, the boys winched and struggled, cursed at each other and giggled as they shoved the piano from the Hodges' parlour. Mima, Millie and Eddie stood by the fireplace howling. Edna and Esther, too embarrassed to watch alongside them and too devoted to the piano to see it leave forever, locked themselves in the kitchen.

* * *

We come now to one of the most difficult chapters in my mother's life, and one which she only ever alluded to. I've put the pieces together from the few details she let slip, or confided in me. She would return to those few months many years later, as I prepared to make my entrance into the world. It helped her, I imagine, to remember the most painful thing she'd ever willed herself to do.

Following Tommy's accident the Hodges sank further into poverty. Edna, so bright and brilliant, so mathematical and musical, was sent to Cardiff, where a middle-class family — landed gentry, no less — required a scullery maid.

"Is there nothing more... local?" she'd pleaded with Esther, but the decision to send Edna was strategic on Esther's part. The younger children needed a great deal of attention, especially since the accident, and Esther was concerned that her eldest daughter was taking on too great a burden alongside her studies. "Take your books," said Esther. "Make some money, and practise your schoolwork in the evenings. You'll have bed and board there, it'll be a good opportunity for us to save, and you'll be back in no time."

She was indeed back within just a few short months. The work was long and hard — endless mopping, dusting, scouring, cooking and sweeping. She rose at 4am to empty out the bedpans, refill the coalscuttle, boil the endless pans of water required and polish the brass step. She was also tasked with taking care of Master Jack and Miss Millie, the couple's children. She enjoyed the midday walks to Sophia Gardens with the pair, who were sweet and taciturn, so quiet and polite compared to Edna's own siblings. Their accents were clipped and British-sounding — they never spoke Welsh.

Edna imagined it would be a haven, but instead the silence was oppressive. She'd never known anything like it. Sometimes, in the dead of night, she'd lie awake thinking that perhaps even the sounds of her father's screaming would be preferable to this terrible quiet. And then she hated herself for even contemplating such a hideous notion. She had a busy mind, Edna, and no amount of scrubbing or polishing seemed to calm it.

It was on one of these dark, silent nights that Edna crept downstairs, filled the large tin pan and began to boil water. All my mother ever told me about the master of the house – a man with squinting eyes and an imperious manner – was that he "wasn't very nice to her."

We can only imagine what that meant, given what she was about to do.

There she was, two o'clock in the morning, watching the bubbles rise and taking off one of her stockings. She waited and waited. Then she lifted the pan and, before she could give herself a moment to hesitate, poured half of it straight down her leg.

The pain was blinding. When Edna opened her eyes, she was lying flat on her back and the master's wife, a kind woman with concerned eyes, had placed a small bottle of something strong-smelling beneath her nose. Edna looked down and saw the blistered welt running down her lower calf.

Later that day, she was packed into the master's horse and carriage and driven back to Sunnyside, back to Esther and Tommy and her siblings and their noise. She didn't return to school, and the scars from that boiling pan – used to escape, for what else could she do? – never quite faded, right through into her old age.

* * *

It was hard at home, with so many mouths to feed and so little money. Brinley and Robert continued to go down to the pits, and Esther watched – each evening from 4pm – as the men emerged from the shafts across the field. After a year, Tommy returned to work.

By 1926, just weeks after my mother's 17th birthday, the country is thrown into panic on a chilly January evening. Families huddled around the wireless were growing increasingly disturbed by the reports being broadcast from the BBC. According to the newscasts, the National Gallery had been razed to the ground, Big Ben had fallen 320ft to the horrified crowds below, trench mortars were firing at the Houses of Parliament and the Savoy Hotel – that bastion of Britishness – had been completely blown to pieces. People emerged terrified from their houses, gathering their children and preparing to flee the city.

It was barely a decade since the Great Terror in Russia, the revolution that had seen the capture, imprisonment and eventual execution of that country's monarch and his family, along with over nine million citizens. Tensions were running high across Europe, and it seemed as though the culprits in this case – unemployed, dissatisfied workers – were fast gaining the upper hand over authorities. When it was announced that a minister of traffic, Mr Wurtherspoon, was caught while attempting to escape in disguise and subsequently hanged from a lamppost in Vauxhall, panic reached its fever pitch. The BBC were forced to intervene. The news bulletin, it transpired, was a hoax: part of a comic skit written by a Catholic priest called Father Ronald Knox, a segment from a piece called "Broadcasting the Barricades" which focused on a completely fictional "red riot":

"Some listeners, who heard only part of Rev. Father Knox's talk at 7:40 this evening, did not realise the humorous innuendoes underlying his imaginary news items, and have unease as to the fate of London, Big Ben and other places and objects mentioned in the talk.

As a matter of fact, the preliminary announcement stated that the talk was a skit on broadcasting, and the whole talk was, of course, a burlesque, and we hope that any listeners who did not realise it will accept our sincere apologies for any uneasiness caused. London is safe. Big Ben is still chiming, and all is well."

It took several hours, in some cases days, for the furore to die down. Bad weather across the country delayed the delivery of the next day's newspapers, meaning many people who'd heard the original broadcast found themselves in the dark as to its true nature.

It was a momentary flare-up, a storm in a teacup, but Knox's satirical jab had come, as all good state-of-the-nation comedy must do, from a very real, very tense atmosphere experienced high and low along the length of the country. 1926, as they were all to discover, was to be a seminal year. In April, the Duke and Duchess of York welcomed their first child, a daughter, and named her Elizabeth. Here was an infant set to grow up in the very lap of luxury, far removed from the common plights of the Crown's subjects. The divide between those who had, and those who had not, was growing ever wider, and the people had had enough.

Trouble was brewing. The miners were galvanised. Tommy's plight was just one example of the horrors the men faced each and every day when they entered the pits – it might be worth it if they were still able to feed their families. Back in Cardiff, Edna had lived on the same leafy street as the composer Ivor Novello, whose song "Keep the Home Fires Burning" had provided such solace and vitality during the war years. It all felt a long way away now, and the very men who'd kept those fires burning were at breaking point.

The General Council of the Trade Unions Congress called a general strike on 3 May 1926. Tommy, Brinley and Robert had heard whispers of the approaching action for months beforehand, and were determined to take a stand. After the Dawes Plan of 1924, which saw the reintroduction of German mining and a system of "free coal" sent to Italy and France – as reparations for the war – coal prices had fallen, but mine-owners were hell-bent on maintaining a profit that couldn't be achieved. The seams had been heavily depleted since the end of the war. Men were required to work longer hours, and wages had fallen from £6 to just £3.90 over the past seven years. And it wasn't just the miners: all over the country, workers from all industries joined in protest. From railway and dock workers in London to electrical engineers, printing presses and ironworks in Inverness, industries stood beside the miners. On 4 May, almost two million people were out protesting on the streets. Prime Minister Stanley Baldwin saw the strike as "a challenge to Parliament," claiming it as a "road to anarchy and ruin." King George V, however, seemed sympathetic: "Try living on their wages before you judge them."

I feel so proud of them today, thinking of my own dedication to and gratitude for UNISON and Unite who continue, now, to provide essential support for NHS workers. It was Martin Luther King Jnr who stated, so truthfully, that "Our lives begin to end the day we become silent about the things that matter."

The Hodges marched through the streets with the rest. They campaigned outside the pits and in the streets, banging tin cups together, beating drums. Their constant refrain was simple: "Not a penny off the pay, not a minute on the day." Enough was enough.

One of the most challenging aspects of the strike was the division created between families who had helped and cared for one another for generations. Mr Williams, the next-door neighbour who'd worked so hard to get Tommy out of that pit, ranted and railed at the Hodges. "It's no use, Tom!" he bellowed, after Tommy had asked him to leave. They'd been quarrelling about the strike for hours. "They'll not change now, and all you're doing by carrying on with this is denying the rest of us the chance to make a living. I'd have thought, with all these children—" He stopped and huffed off home after catching the look on Tommy's face from the parlour window. The Williams and the Hodges stopped speaking.

The eight-day strike – which ended without restitution for the miners, after secret talks between unions and mine owners – had a lasting impact on the history of my family. The miners had mostly all returned to work by November, without an increase in pay and with an extra hour added to the working day. Though miners were expected to return without incident, many owners – the heads of busy, over-populated pits – refused re-entry to some of the most ardent strikers.

In the past six months, Edna has never seen so many homeless families on the streets of Swansea. When she accompanies Esther into the city once a month, to deliver the dresses and make job enquiries, she can barely cross the road without seeing a family huddled under a doorway, a pair of freezing children perched on the steps of a townhouse by the seafront, a group of women fighting over the last ream of reduced-price material in the sewing shop. Soup kitchens have been set up by local women, and men – those who haven't already been arrested, imprisoned or fined – dart out at night to steal coal off the tips. It will have enormous consequences for the people of South Wales: by 1927, when the trade unions get involved, many have already left their homes and settled elsewhere.

Edna scours the local newspapers each week, when she can find crumpled copies on the back pews at church. There is nothing to be found, nothing worth pursuing – short-term cleaning duties bridge the gap for a little while before she's unemployed once more. Esther is growing impatient, though she doesn't mean to be. It's easier for Brinley and Thomas – and Eddie, once he's old enough – to find permanent work in the pits, even if it's the very work they've campaigned so hard to change for the better.

Just like her grandfather all those years ago, setting off for Wales with her great uncles, Edna comes to a decision. She will leave Glamorgan, leave her beloved homeland altogether, and go to the only place she knows work is virtually guaranteed. She will go, as so many have done before and since, to London.

* * *

On the morning of her departure, she crouches down to say goodbye to her sisters, to Eddie, Brinley and Robert, and lastly to Tommy and Esther. In her hands she holds a small cloth bag containing three changes of clothes, sandwiches prepared by her mother, and a week's worth of Tommy's wages. "Here you are, pet," he said last night, pressing the money into her hands. It was a lot, too much, and she considered giving it back – leaving it in the kitchen cupboard, or giving it to Esther in secret – but then the thought of the journey she is about to undertake flits across her mind, and she holds the tattered envelope inside her pocket as she walks towards the train station. Goodbye old life, she thinks, and hello world. Whatever she's headed towards, it has to be better than what she has left behind.

Some 30 miles northwest, not far from the Brecon Beacons in Cefneithin, Carmarthenshire, Willie Rees − now 21 − is also preparing to leave Wales, perhaps for good. Along with 12 fellow miners, he has decided to test his fortune elsewhere, too. He'll do anything, he thinks, anything at all to avoid going back down into those pits. His mother, Mary, has been dead for almost 20 years, and his father's second marriage has brought him much sadness. His half-sisters, Rowena and Bessie, are adored by Philip. His stepmother brought her own children into the marriage, and along with Philip and Mary's kids, the house is permanently crowded, too filled with conflicting loyalties and fights and his father's hideous, hacking cough.

So, just as Edna May Hodges steps onto the train at Swansea and begins the journey east, surveying a list of employers forwarded by a cousin, Willie and his friends begin the week-long walk into England. They sleep under the stars, in deserted farmyards, in bushes when it rains. It's balmy and warm, and many labourers they meet along the way become allies, taking them in for the night, listening to their stories of the dirt and soot and the fact they've escaped. "What will you do next?" asks one man, in the North Wessex Downs. He's a sheep farmer, and the men sleep coddled in thick woollen blankets softer than anything they've ever known.

Willie shrugs, smiling with his young, optimistic confidence. "Anything. We'll do anything."

It's a funny thing, fate. The strike, which caused so much hardship and conflict, was about to unite my parents. They were barely adults, these two, travelling in tandem to a new place, but they could have no idea just what their meeting would mean, and just how significantly their lives would soon be altered.

TWELVE
FINDING A WAY

Willie has never felt so exhausted in all his life, and that's saying something. It feels as if they've been walking for years. His feet are blistered and raw where the walking boots Philip gave him – his own, and a size too small – have cut into his heels and toes. It doesn't help that they spent quite so much time in the public house last night, either. He wishes he'd turned in a little earlier, but even as he thinks this – with the sun beating down on his head – he can't help but laugh to himself. Turn in where? They slept in the old horses' stables behind the pub, after closing time, and only started so early this morning because the landlord's wife, a woman Willie last saw at 3.30am singing "Tipperary" on the long bar, came stomping outside to see why the stable door had been left open. They'd left in a bit of a hurry.

They're feeling grumpy today, the 12 men walking. Willie considers taking his boots off, but the ground is so jagged and covered in stones he thinks he'd just make matters worse. He can't afford to get an infection, not when he'll soon be looking for work in London.

While he's considering this, Edna May is glancing from side to side at Euston Station, anticipating pickpockets, murderers and conmen watching her. The thick, cloying air sticks in her lungs – she needs to get out of here. As she spots her cousin in the crowded throng of commuters and people waiting to greet their friends, she feels a little safer.

When Willie and his friends arrive just outside Basingstoke, they manage to book two cheap rooms at a small lodging with a decrepit-looking "Rooms Available" sign hanging in the front window. It's here, over a dinner of eel pie and mashed potato, that their host overhears them discussing their plans for London. "I wouldn't go to the city, boys," he says jovially, pushing his chair back from the table and lighting a cigarette. "It's been terrible since the strike. Shops cleared out, dock workers on leave. It's not a pretty place to be right now."

"We need work," says Willie shortly. "There'll be something we can do." "Miners, were you?" says the landlord. He looks at them shrewdly. "Good on ya. I thought it was a travesty myself, what they done to you. An outrage." The men murmur in response, looking down at their plates. There's still an odd sense of shame about what's happened recently. It's a strange balancing act of pride and guilt they're all walking, right now. On the one hand they know they were right to demand something better, to seek change. On the other, they've walked away from family traditions, from jobs their fathers and grandfathers did before them. A large part of them feels spoilt, babyish, like they couldn't hack it and can never return to the villages and towns they've deserted. The country, they know, needs coal – and they are just a few of the hundreds who've downed their picks and shovels for the last time. No wonder London is in such a terrible state. "There are other things you could do…" says their landlord, thoughtfully.

He tells the men about Park Prewett nearby. Founded in 1917, it served as a military hospital for Canadian servicemen until the end of the war, and by 1921 it had reopened its doors. Their host puffs out his chest as he tells Willie and his friends that he worked on the wards during the war.

"You didn't enlist?" asks Sam, one of the men travelling with Willie.

"Couldn't," he says simply, and points to his leg. None of them have noticed it up until now, but his right foot is bent to the right at an impossible angle. "Born with it," says the landlord. "Keeps me out of trouble, at least."

They feel a certain affinity with him, then. Here is this man who, like them, was unable to fight and probably encounters questions like Sam's every day. His reasons for staying home when the other boys went off are more obvious, though. There have been days when Willie feels so furious, so helpless in the face of his inability to go to war that it feels unbearable. It's a hard thing to comprehend now, perhaps, since the end of the second war. But during Willie and Edna's lifetimes, everybody enlisted. Everybody turned up. Unless you were a conscientious objector, a plain "coward", disabled in some way, or a miner like Willie, everybody went off to defend their country. Although

Willie's contribution to the war effort was enormous – those long days and often nights spent shovelling, hacking away at the tunnels and the earth – it doesn't feel like that to him.

The landlord seems to understand the subdued mood that comes over the men at this point in the conversation.

"Look, lads," he says, leaning forward again. "It doesn't much matter what you've done before – it's about what you'll do now. And mark my words, the capital isn't the best place for quick work. You'd think so, but I've seen more groups of boys just like yourselves leave as quick as they came. There's no guarantee."

"So what do we do, exactly?" says Sam. His face is growing dangerously red. Sam's father was crippled shortly before the strike, and has been bed-bound since. The family have had to move to smaller lodgings outside the village. There are rumours, though Willie doesn't believe them – doesn't want to – that the evenings Sam's wife spends down in Swansea are less innocent than she, and Sam, are making out. How else are they bringing in what little money they have?

The landlord keeps talking. He mentions the farms dotted around the Downs, the country families here who lost sons and brothers, uncles and cousins. "There's a lot of land going untended," he says. "This is where the real money is, the fields. Take a look around you tomorrow. It's everywhere. You can find something short-term here, something seasonal."

The men nod and grunt and some look relieved at this news. But Willie's attention is caught more by Park Prewett. A hospital isn't seasonal, there'll never be a time when people don't need help. He's used to shift work, too. It might suit him. He has no training, and he knows the chances of progressing beyond a cleaning or caretaking role would be minimal. But he likes the thought of a job where he's interacting, not bowing over a hedgerow or scooping to gather crops, wielding great instruments such as he's already wielded down in the pits. It feels too similar, the idea of farming, to what he's done before – even though it'd mean being outside every day, come rain or shine.

Over in southeast London, Edna has spent the past four days applying for the roles her cousin suggested. She's surprised to find she's not getting anywhere. Mostly her prospective employers are simply not responding to her carefully worded letters. She drops them through letterboxes, sticks stamps she cannot afford onto thick cream envelopes. But on the third day a letter arrives and she hastily arranges an outfit mostly filched from her cousin's closet.

"Wrap this around the collar," says Susan, tossing a thin kerchief over to Edna, "It'll smarten it up, the whole look."

A couple requiring a maid sit opposite her in their large Clapham townhouse and ask more questions than she ever thought possible for a job so simple! She answers as fully as she can, feeling awkward about the Welsh lilt tripping over her vowels, spends over an hour with her prospective employers, leaves feeling hopeful, and never hears from them again.

After two weeks, she takes her cousin's advice and starts searching through leaflets. There are vacancies, plenty of them, but none in London – or at least, none that she could get to easily from Lewisham. And then, on a rainy Friday afternoon, on the very last page of the pamphlet she's been flicking through, its advertisements a little thin on the ground, she spots something. Park Prewett, Basingstoke. She grabs her cousin's map and flicks through until she finds the city. It isn't far, nestled beneath the Downs, and feels a little nearer to home: closer to Tommy and Esther and Millie and Mima. She's been shocked to discover just how much she misses the girls, especially when they give her such grief and need so much care and attention. But then, she thinks, hasn't her role in the Hodges family equipped her quite perfectly for a job looking after the sick? Would she not be quite qualified for work just like this?

In June 1926, my parents arrived at Park Prewett. Willie on 6 June, and Edna – a little later because they'd had to save for a train fare – on 18 June. Two days later, they met.

* * *

Park Prewett was a psychiatric hospital. It housed over 800 patients, and both Willie and Edna were employed as nurses, receiving training on the job. The state of mental-health provisions in England at this time was dire. They had been scaled right back, partly due to a perceived decrease in demand. After 1918 many mentally unwell patients had been displaced to make room for the casualties of war. Some had chronic psychiatric problems, others were simply old, or suffered from long-term illnesses that were little understood.

There were several other well-known psychiatric wards at that time, and most carried grim reputations. Colney Hatch in north London boasted the longest corridor in the country; it housed over 2,500 patients at its height, and the wards took two hours to navigate. In 1903, a fire broke out at one of the hospital's makeshift buildings and took the lives of 52 female patients. So-called lunatic asylums had only existed since the mid-19th century, and before then those with mental-health problems were often to be found under the Poor Law's workhouse system or in prisons. Conditions were dire, with common treatments – leftover from the 1800s – that included carefully controlled and frequent baths, straitjackets, isolation in padded cells and, later, psychosurgery, more commonly known as lobotomy. Years later, through my own work, I'd encounter the horrors of the "spinning chair", a rotational device used to release madness from patients.

Neither of my parents had been made aware of the true nature of the work advertised until they arrived. Edna's cousin had never heard of the place, and Willie's landlord – perhaps spotting the glint of interest in his eyes and not wanting to put him off – had failed to mention it was a psychiatric facility. But neither of my parents were perturbed by the very different set of skills required to work in such a hospital. They had both seen their fair share of broken minds – people forced to the point of mental collapse by circumstance, poverty, or a mixture of both and many other things besides. The work itself required a level of respect and dignity for those whom society infrequently observed – and then only with pity or repugnance.

Willie worked on the male ward and Edna on the female, though these two sections – or at least the staff in charge of them – had frequent opportunities for interaction. The medicine cupboards were placed under strict lock and key on the corridor linking the two wings. For the first week, although they nodded and smiled at one another, both were too busy to take much notice. "Hodges!" came the bark of the ward sister, when she spotted Edna chatting or staring out of the window. It was a strange new life, this. There were medicines to administer – antipsychotics, heavy, dulling opioids for the most disturbed, and gentle relaxants for those who needed less help.

Edna quickly realises the enormous spectrum of possibility for error that exists in the human brain. The vast potential for things to go wrong, or shatter completely. She'd never heard of depression before arriving at Park Prewett, but it's astonishing how many of her patients suffer from it. The worst can barely lift their heads to greet her in the mornings, and have had their shoelaces and ties, their scarves and sharp things, pencils and scissors removed in case they attempt to hurt themselves. Then there are schizophrenic patients, who grab Edna's hands and implore her to listen for the shouts, cries and whispers they hear. There are plenty of "hysterics", too, especially on the female ward. Edna sympathises most with these women, who are often sedated but who cry and shudder with sobs in the longer gaps between doses. She chats to them and they are always the most lucid of her patients. "I'd just had enough, I'd had it up to here," says one, looking sadly at her hands.

At lunchtimes and before dinner the patients, male and female, take exercise in the courtyard outside. They can see but not touch one another, separated by a chain-link fence and uniformed guards. Sometimes they shout jokes across. "Why are young ladies like arrows?"

There's muffled laughter, suggestions thrown across the fence, some lewd. "Because," says the comedian, "they're all aquiver when they spot their beau!"

Edna and Willie have both noticed how often they smile at one another. True, Edna smiles at everyone, but Willie is shier. And yet she notices that he doesn't flash the same small grin at the others, that he reserves that slight toss of dark hair and, once, a wink, for her. At first, she doesn't know what to make of his obvious interest. And then, at night when the screams and calls of the women tend to worsen, she remembers home. She thinks of her time in Cardiff, and of her father's accident, and for once she decides to pursue happiness. She's spent so long expecting it to be denied her. Why not switch things up a bit?

When Willie asks her to one of the dances held for staff at the hospital, her first instinct is to laugh. "What's so funny?" he mutters, looking hurt. This makes her laugh even more. She simply can't believe her luck – it's too perfect. She agrees on the spot, chuckling to herself as she walks away. Edna's never kissed anyone before. She wonders, all the way through the dance, how it'll be – whether it'll now be his turn to laugh at her. "Do you like it here?" she asks him, as they walk back to their living quarters, arm in arm. It was hot inside the ballroom, but now that they're outside and the nights are drawing in, they're both shivering.

"I didn't think I would," he twinkles down at her. She's so much shorter than he is, he almost has to stoop. "But it's been better than I thought. Beats home, anyway."

"You're from Wales too, aren't you?" Of course she can hear it in his voice, but there's also something about the way he moves, a loping gracefulness, that reminds her of the young men she'd see heading off to the pits in the morning. He nods. They've reached Edna's dorms, and a gust of wind buffets them against the door. "Well then, Edna May," he says shyly, "Goodnight to you." "Goodnight, Willie Rees," she says. And then she surprises herself by standing up on her tiptoes and kissing him. "Sleep well," she whispers, and then she's gone.

* * *

Telegrams never bring good news, especially when they cost so much to send. Nobody is going to write to Edna to ask her how her breakfast was, wish her a good day or enquire about the weather in Basingstoke.

She writes to the girls and her parents and receives slow, laboured responses on what little paper they've been able to purchase. When she begins her morning shift, hurrying from

the nurses' quarters at the hospital, past the red-brick buildings and the clock tower, and arriving breathless on the main
corridor, a member of staff calls over to her. "Go to the office,
please, Sister Hodges. There's a telegram for you."

They never bring good news, and this one is no exception.
Come home immediately, it reads. *Mother is dying.* Edna stares
down at the leaf of paper in her hands, swaying slightly on
the spot. It takes a few seconds for the words to rearrange
themselves in her mind, so that she understands them, and
yet she still doesn't truly feel their impact. She simply frowns,
walks slowly to the auxiliary nurse and shows her the telegram.

"Oh, Edna," says the nurse, sighing. "You must go. We'll
give you this week's wages in advance for the journey."

Edna nods, and within an hour she's changed into the
dress she arrived in, clutching a brown bag to her chest as she
walks down the drive towards the bus stop.

Time is of the essence. She finds Willie in the yard,
supervising patients as they walk the perimeter, taking fresh
air. That first dance, just a fortnight ago at the ballroom
adjoining the hospital, suddenly feels like a lifetime ago.
How handsome he'd looked then, with his Anthony Eden
hat and bright dickie strung carelessly about his neck. They'd
moved from a fast-paced, breathless Charleston to *Moonlight
and Roses*. Neither could quite believe their luck. And now
Edna is leaving. The telegram offers no other information, no
indication of time, of how Dad and the boys are coping, of
how Mima and Millie are taking the news. For all she knows,

Edna might never return to Basingstoke. As soon as he sees her face, Willie reaches for her shoulders and draws her close. She says nothing, but simply shows him the telegram, and then he holds her closer. "I'll wait for you," he says into her hair. "Just you stay strong now."

Two buses, two steam trains and a long walk later, Edna stands outside Sunnyside. She's exhausted and the air is close; her shirt sticks to her back. She takes a deep breath, climbs the stone steps and pushes open the front door. It is completely silent inside, too quiet. A different house entirely to the one she left all those months before.

"Hello?" Her voice sounds younger, tentative, unlike the soothing, authoritative tone she'd cultivated at Park Prewett. She sounds like Mima and Millie – her sisters, just 14 and 11 years old. She moves through to the parlour and there she finds Mima, asleep beside their mother. Esther is awake, but only just. She raises her arm towards Edna and the motion wakes Mima, who flings herself into Edna's arms.

"Oh, mam," says Edna, and then finds that this is all she can say.

Esther has stomach cancer, though they don't know this yet. There are no tests, no diagnostics. Since the strike, the Hodges have been harder up than ever before. Tommy, Bryn and Robert do their best, but their wages are barely enough to cover the weekly essentials. There is no money for a doctor and nothing, now, to sell. The girls and Eddie watch over their mother during the daytime, trying to ease her pain by massaging her legs, her arms, bathing her temples in cool water. But Esther's pain is constant. Her cheeks are indistinguishable from the starched white pillowcase supporting her head. She looks utterly wasted. She cannot eat and even water seems to cause her pain, when they can get her to drink it. Mima, too, has lost a great deal of weight. Her eyes look sunken, blank and staring.

The boys and Tommy do not seem surprised to find Edna there, at Sunnyside, when they return that night. They knew she would return. There's no time or energy for welcoming, no time for questions about her new life. Esther slips in and out of consciousness as Tommy wrings his hands. That night, he walks across to Cymmer and makes enquiries about pain relief – he goes to the little pharmacist's office and attempts to barter. He goes to the church, where an evensong is taking place. Nobody can help, not without substantial money that Tommy doesn't have. His leg aches as he crosses the fields back to Sunnyside and he curses the sale of the piano. His leg would surely have survived the accident. Why did they sell it then? Why is there nothing anybody can do to help them?

After a week, Esther turns delirious with the pain. In her lucid moments she calls the children to her, one by one, and asks that the parlour door be closed. She begins with Edna. "Be good, sweet girl," she says, "And let who will be clever." Edna blinks down at her, holding her withered hands. So cold they are, like the twigs they snap down from the trees in the early mornings, to burn through the day. Edna squeezes

Esther's fingers and whispers to her, stroking the hair off her mother's forehead. We will leave them to their last private conversation.

* * *

That Sunday evening, Esther lets out a long sigh. "I am crossing over the banks of the River Jordan," she says, slowly, and closes her eyes. Eddie, sitting closest to her, leans across her chest and tries to push them open, crying for Esther to wake up. Edna pulls him back, gently. Tommy, kneeling by the bed, puts his head on his arms. "I love you," he says, "I always have, I always will. I'll take care of the children." Edna's mother lets out a long breath and grows still. It's over.

For three days, Esther lies in the parlour inside the thin wooden coffin provided by the church. Eddie and Millie, too young to understand, are bewildered by this. They continue to dart inside the room when they think Edna isn't looking, to speak to their mother, tell her about their days or show them a picture they've drawn. Edna has explained the situation to them, but Eddie in particular seems to have closed in on himself, resisting the truth as a means of self-protection. Mima has managed, however, to marshal the two younger children in Edna's absence, creating a game of sorts to make the endless chores a little more palatable. She has drawn pictures of two highly coveted toys and pinned them to the kitchen wall, scratching little tallies into the paint whenever the younger ones bring water from the well, gather firewood or prepare the morning porridge without incident. When they've accumulated a certain number of strikes, Mima has promised them a trip into town to purchase the toys. Secretly, she frets each evening about how she'll keep this promise. She tries to avert her eyes whenever she passes the parlour.

For Edna, the loss is unimaginable. She cannot quite understand the events that have led to this moment, and though she presses Bryn and Robert, they too seem unable to comprehend it. Esther had complained of stomach pains on and off for years, but only very occasionally. She'd never let on how bad they had become recently. Then she stopped eating, and within the week it had become apparent that she was dying. It is grotesque, to Edna, that somebody with so much vitality, so much love and energy dedicated to this house and its inhabitants, should wither and disappear so suddenly.

She tries not to think about Willie Rees too much. It's not just him she misses, but the whole life she had created outside these four, sad walls. On the fourth day after Esther's death, the boys bend to lift the coffin onto their shoulders alongside Tommy, and the Hodges walk up the hill towards the little church overlooking Afan Valley. Here, they say goodbye to Esther for the last time, and trudge back down to Sunnyside one member short − the most important, most sparkling of their number extinguished forever.

Edna tries to adapt. She has heard from a cousin that Willie has started taking another girl to the Park Prewett ballroom dances. She tries to ignore the well of sadness opening like a chasm inside her chest, and is distracted by the constant cleaning, tidying, washing and baking required to keep her father and siblings afloat in this dark sea. The seasons change and their first Christmas without Esther comes and goes in virtual silence. And then, on her birthday, a letter.

To Edna, it reads, *Love will find a way.*

THIRTEEN
THE BIG SMOKE

Years later, long after I'd grown up and thought I'd heard all my mother's stories, she confided this last one. I knew she'd left Wales when Willie came for her, knew they'd married in London and started their small family in the capital. What I didn't know, and what she suppressed for many years, was the nature of that departure.

Everything Edna May Hodges had experienced, up to this point in her life, had been decided for her. Her schooling, her responsibility towards the younger children, the move to Cardiff, Tommy's accident, and her work in Basingstoke. By the age of 18 she'd never been able, never been permitted to choose anything for herself. Options were for the wealthy, after all.

Willie Rees, grandson of the midwife Hannah and son of Mary, was no stranger to hardship. He knew how quickly fate could turn its back on a family, how swiftly all semblance of normality could be extinguished. He wrote to Edna, asking her to meet him at Swansea Station in a fortnight's time, when he had some leave from Park Prewett. He didn't much want to return to Carmarthenshire, to his father and stepmother and the half-siblings they favoured, so it was to be a brief visit, and more importantly he wanted to see Edna.

Willie couldn't remember his own mother – he was too young when she died – but he knew what it felt like to have the rug pulled so spectacularly from under your feet. He remembered the long years following Mary's death, his father's dejection, the dark, still atmosphere that coursed through their small house like poison.

When Edna travels to meet Willie from the train station, they've not seen each other for a full year. Yet nothing seems to have changed between them.

"Hiya, kid," he says, grinning down at her. My father is 6ft 1, towering above Edna, who at 4ft 9 fits neatly into the crook of his arm. She cannot believe how much has changed since she last saw this man. Willie notices the depth of the bags under her eyes. Their sparkle seems to have been extinguished. They sit over steaming cups of tea in the station café, and later take a room at the Mackworth Hotel. "You can't keep this up," says Willie, as he closes the door. She knows what he means. She is so excited to see Willie, but can see he's noticed her exhaustion, how quickly she runs out of steam when they're talking. "It's not up to you to fix this, Edna," he says. He helps her with her coat and they perch on the edge of the bed, not looking at each other. "My sisters raised me, after Ma died," says Willie. He's become very interested in his shoelaces, Edna notices. "Of course, I'm grateful to them.

Wouldn't be here without them. But it took its toll, Edna. They were mothers to me long before they ought to have been. And it drained them of all their energy before they'd had a chance to live their own lives."

Edna rubs her arms. It's cold in here, all of a sudden. She thinks back to yesterday morning. Since their mother's death, Mima, Millie and Eddie seem to have reverted to their old ways – it's as though Edna's return has granted them permission to become children once more. Mima mopes in their bedroom for hours on end, refusing to help with the most basic of chores. Millie and Eddie, starved of stimulation and testing out the limits of Edna's patience, fight almost constantly. Eddie came snivelling to her yesterday with a black eye, a cut lip and his shirt torn – his last shirt. Edna stitched it up, all the while trying to bathe Eddie's eye in salt water, only for another fight (this one definitely started by Eddie) to break out and cause the material to rip wide open once more. Millie refuses to eat at the moment, telling Edna she's not hungry, and then saunters down the road to the Bakers' cottage, where she devours bread and jam. Mrs Baker has taken to giving Edna reproachful looks, as though she's somehow neglecting the children. And every night, without fail, Eddie wakes the whole house when he wets the bed. Bryn and Robert deposit their brother sleepily in the bed Edna still shares with the girls. They have to be up in three hours, they mutter. You take him, Edna.

"If you carry on like this," Willie is saying, "you'll get sick yourself. There'll be nothing anyone can do. Can't you see,

Edna? This is the cycle we're in. Work, work, work, get ill, die. But you can break it, my love."

Edna stares at him. "How'd you mean?" she asks slowly.

"Come away with me," he says. "I'm leaving Park Prewett. There's more work opening up in London now. Better pay, and it'll be fun. Things are changing. Come with me."

"And leave the children? My father can't cope with them on his own. They won't manage."

"Edna, when you came back from Basingstoke, they were managing just fine, weren't they? The girls were tending to your mother. Your father and brothers were working. It was hard, but they were doing it. They were all mucking in. But now it's fallen to you. It'll kill you, Edna. Think of both our mothers. Dead at 33, mine was. Yours at 44. You need to get out while you still can."

It's a horrific thought, all the more so for how utterly captivating it sounds to Edna. Leave Sunnyside, with its stale air and weeping, with its memories of Esther and the piano and Tommy's accident and the children tumbling over one another. As she turns to look at Willie, she knows – from the feeling in her chest – that he is right, but she also hates him for drawing her attention to such an inescapable fact. If she stays put, and takes Esther's place, she will die just as young and wracked with pain as her mother. The two seem so connected in her mind. The responsibility of these children, this household, it needn't be hers. She could leave with Willie, make some money, send it back. She could attempt to make things better for them all. It would hurt in the short term, of course it would. But she doesn't see what else she can do, without sacrificing herself to an already sinking ship.

And so they leave. It's 1928. Just a few months ago, they both listened in horror to stories of the Thames' flooding. Over Christmas, snow fell heavily through the Cotswolds, at the river's source, and its thawing over the new year – coupled with high spring tides and an unusual storm surge in the North Sea – saw water levels rise to 18ft above the datum line.

All along the banks of central London there was chaos and destruction. The collapse of Chelsea Embankment saw the waters rushing into the Tate gallery, where many paintings were damaged. The down-at-heel areas surrounding Lambeth Bridge were some of the worst affected, with eight tenants drowned in their basement flats.

So Edna and Willie learn, as the villagers discuss the flooding in hushed tones, that London has the potential to be just as deadly as the place they're planning to escape. In February, just weeks after the flood, the Cumberland Coalfield suffers a devastating loss when an underground explosion kills 13 miners at Haig Pit in Whitehaven. Willie buries his face in his hands upon hearing this – there is no worse way imaginable to die. Those not immediately beside the explosion would be dreadfully aware of the consequences. The air would have crackled with trapped heat, the smoke thick and dense. While the floods in the capital are visible, loud and wild, the fatalities that happen each and every day down in those mines are quiet, barely causing a tremor on the earth above them. They're often under-reported, the lives lost a complete waste. But for both Edna and Willie Rees, the capital represents a second chance, opportunities and freedom. If he had to choose between drowning in his bed in a London basement and being blown apart in some quiet cave underground, he knows which one he'd go for.

On the morning of their departure Edna waits until Tommy, Bryn and Robert have left for the morning's shift down at the pits. She boils the pan of water, ready for the porridge oats, and lays the table for Mima, Millie and Eddie. They're all still asleep upstairs. When the porridge is cooked, she places the dishes on the table, picks up her bag from the hallway and looks around her one last time.

On her way down the street she tries not to look back, but at the end, just as she rounds the corner, she spots Millie from an upstairs window, beating a small fist on the glass. Edna tucks her head down into her scarf and walks forward with more purpose than she's ever walked before. It's now or never.

* * *

As their train pulls into Paddington Station, Edna leans closer into Willie. They've barely spoken since leaving Swansea. Something about finally departing, finally deciding, has exhausted Edna – and Willie can feel it. He, too, is glad to be leaving Wales. Such a trip would have been unthinkable for Edna's ancestors, those boys crossing the Severn all those years ago. London would never have been an option, yet now, as they trundle along past fields full of cows and sheep, it's their final destination. They could, perhaps, make a life for themselves here.

"Into the den of sin, then, kid," says Willie. "Let's see what she throws at us."

Paddington is all noise and bustle, smoke and laughter and yells across platforms. Edna doesn't know whether to giggle or cry. It's such a world away from anything she's ever seen before.

They leave the station and Willie turns to her. "First bus we see, we'll hop on, ok?"

She nods. The first bus is the number 76, going to Willesden Green. Neither of them have ever heard of the place, but it's a start, surely: they can't stay at the station forever.

The next morning, after a night at a local boarding house, they buy newspapers. They're in luck! There are positions advertised for handymen – perfect for Willie – and cleaning posts for Edna. It's a start. Later that day, they head down to a small terraced house near Gladstone Park and sign the necessary papers for a couple of attic rooms available to let. It's leafy and calm here – so unlike the London Edna had been expecting. And there's a far greater sense of community here, too. People stop and chat to one another in the streets, doff their caps and smile at you, even if they don't know you.

Willie is employed as a labourer. He's ecstatic about that, especially as the days start and finish early, and all the work is outside. He gets up and walks the few streets to the bus stop where he catches the bus to Waterloo. Willie, like hundreds of other men, young and old, is helping to build what now stands as the modern Waterloo Bridge.

Edna, for her part, arrives at the home of her prospective employer and is surprised to discover that she knows him already. It's Ian Hunter, the actor, a man whose face she's seen splashed across newspapers and over billboards. He's a kind man, enquiring about her family back in Cymmer, sitting down with her for a cup of tea before she begins her cleaning duties in the pinafore she packed into her satchel that morning. Ian makes Edna believe, for the short hours that she's with him each day, that there's no difference between them – that they have more in common than she might anticipate.

"Tell me again about Cymmer," he asks her. It turns out he holidayed in Wales as a child. He loves to hear stories of the brook at the bottom of Sunnyside, the lush fields, the lilt of her accent. Edna is both amazed and relieved to have landed on her feet quite so firmly. When Tommy writes to say that Eddie's skin condition is flaring up once more, Edna spends two days' wages on the best ointment she can find, at the fanciest pharmacy in town – the one that stocks everything from bandages and plasters to cough lozenges and camphor. She's never seen so many different remedies, for illnesses she's never heard of, all laid out before her. She tries not to think about how a shop like this might have helped Esther, in her final days – but then, what would be the use if they couldn't have afforded anything inside?

One morning, turning sleepily towards her as the sun filters in through the tatty old curtains, Willie takes Edna's hand. "Fancy getting married today, kid?" he asks. Edna stares at him. They've been living in their attic rooms for some months, no questions asked or eyebrows raised. There's no necessity for them to get married but, as she looks up into Willie's face, Edna realises she knows what she wants, very strongly, for the first time.

"We haven't any money, Will..." she begins.

"We've enough," he says. "We'll go down to the register office. Come on now." He stands and pulls on his work trousers. "I'll have a shave, you run a comb through your hair, and we'll be off, Mrs Rees."

They marry two days before the Wall Street crash, as the newspapers carry terrible stories of stockbrokers jumping to their deaths from New York high-rises. The world keeps turning and none of it is good, but for a while, at least, the newly formed Rees family shut themselves off from it.

FOURTEEN
DECISIONS, DECISIONS

From X-rays to Teflon, microwaves and the Slinky, many useful and not-so-useful everyday items and appliances were discovered quite by accident. And by the end of the roaring twenties, the medical presses were gripped by the revolutionary news of one Alexander Fleming.

Fleming, a bacteriologist who worked in the inoculation department of St Mary's Hospital, was working on the then-deadly influenza virus when he left the lab for a two-week holiday in Scotland. On returning to examine his cultures of staphylococcus, he noticed the growth of a mould on the plates containing the colonies. There were no further growths of the bacteria anywhere near the mould, and on creating a meat broth through which he passed this same substance, found that germs were dying on coming into contact with it. It wasn't until 1942, after years of attempting to extract "pure" penicillin into its crude form, testing it on mice and subsequently adapting the dosage to meet human needs, that Anne Miller, a woman suffering from a serious infection caused by a miscarriage, was successfully treated with the drug.

Fleming, completely by chance, had found something set to save millions of lives: he'd ushered in the age of antibiotics.

I imagine, when I see Edna – cigarette in one hand, cup of tea in the other – that such news would have been bitter-sweet. The discovery of life-saving medicine could never be anything other than cause for celebration. It felt almost divine in its power, this new addition to a doctor's arsenal against otherwise deadly disease. And though Esther died of cancer, Edna did not know this yet. To her mind, the headlines and television interviews heralding the discovery of this wonder drug had come too late – they were unable to save her mother.

The seasons turn and change and one day, in early 1932, Willie finds Edna staring out of the window when he returns from work. They've both been up since 4 o'clock that morning – Edna's shirt and skirt smell of furniture polish. Mr Hunter has guests arriving for the weekend, and she spent the morning dusting every surface in his considerable house.

"What's up, kid?" he asks. His throat is stinging from the brick dust that flies into the mouths of the labourers from morning to night.

"Oh, nothing," says Edna, looking out at Gladstone Park. The plane trees on their clean, well-swept street are steadily losing their leaves. Soon it'll be winter. "I was just thinking about Mam."

Willie comes to sit beside her, taking her hand in his. He doesn't need to say anything.

It's Edna who breaks the silence, eventually.

"Will…" she begins, and he cocks his head to one side. "I'm pregnant."

She isn't sure how he'll react to this. They're bringing in money, but it's never quite enough, and surely it won't cover the endless litany of items a baby seems to require. Edna remembers how Eddie's birth meant Bryn having to go into the pits early, just to bring that little bit more cash into the household every week.

Willie grins at her. "Is that so?" he says. "How in the world did that happen?" He catches the worried look on her face and, in his characteristically laissez-faire way, tells her they'll manage. "We'll be fine, Edna." His face sets a little stubbornly. "Babies are easy, aren't they? They're only small."

He then stands up, looking a little taller than when he came back from the bridge. His clothes are tatty and filthy, his hands chalky and calloused. As he looks down at Edna it's as though, besides the money, he's actually started to realise what she is telling him. A baby, their baby. He's surprised at how happy he feels, how right this must be…

My sister Marilyn is born two days before Christmas in 1932, followed two years later by Beryl. Edna cannot believe the changes her body undergoes each time. The terrible sickness, the feeling of tightness in her ankles, the incremental ballooning of her small waist until nothing fits her any more and she can't bend down.

She is also amazed, on the night of Marilyn's birth, to find just how naturally the whole process comes to her. The complete inevitability of the desire to push, the flood of relief and the joy that courses through her as sweat pours down her face. It's entirely the opposite of what she'd expected, given all those times her mam had fallen pregnant. She doesn't know whether that's because Esther was more frail, generally, than Edna, or because here in London Edna knows things might go wrong, but they are at least surrounded by people. The possibility of help is so much more visible, behind every curtain looking onto the street.

Edna and Willie rented a larger house on Churchill Road. Sarah, known as Sally, followed Beryl. "Another bloody girl!" chuckled Willie, as she came shrieking into the world. Born at home, Edna and Willie were intensely aware of the mounting costs not only of the babies and their welfare, but the actual process of giving birth itself. With each new child came the bills: the midwife's fees, the cost of medicine for pre- and post-partum care, the fact that first Marilyn and then Beryl and now Sally all suffered badly from croup, a type of whooping cough only exacerbated by the city's harsh fumes.

Unemployment was, by this point, creeping through the country like a cancer. Coupled with the intensity of the London smog, money was tight and it felt like things were only set to become darker, less enjoyable, more difficult. On Sunday evenings, when Edna joined Willie for a drink at the local public house, she'd smear a little custard powder on her cheeks, to make herself look paler, when the money for make-up ran out.

A quarter of England's citizens had nothing to wake up for the next morning, no ringing bell or shift and no hours to clock up for a week's wages. The situation was as stagnant as it had been during the years of the strike, and showed no signs of abating. Willie continued to find odd jobs when they arose. He'd walked the length and breadth of the city searching, often posting little cards through the doors of well-heeled neighbourhoods in the hope that somebody might hire him. Over the course of the 1930s, too, refugees began to arrive in England. Landlords, seizing the opportunity to capitalise on a brewing housing crisis, began to extract more rent from families who could hardly afford the weekly groceries.

In 1937, the family of five still lived in the leafy streets of Willesden Green. Edna would thrust on her so-called "thinking cap" every few months to draw up plans for the little money coming into the house. After dropping the girls at school one morning, her eye was caught by a sign hanging in a shop window on the high street. *Mother's help needed*, it read. *Enquire within*. Within a few days, she was working for a Mr and Mrs Cohen, a kindly Jewish couple. But, as with Tory, and Hannah and Mary and all the women of their combined families before her, fate so often had its own ideas about Edna's careful scrimping and saving. Not long after she'd secured her new position, my mother felt the first tell-tale signs of something dreadfully familiar. She found the taste of her morning tea repulsive. After three pregnancies, she barely needed confirmation, and couldn't hold back the tears as she worked at the Cohens' that morning.

"Oh, Edna, I'm so sorry," said Mrs Cohen. She came towards my mother, offering her a clean handkerchief and rubbing her back. "I know the timing is awful. No one wants to bring another baby into the world right now. I'd be just as upset as you."

Edna continued to cry. She thought of the girls, of how much they needed already and how much more they would need in the future. Marilyn's shoes were already a size too small, and cut into her heels when she walked. Sally's nightdress – a hand-me-down from Beryl – trailed the floor when she walked about in it, catching dust motes from the floor and making her sneeze.

They were just about managing, the Rees family, but how would they cope with yet another child?

"There are… ways, Edna," said Mrs Cohen. She closed the door of the shop and flipped the sign in its window to *Closed*. Edna stared at her. She wasn't sure she knows what Mrs Cohen meant, but she had a suspicion.

"I know a lady who's been in the same position," said Mrs Cohen, breathlessly. She looked half frightened, half uncertain. "She couldn't afford another either. Not that she didn't want him, mind. She did. But they just couldn't cope with it. So she went to see Mrs Greenlay in Homerton. It was horrible, she said, but it did the trick."

"Who's Mrs Greenlay?" asked Edna, though she knew the answer. She'd heard whispers about the woman in the East End, the one who made unwanted babies disappear.

"She's been doing it for decades," said Mrs Cohen. "And I know a lot of folks hate it, and wish she'd stop – some have even reported her for it, but they never found anything in the flat – but you can't deny that she's helpful in a fix."

Edna returned home to Churchill Road that night, determined to come to some sort of decision. She remembered the terrible talk after Ginny, a childhood friend who'd also lived on Sunnyside when Edna was small, had deliberately thrown herself from a tree, and fractured her collarbone. How a friend of Esther's had sat above a boiling pan of steam for several hours, and how another had drunk a bottle of gin every other day for a week. This last, a tragedy, had given birth to a girl nonetheless, but one born with such terrible deformities that she lived just a week before being buried in an unmarked, unvisited grave in Cymmer.

There is no end to the ways women have historically attempted to rid themselves of a baby that cannot be born. Throughout the Victorian era and well into the 1920s, products claiming to "restore feminine regularity" lined the shelves of pharmacies – from Hardy's Woman's Friend, Lydia Pinkham's Vegetable Compound, Farrier's Catholic Pills and Dr Peter's French Renovating Pills. Many of these contained abortifacients like savin and tansy – herbs known to induce termination. Pennyroyal, however, was only effective at high enough doses to cause irreversible kidney damage.

Dr Patterson's "Famous Female Pills" claimed to contain "no irritative or dangerous drugs", and proclaimed itself as "the great remedy for irregularities of every description, from any cause whatever". Until the Abortion Act of 1967 came into effect, hospital emergency departments found themselves inundated on Fridays – payday – when pregnant women would seek out backstreet abortions. Thousands died attempting to end pregnancy themselves – some of the most commonly used methods were hot baths, falls and even bleach. Spoons, knives, Roman Catholic candles and coathooks were the preferred instruments.

Although it was demolished in the 1920s, the Foundling Hospital in London's Brunswick Square is now a museum. Unwanted children were housed at the Foundling between 1739 and 1951. They had been deserted by their mothers, often because they were illegitimate. Edna would have been aware of the place, and the possibility of carrying her child to term and then placing him or her up for adoption. Small objects were often left alongside the children – tokens and talismans that would serve as identifiers if the parents were ever able to reclaim their offspring. These ranged from coins to jewellery, slips of paper, medals, buttons, pieces of ribbon, tickets and scraps of lace. Perhaps this alternative crossed my mother's mind. I wonder what she'd have left behind.

* * *

Edna cannot quite believe she is dressing up to visit Mrs Greenlay. She has ironed her skirt and blouse suit crisply and evenly, as though arriving with respectability and cleanliness will somehow make the whole situation easier.

She's never been to Homerton, and after church the following Sunday it takes two hours and four buses to reach this run-down corner of the East End. Children in torn shirts and muddy feet sit perched on the stone steps to tiny flats; they tear through the narrow streets, skipping ropes fashioned from old bits of hemp from the docks.

By the time she reaches Tudor Road, her stockings are splashed with mud from the puddles ground deep into the roads. She has never seen so many policemen wandering about, twirling their batons, stopping to chat with women hanging out the laundry. There is so much washing strung between windows the place has a bright, colourful air despite the poverty. Men stand in clumps, smoking and chatting, it's the weekend, after all, and they shout and jeer at one another, all flat caps and fanfare. There are public houses on every corner, it seems, and though she cannot see inside them Edna knows they are full, dark silhouettes in the windows betray the cluster of many bodies, packed to the rafters like sardines.

She rings the bell to number 56, just as Mrs Cohen advised her. There is a short delay, a silence so complete Edna wonders if she's got the right address. The street is particularly narrow. From where she's standing, Edna could touch the windows on the opposite side. She thinks of Beryl and Sarah and Marilyn, her daughters, back at home with their father. They are everything to her. Their tiny hands and feet, the small snores from the bedroom when she comes to wake them in the morning. She feels a swooping sensation in her belly, anxiety, or the baby? Or both?

A woman answers the door, peering through the crack. She is older than Edna expected – in her early 70s, at least. "Mrs Cohen sent me," Edna says, looking up and down the street. The woman gives a small nod and opens the door.

* * *

"When did you last bleed?" she asks Edna, as they sit in the small sitting room. It is a perfectly ordinary house, not unlike Edna's own. The floorboards are covered in a threadbare rug, the mantlepieces are clean and covered with tiny photographs in wooden frames. There is a crucifix hanging above the fireplace. Mrs Greenlay is a no-nonsense sort of woman. Edna likes her immediately. She appreciates the quiet calm of her, the lack of judgement in her eyes.

"Around six weeks ago," says Edna. "I know it's early still, but I know."

"When you know, you know," says Mrs Greenlay, calmly. "And what has Mrs Cohen told you about the way I work?"

Edna hesitates. The answer is she doesn't have a great deal of information. This was partly deliberate. My mother would rather not be made aware of the exact details – and who can blame her?

"I've procured many miscarriages," says Mrs Greenlay. "It's certainly easier if you're not too far along. I suppose you know about the complications that can occur. It's not risk-free, this sort of thing."

Edna nods. "Neither's having them, though, is it?"

"Quite right," says Mrs Greenlay.

"How many…" Edna pauses. "I mean, if it's not offensive to ask. You said you've done this many times. How many?"

"I don't keep an exact count," says Mrs Greenlay, slowly. "Around twice a month for the past 15 years."

"Why?" Edna surprises herself with the question.

Mrs Greenlay considers this for a moment. "I'd six myself," she says eventually. "I lost four. It's a terrible thing, losing a child. My mother-in-law helped me, before my husband's death. She knew we couldn't afford any more. We never told Jim. It was either me or the babies, by the end. That's what the midwife said, anyway." She pauses. "In the end, I chose myself."

Edna nods. It feels wild, almost blasphemous somehow, to hear such talk. But she understands it. She wants to live for her girls, for Willie, for herself.

"How can it be done?" she asks. This is what she's been dreading… The long needles, the prodding, the blood.

Mrs Greenlay's eyes flick to Edna's belly. "You're early enough that we can give you something to drink. There'll be pain, but not much. And then it will pass. Just like a monthly. You'll need to rest for about a week afterwards."

Edna thinks of the walk to school, the washing and cleaning. The tasks she cannot neglect, the endless rounds of caring, darning, mending. She thinks of Mr and Mrs Cohen, briefly, wasn't it Mrs Cohen who suggested this in the first place? A week's missed wages will be nothing to the money they'd lose if Edna sees the pregnancy through. Surely it's better this way.

"Mrs Hodges," says Mrs Greenlay, more gently now. "I would like you to go away and think this through. We have some time before more invasive measures would be your only option. You are not far along. You can take your time. Speak to your husband about it."

"To Willie?" Edna's head swims at the thought. "He doesn't even know I'm here. He'd be devastated."

Mrs Greenlay sighs. She has heard many women say the same thing. It never fails to make her feel tired, to wish there was some way to eradicate the fears these women so often feel. They gradually realise that though it takes two to tango, only one person will go through the ordeal of carrying, bearing and – let's face it – raising these children. The majority of the women who come to see her are not about to become mothers for the first time: they're usually on their fourth, fifth or sixth pregnancy, and they know they cannot bring another child into the world. There's no money, no time.

Now she leans in closer to Edna, her elbows planted squarely on her knees.

"It's not Willie's body that will go through the ordeal – whatever you choose. It isn't Willie who will either take the medicine I am offering you, or else give birth to a fourth child. You must try and explain this to him. But unless he's a violent man – unless you need help – I would recommend talking it through with him."

"I'll try," says Edna. She picks up her handbag, smooths a crease on her skirt and attempts a smile at Mrs Greenlay. "Thank you."

Outside the sun is setting and the streets have turned moody, gloomy. Edna buttons her coat and steps out into the road, feeling dizzy. Mrs Greenlay is a good woman, she knows this. A kind woman, determined to do what she can to help. She's reassured to know that people like her exist, that there are options, choices to be made. She's glad, too, that she knows her body well enough to have spotted the signs of this pregnancy early, and that any procedure designed to stop this needn't be as invasive as she was expecting.

On the long journey back to Willesden, she tries to put the thought – the decision – from her mind. She wonders what she can make the girls for their tea. It's a soothing thought, a normal thought.

* * *

"Edna, it's impossible," says Mima, her mouth full of toast. Her tiny son toddles around the chair legs, grasping at his mother's legs through her skirt. Mima and Millie arrived in the city after Beryl's birth, one suitcase between them. Since then they've grown and married and had children of their own. Edna can scarcely believe it, when she sees them lifting the children into prams, tucking bibs into the collars of tiny shirts. Her sisters, all grown up. Mima, this morning, is in full flow, a cigarette dangling from her lips.

"You can't do it," she's saying. "It's too much. That woman was right."

Edna has told them both about Mrs Greenlay, but hasn't felt able to broach the subject with Willie. Not yet.

Millie sighs and frowns, looking at Edna and Mima. Millie's first pregnancy was an ordeal, and Edna has always wondered if her little sister decided, there and then, not to have any more. Anita is almost five now, after all, and Millie shows no sign of considering a sibling for her.

She's a sweet but naughty child, and needs a lot of attention. A crash from the girls' bedroom upstairs at Churchill Street announces she needs just such attention at this moment, and Millie bustles off. Edna wonders whether she has ever visited a Mrs Greenlay, whether she has lain awake at night wondering what to do.

Mima spears another piece of bread on the fork and holds it over the fire's flames – the woman's appetite knows no bounds. She works at the candle factory in Battersea, telling her sisters it's nice and close to the train lines at Clapham Junction. "So?" says Millie. "Where you planning on going, then?" And Mima produces a good-sized loaf from her pocket, grinning. "I'm not going anywhere, but the bread train is. It pulls in each morning at half six for the local caffs. They're so clumsy, the boys unloading – there's always bread there for the grabbing."

The room is momentarily quiet, just the sound of the tap dripping in the corner breaking the silence. "You know it'd be too much, Ed," Mima says again. She looks sad.

Edna stares back at her, her hands on her belly. It's been 10 days since she went to Homerton, and still she feels as adrift as she did then.

"A part of me knows it'll be too much," Edna says slowly. "But then, I always wanted a big family. I always wanted lots of children. It's just the risks of having more. The sickness, the fact we're barely managing as it is. The cost. And it feels terrible to admit that, to say it out loud."

Mima nods. "When Anita was ill…" she begins. Millie's daughter spent much of the previous six months wracked with fever, on and off, her body convulsing with terrible hacking coughs. Millie was beside herself. The doctor's fees were so enormous by the end of her illness that she and her husband had been forced to wait in line for food at the Salvation Army canteens for a month afterwards. Every pint of milk, or scrap of bread, went straight to their daughter. Millie is still attempting to gain weight – in typical fashion, she never told Edna or Mima about their troubles. They assumed she'd been busy taking care of Anita. They never knew just how bad it had been until the bill was paid off and it was over. Sometimes London has this effect. It would never happen in Glamorgan, this ability to disappear and lie low.

Mima continues. "You are so lucky, you have three healthy girls, a decent wage coming in. Willie is doing well. You have enough space here and enough food. A fourth child could throw all of that out the window, you know that."

Edna knows it and yet, a week later, it doesn't seem to matter. She feels powerless to resist the lure of this tiny thing inside her, still no bigger than an apricot.

"I went to see someone," she tells Willie, once she's sure. "I didn't know what else to do. I was worried about another mouth to feed, another set of clothes, school books, everything. I was so frightened, Willie."

He stares at her, incredulous. Part of him feels such sorrow at the fact that Edna was forced to consider an alternative. He wishes it wasn't like this. He knows how much she loves their children, and he's concerned about how they'll make his wages stretch. There's a lot going on in his mind, but he speaks calmly.

"You'll make a wonderful mother to him, Edna," Willie tells her. "A boy, I'm sure of it. A little brother for the girls. You did the right thing by questioning it. We don't have the money for it, so I understand."

Edna smiles at him, weakly. She feels more free than she has in a month. "I'm going to have the baby. Yes, I'll do it. We'll manage together, won't we?"

He turns to her, smiles and carries on rubbing ointment onto his chapped fingers. His response is characteristically optimistic. "We'll make it work, kid," he says. "We always do."

FIFTEEN
THE MIDNIGHT FLIT

The baby is born just after Edna's birthday, on a freezing January night at the outset of 1938. For most families across the country, this is to be the last Christmas of relative normality for some time. Disturbing reports filter from house to house, newspapers warn of increasingly austere times to come. War is marching inexorably toward them.

Millie is sent for and arrives, breathless, ready to take the girls home with her while the baby is born. As with all my mother's pregnancies until the very last one, this baby is born at home, in Edna and Willie's bed.

"Call him Phil, after Dad," says Willie, when my first brother – Phil, Will, Billy, depending on how he felt – enters the world.

Edna cannot believe she ever considered a world without little Billy in it. He's a golden-haired, blue-eyed child with an infectious giggle. He is soon the darling of Marilyn, Sarah and Beryl, who fuss around him, clamouring to be the one to bathe him and spoon Horlicks into his mouth before bed.

For a matter of months, the Rees family mull along much as before. Edna often feels, now she thinks about it, that it's not the first weeks or even years with a new child that leave their mark, but the difficulties once they reach seven or eight. Marilyn and Beryl seem to take up so much more space now, and Sarah never stops eating. Their clothes grow dirty so quickly, from hours spent playing with the neighbourhood children outside in the thick, sooty London air. It is not, she reminds herself, Billy's fault that things have become so tough of late. It's no one's fault but hers and Willie's. She knows they must work harder, but cannot think where the extra hours per day will come from.

By April of 1938, Willie is desperate. He's had no work in a month, the cupboards are bare and Edna has had a nasty infection, which has prevented her returning to Mr and Mrs Cohen's employment yet. As the sun sets one evening, he turns to his wife, nursing Billy in bed.

"Edna," he begins. She can tell by his tone of voice that he cannot have anything good to impart. "We're going to have to leave. We can't afford the rent next month. I've added it all up, and it won't do. We're well short."

The baby gurgles on Edna's breast, his eyes closed. He has been chilly all week, his fingers and toes needing extra socks, blankets and mufflers. Years down the line, tiny plastic sticks will give more-or-less accurate readings of temperature, but we're not there yet. Edna remembers those chilly evenings when she was a girl, trying to keep the younger ones warm. The way they'd tentatively feed the fire until there was no wood left to burn. Why is she thinking of this now? It must be shock. She clutches Billy's tiny feet to her and turns back to Willie.

"Where will we go? When?"

"The midnight flit, kid," he says, grimacing.

"What, leave now? Just pack up and leave?"

Edna knows he doesn't like the idea any more than she does. It's stealing, after all. But as she looks into his eyes she can see his exhaustion. She knows that if he remains here, in Willesden, and explains to the landlord that they cannot pay, he will serve time in prison. Not long, but enough. And in that time, who knows if Edna's health will remain stable, what the girls and baby Billy will need – and where they'll live.

"Milly and Mima could—" she begins.

"I already spoke to your sisters," he says gruffly. "Mima's all the way on the seventh floor in Camberwell, miles from any work, and Millie has space but only for three extra. We're a family of six now, Edna. There's few who'll have room to take us in.

I'm sorry, my love, we've no other option, y'see."

She nods, readjusting the baby on her chest. She hopes tomorrow night is not as cold as tonight.

* * *

Edna closes the front door for the last time, passing the bag of sandwiches to Sarah. Tripe: the kids will scream even more when they find out. She hopes they won't need them, that the first shelter they come to has space for them.

The street is utterly silent. Up ahead a fox crosses the road, his tail aloft. He gives them a cursory glance, this motley crew of adults and children, suitcases and shawls, coats, hats and scarves. Everything the Rees family owns is currently on their backs. One look at Willie would tell anyone peering down from their window exactly what was happening – at Edna's insistence, he has lugged the kitchen table onto his shoulders and is groaning under its weight.

They walk for what seems like hours. The night isn't particularly cold, but it seems to chill with every passing hour and every shake of a head in a doorway. Austerity has hit the city hard, and the homeless shelters are at full capacity. There's nothing to be done but keep going and keep hoping. As they walk past the gates to a huge park, Willie jerks his head at Beryl, who appears to be dozing on her feet. "Kids need to kip, Edna," he says. "We'll head in there."

In the dead of night, and somehow without waking Billy, my parents and siblings manage to pass their possessions over the railings and into the park. They huddle together on a bench, eating the sandwiches and shivering as dawn breaks. Willie hears the tell-tale tinkle of the milk truck and dashes off, coins jangling in his pockets, to fetch some. They sit in contented silence, there on the bench, passing the glass bottle back and forth between them.

There's a certain amount of placidity that that kind of early upheaval lends a person later in life. My mother had suffered greatly, by the time she sat on that bench, with three daughters under eight and a baby in her arms. But they were all there, weren't they? They were healthy, they had sandwiches and milk. It wasn't cold. If Edna had learned anything from her life so far, it was that such things should not be taken for granted.

PART FOUR

CHANGING TIMES 1938-1948

SIXTEEN
LAND OF MY FATHERS

As with the lives of all who'd come before them, my parents could never rely on security of any kind. From 1936, British shops were being stocked with an increasingly popular import from the United States: a game called Monopoly. If there was ever a reflection of the turbulent times in which they lived, it was this. Life was a series of ups and downs to be navigated with as much joy, as much humour as was humanly possible.

For a time, following that night in Hyde Park, they were on an up. They found temporary lodgings in Kilburn when Willie's work picked up. Their new rooms were furnished; all they'd had to do was claim two children, instead of four (Beryl had hidden round the corner with the baby as Willie and Edna discussed the terms with their new landlady).

"We're Welsh," Willie told her, as she unlocked the doors at the top of the house. "From Glamorgan, ever heard of it?"

The landlady shook her head. "I'm from round here myself, never left London, truth be told." She smiles down at Sarah, always the cutest child and the one my parents pushed forward if a toothy grin was required. "Most people round 'ere are Irish. Funny how different folk settle down in different bits of the city. Where are the Welsh in London, eh?"

"There aren't many. Wales is a hard place to leave," smiled Willie, and he meant it.

It's a different atmosphere to Willesden, but not in an unpleasant way. It's a new part of the city to explore, even though it's barely any distance at all.

Willie goes off to work in Cricklewood and Acton each morning, past buildings with open-plan offices which are rearing their heads in the north-London suburbs. He returns in the late afternoons swinging his tin lunch box and singing.

"Dad, will you teach me some of the words?" Marilyn, aged seven, asks her father. Willie chuckles. "Don't tell your mother. Of course I will, but they're in Welsh, and…" he leans down conspiratorially, *"they're rude."*

By the end of the following week, Marilyn's teacher has written a note full of lavish admiration home to Willie and Edna, praising the linguistic skills of their eldest daughter and encouraging them to keep up with Marilyn's blossoming Welsh. The teacher, a Londoner just like the Hodges' landlady, will never know that the song's final verse is dedicated to the nether regions of an old goat.

Things are looking up. So much so, in fact, that Willie comes home one afternoon holding a beaten box, handing it over to Edna with a flourish. "For you, madame," he says, and sits down to watch her open it. Inside there is a wireless! Deep brown and slightly worse for wear, but it crackles merrily into life at the push of a button.

"Oh, Will…" Edna turns it over in her hands, marvelling at the sound blasting from the tiny speakers. Noise, distraction, jokes and music – it will transform her days in with the baby, the long nights between feeds.

The wireless begins as a symbol of hope, of prosperity for my family, but quickly acquires darker undertones on a quiet September morning later that year. Sarah and Marilyn are playing in the corner of the room – there is nothing so coveted, right now, as the Shirley Temple doll Beryl found (she claims) in the park last week. The doll's face was smudged and dirty, her ringlets tumbling out of shape. But the girls have worked hard to restore her former glory. Sarah, barely four, has begun surreptitiously taking Edna's sewing needles when she thinks her mother isn't looking. Marilyn, using scraps of old curtain from the local dump, is making clothes for the doll. Billy has been asleep for half an hour: they still have some time before he wakes up.

It's Sunday. Edna and the girls went to church at 10 o'clock and have only just arrived home. Willie stayed behind with the baby. There's a slow, lazy feel to the day; Willie has suggested going for a walk up to Alexandra Palace later on. Tonight the children will have a bath in the large tin bucket kept under the sink. Tomorrow the new school year begins. It will be Sarah's first day.

"Blasted thing," says Willie now, moving over to the wireless. It's been playing up all morning, dipping in and out of range. It's crackling away now, spluttering into life briefly for a snatch of song or a low, monotonous voice, and then silence again. Willie ruffles Beryl's hair as she comes into the room: "Bash the box, will you, love?" he asks, and taps the ash from his cigarette into the tray beside the chair. Beryl obliges, giving the top of the wireless a resounding whack.

The noon-day sun is trickling in through the windows as a voice begins, at last, to speak. Beryl's thump has worked its magic. "That's Chamberlain," says Willie, stubbing out his cigarette and leaning forward. "Sounds like the wall's come tumbling down…" He looks agitated. Marilyn looks over at our father, sensing something is wrong. Seizing her opportunity, Sarah takes Shirley Temple and scurries off to the kitchen with her before her sister can act.

The voice speaking to the Rees family is also speaking to thousands around the country. Anyone who can afford a wireless has it on almost constantly in the evenings and on weekends. Chamberlain's voice, from Downing Street, is strained and he is trying, with all his might, to contain it.

"You can imagine what a bitter blow it is to me, that all my long struggle to win peace has failed. Yet I cannot believe that there is anything more, or anything different, that I could have done and that would have been more successful." Edna gasps. She looks up at Willie, whose head is in his hands.

"Up to the very last it would have been quite possible to have arranged a peaceful and honourable settlement between Germany and Poland, but Hitler would not have it."

"What's happened to Germany and Poland?" Marilyn asks, but no one answers her.

"He had evidently made up his mind to attack Poland whatever happened; and although he now says he put forward reasonable proposals which were rejected by the Poles, that is not a true statement.

"The proposals were never shown to the Poles nor to us; and though they were announced in a German broadcast on Thursday night, Hitler did not wait to hear comments on them, but ordered his troops to cross the Polish frontier the next morning."

Willie groans. Marilyn looks seriously frightened now. Her father is never despondent like this, he never sits as he sits now, hunched and exhausted-looking. Edna looks at her daughters, and at Billy sleeping in his cot. She feels, quite distinctly, that they are enjoying the final moments of something rare and precious here in London, as the voice drones on from Downing Street.

"His action shows convincingly that there is no chance of expecting that this man will ever give up his practice of using force to gain his will. He can only be stopped by force, and we and France are today, in fulfilment of our obligations, going to the aid of Poland, who is so bravely resisting this wicked and unprovoked attack upon her people. We have a clear conscience. We have done all that any country could do to establish peace. The situation in which no word given by Germany's ruler could be trusted and no people or country could feel itself safe has become intolerable.

"And now that we have resolved to finish it, I know that you will all play your part with calmness and courage."

"We're at war," says Willie, in a hollow voice. "At bloody war again. I promised myself—"

He seems unable to finish, and stands up, his hands screwed into his eyes. Sarah comes in from the kitchen, holding Shirley Temple aloft, but nobody looks at her.

From where she is sitting, Edna can see down into the street below. The Prime Minister's words have had an immediate, devastating effect. In the distance, a loud wailing noise has begun – a siren. A man runs past in his Sunday best, clutching his bowler hat to his head. Two women are dashing along the cobblestones, clutching their prams and giving frightened glances over their shoulders.

Sarah clamps her hands over her ears, looking terrified. She climbs onto Edna's lap as the baby starts to howl. "What's that?" she shouts, "What's that noise?"

Later, once the deserted streets begin to fill once more, it will transpire that friendly aircraft – mistaken for enemy planes – had returned to UK airspace across the Kent coastline, on hearing the announcement. A false alarm, but an ill-timed one. The sirens won't be heard again until the following June – a calm before the storm of the Blitz.

Willie and Edna allow the children to go and play in the street, once they've established the all-clear. They sit together on the sofa, the baby between them. His legs are high in the air, and he's chewing on his toes. "We can't stay, Will," she says. "You know it'll be different this time. It'll be worse. The Smiths down the street are saying London will be in ruins by next summer."

Willie nods. He had made up his mind the moment they'd first heard Chamberlain's voice, but he wanted to hear Edna say it first. "We'll go back," he says. "Back home."

* * *

In the six hours since war was declared, Willie has sold a watch, collected his week's wages in arrears and arranged for a transfer of the deposit from their landlady. She comes into the room to check the furniture against the inventory, shaking her head sadly. "All this fear, and for what?" she says, lifting the beds to examine the frames. "There they went, saying the last one would be the war to end all wars. That wasn't even 20 years ago."

Edna nods and makes a noise of sympathy. "Course," says the landlady, "You'd be too young to remember much of it."

"That's true," Edna says, "I was quite a young child during the last war. About Marilyn's age, maybe a bit older."

"I lost my David during the Somme," says the landlady. "Never found his body. He's buried somewhere in France, but I've never had the money to go and visit the grave." She shakes her head again. "Not sure I can see the point of it myself. Going at it all over again." She spots Billy sleeping in the corner, the baby she didn't know was living here. She says nothing about it, though, and turns back to Edna. "You've got somewhere to go?"

"Willie's sister, in Wales. She doesn't know it yet, mind."

The landlady chuckles. "That's as well, with your brood. But there's no refusing a family from London, not in times like this."

With the scraped-together cash from his afternoon's sales, Willie purchases six tickets from Paddington. My parents are not alone in this decision. As they wait on the platform they see mothers and fathers just like them, with tiny children in tow. One woman brushes past Edna, an infant on her hip, a toddler holding her hand. She has a briefcase overflowing with letters and photographs dangling from her elbow. Her elder child begins to resist when they approach the train doors. He's shouting, then screaming for his father. "He has to stay here, Henry," says her mother. She tries to manoeuvre the boy up the steps, but he won't budge. "Here, give the other one to me," says Edna, and the woman – with a look of mingled gratitude and relief – hands over the baby to Edna. Beryl chuckles at her mother, stood in the midst of all this bustle with Billy on one hip and the woman's baby on the other.

At seven o'clock the train rumbles into life. It seems like madness that 12 hours before they were sleeping soundly in their beds in Willesden. Now, they will likely never return to London – or at least, not to any London they recognise. As the tracks snake their way through the outer suburbs of the capital's north-west ring, Beryl and Marilyn press their faces to the glass, looking out. Marilyn wonders, though she decides not to ask the question, what will happen to the other children in her class at school. She never sees any of them again.

* * *

My parents and siblings arrive at my Uncle Owen John and Auntie Hannah's farmhouse in the early hours of the next morning. It was a long, wearying trip on an already overcrowded train, where shouts and whispered discussions jostled for precedence. Some of the young men Edna has seen look truly wretched – she wonders how many of them are returning home, back to Wales, to say goodbye to their families before the mandatory enlistment begins. Willie's family are tickled pink by the girls' Cockney accents – their short, clipped London vowels.

Two months after they left, the first bomb to fall on the UK was dropped in Shetland, with just one casualty: a single rabbit. This gave rise to the song *Run, Rabbit, Run* – and, for a time, the population was mollified by the idea that perhaps these German fighter pilots had less sting than they'd imagined.

It's easy, now that they're out of the city, for my parents to at least try to pretend that life will continue as normal. Gone are the paper-boys and the sirens, the whispers across narrow streets.

Drefach is a gorgeous village. It was then and it remains so to this day. It's a corner of Carmarthenshire that seems untouched, unaffected by the events of the world outside. Willie returns to the colliery – he'd never have believed it possible, after those years in London, where there was so much work to be found above ground. But even Owen cannot afford to pay another employee on the farm, and he can either return to the mines or enlist. Willie will not go to war and be blown apart, leaving Edna and the children, just another statistic in this country's mad war games. He will keep his head down – quite literally – and try his best to see this through to the end. Perhaps, at the end of it all, they can go back to Willesden. He daren't hope too hard, though.

At first, Edna misses the city. It had never been easy, but it'd become a home, a community. She brought the wireless with her, and every evening she, Willie, Hannah, Owen and Marilyn gather round the fireplace to listen to the day's reports. By the summertime, they are resisting the evening's bulletins, though Edna forces herself to sit down and bear witness, if nothing else. She hears about the men, women and children crowding into Anderson shelters night after night, about the terrible wailing sirens, the houses razed to the ground. On weekends she hears that families have braved a balmy evening for a walk to the pictures at Putney. The reel starts and the crowd hushes, finally – some sense of normality! The hero is preparing to put his rescue mission into action: he'll save the woman he loves, dashing through the Amazon as the tiger he's fought so hard all this time gives chase... And then the screen goes blank. One hour in, the traffic lights go up.

At cinemas, the lighting system beside the screen is used to indicate enemy attacks. Green means there is no threat, amber means enemy planes have been spotted passing the Kent coast, and red means imminent danger: planes directly overhead, take cover, run. The amber light sputters into action as the audience begins to groan. The theatre is evacuated, though the Luftwaffe are not heading down to Putney. They won't intend to hit there, anyway.

Edna sighs as she listens to the broadcasts day in, day out. It's a terrible business, but the devastation being wrought across the streets she once knew is enough to convince her that they're better off where they are. She hears about the reams of black-out material being delivered to households across the major southern cities and shakes her head. It'd be typical of Marilyn, on hearing the noise at night, to rip back the curtains for a proper look and expose their tiny orbs of candlelight. It would be like living in a mausoleum, even in the summer. She's glad to wake in the mornings and feel the breeze of the valleys on her face. She hadn't realised how much she missed it here, until she returned. Marilyn, who would go on to train at opera school in her teenage years, meeting her beloved Johnnie boy whom she would marry and live happily ever after with for over 60 years.

Hannah and Owen are good people, and my parents are grateful to them. But as the months go by, and the house seems to grow ever louder – the couple have two small children of their own – Edna begins to wonder how much longer they'll be staying. As though he's read her mind, Willie sidles up to her one morning, before he leaves for the pits.

"Ey, kid," he whispers.

She's milking the cows – something that seems so alien and removed from her life in London she sometimes finds herself laughing. "What's the matter?"

It's not quite five in the morning. She wants Billy to sleep a little longer. Soon she'll need to wake Marilyn and Beryl for school, they'll need to muck out the horses before they leave. "I think I've found us somewhere. Somewhere to live." Willie's eyes are shining in the darkness. Edna looks up at him as a smile begins to creep across her face.

Rises and falls, ups and downs. One moment you're in Hyde Park, freezing, and the next you might just have a place to call your own. In 1941, UK Secret Intelligence Services commission Monopoly's manufacturers to design a special edition of the game, one sent to prisoners of war in Germany. Stashed away inside them are real bank notes, compasses and maps, all designed to help the prisoners escape the Nazis. Sometimes the light at the end of the tunnel might not seem obvious – but look a little harder. It's there to be found.

SEVENTEEN
YOUNG MAN'S GRAVE

There were two options available to sick patients in 1939: voluntary hospitals, where medical assistance was billed, and where patrons often donated funds for maintenance – or infirmaries. Infirmaries were funded by local authorities, and widely feared. Perhaps rightly so, given that they were often built right beside cemeteries, and were not well regarded. Care was so appalling, or so the joke went, that one might as well check in immediately next door.

For the first few months of this much-feared, much-lamented world war, very little changed. Indeed, this period of time and its comparative lack of drama ushered in the idea of a "phoney war." The armed forces estimated 5,000 trained nurses would be needed. This recommendation was changed, of course, come 1940, when the air raids began and the city hospitals were suddenly awash with critically ill patients. Suddenly around 67,000 were required. Night after night the country was bombarded, and emergency services became more important than ever before.

There are few positives to war, of course. Thousands were killed, in fields far from home, in nuclear blasts, in submarines deep beneath the ocean's surface, in detainment camps and in houses across European and Asian cities. Death came for millions during this time. But without this war, the UK's health services would not have seen the vast – and incredibly quick – transformation it ultimately came to experience. Things needed to change. The sheer number of men who'd returned from the first war broken – both physically and mentally – bore testament to this. If that chain of events was to be repeated, then provisions needed to be put in place.

* * *

When Willie returns home to say the lease is available on Rhydycerrig, Edna is stunned, delighted and a little dubious. There is neither running water nor electricity at the farmhouse, just a spring-water well in the front field. At night they'd be using oil lamps. It feels medieval somehow, after their life in London – but there's also the sense that the seven acres of land surrounding the property might provide an even better upbringing for the girls and Billy than anything they'd known in Willesden. Willie signs up to the local Home Guard – mining was a reserved occupation, after all, but we benefited from his inclusion in Dad's Army by sleeping underneath his great regulation overcoat when the weather turned icy.

In the 19th century, Rhydycerrig was stationed on an old drovers' path. It served as an inn, where the drovers could pause along their journeys with the sheep, cattle and geese they were often walking to London or other cities to sell.

Whilst the better-off among them rode horses, the majority set off on foot, usually with their trusty working dogs trotting alongside them. If these marches were wearying for the drovers themselves, it was nothing compared to the impact the walks had on the animals. The geese, for instance, had their webbed feet dipped in tar and then sand, for protection.

It all feels miles away from the nervous atmosphere in London, away from the fretting and the fear and the hand-wringing. Here, it feels as though world wars come and go and leave no imprint.

Years later, when my brother Phil was around 11, his schoolmaster informed him that Rhydycerrig had a dark and dangerous past.

"You've never heard of the Kentish five?" said the man, who had lived in the area all his life, and fancied himself something of a local expert. He had the manner, this Mr Jones, of a modern-day Ripperologist, someone with a deep-seated fascination for all things macabre and an absolute iron will to tell anyone who'd listen all about them.

Phil, always the cheekiest of us, would have stuck his tongue out at old Mr Jones, whom he knew liked him and was unlikely to punish him. "Kentish five? Never heard of 'em."

Mr Jones leaned down next to him and nodded. "You may laugh, lad, but I'll be surprised if you take it so lightly after hearing what happened to them…"

"Go on then," Phil said. "Tell me about the Kentish five. See if I'm a-quivering by the end of your story!"

Mr Jones recounted the lives of the drovers to Phil: the long, isolating walks, the risk of thieves and highwaymen, the hunger and exhaustion and the constant care of the animals often being walked hundreds of miles to market. "This was before the steam trains, you see," said Mr Jones. "Before we even had proper roads around here, tell you the truth. Every day was a hardship, every step a burden. And the animals who weren't sold at the furthest market went straight back walking home again, along with the drovers. Not everyone was kind to them – sometimes they'd be holed up in ditches, sleeping beside the pigs on freezing winter nights."

Eddie's interest would have been piqued by this. An animal lover from birth, he found the notion of spending all those hours with the sheep, pigs and donkeys romantic – perhaps he one day dreamed of becoming a drover himself, if such a thing existed by the 1940s.

"One night, must've been a hundred years ago now or more, the wind was howling something shocking, and the Kentish five – on their way back from the mountains, tired and cold – decided enough was enough for the night. My, they were tired. In the distance, they spotted lights, small orange lamps glowing in the middle of the darkness, and on they pressed."

Phil started to feel his insides squirming: he doesn't like where this is going.

"They pushed on, and soon enough they came to a broken old wooden fence, with a painted sign across the front of it. Rhydycerrig. And they decided, since it was the only place around for miles, that they'd beg a few hours' kip in the stables. It had started to rain by now, and the animals were making a racket behind them. The men went in through that fence around midnight, according to a witness who was coming home from Cardiff in his cart that evening. Their pockets were loaded with gold, spoils from the day's sales. But they were never seen or heard from again. All five of them, gone."

Phil stared at Mr Jones, his brows furrowed. "What—" he asks uneasily. "What happened to them?"

"Robbed, most likely, Master Rees," said Mr Jones, satisfied to have got the desired reaction from my brother at last. "Very common, back in those days. Robbed and buried. Buried right where you and all your wee siblings play in front of the house, and all their animals, too."

My brother Eddie, born as my parents attempted to shift an old horse from the barn – a pregnant horse that wouldn't budge – would never feel quite the same way about the farm he grew up on again, not after Phil told him the story.

When Phil and his friends decide, one day, to find out the truth for themselves, they spend a weekend digging in the furthest, most isolated reaches of Rhydycerrig's limits. Phil is amazed when he unearths a thick gold chain from near the blackcurrant bushes, by the orchard. The smell of lilac is almost overpowering as he gazes in wonder at this treasure, this unexpected thing. He is desperate to show the others, desperate to bring the necklace home to show Edna and Willie, but something stops him. He buries it again, exactly where he found it, resolving to leave it here but show the other boys once they've returned from their own digging. Later, Phil unearths the same section of the ground to find the necklace gone. Despite his remonstrations, none of the boys confess to its theft. It's only years later, as one of their number's life begins a descent down a very dark and slippery slope, that Phil privately wonders whether it was that little boy who had stolen the old drover's neckchain, and was paying for it dearly with every decision he made since.

As the war continues, the country braces itself. There's still not much provision being made for the mental suffering of men returning from the front, but it's all hands on deck as far as nursing is concerned. It's an incredibly intense time to be a trainee. Each and every day people arrive, often on stretchers, some with bodies maimed beyond recognition.

Along with my parents' already significant brood of children, the move back to Wales also sees the arrival of Rosie the cow, Peter the pig, chickens, geese, Jess the dog and Suzie the cat. Life is certainly busy for Edna, dealing with the rabble morning and night. It is noisy, filled with a thousand different needs. Not long after they left London, Edna fell pregnant twice more – Eddie and Maris are born, bringing the Rees children to a grand total of six.

Willie, my father, has returned to the pits. The most notorious, Young Man's Grave, was the only option available to him – all the other mines had no vacancies. Many men, fearing the shellfire and wretchedness of battles fought far away overseas, have signed up to work in the pits – it's the only alternative to enlistment. That and conscientious objection – which scarcely counts as an option.

One morning, just as the crocuses Edna has planted many months before are starting to bloom, the post-boy comes panting up the long walk of the smallholding, clutching a telegram. The sight is a common one around these parts: the Sheldons, who live two miles away, were accosted by a similar sight just a few weeks ago. A notice informed them curtly, dispassionately, of their son's death. Edna and Will haven't seen Mr Sheldon since. Edna watches the child hesitate outside the front door and she dries her hands, readies herself and calls out to him to come inside. She gives him a slice of buttered bread, a glass of cold well water and sends him on his way, only tearing open the slip of paper once he's left. Whatever this telegram contains, it's nothing good.

It's from Will's sister, his favourite sister, the eldest. After the death of Mary, their mother, she raised Willie virtually on her own. They are close, these two. There's an understanding between them, a bond that has only strengthened since Edna and Will moved back to Wales.

"What's up, kid?" he asks that night, his hands and face dusty and lined-looking. The soot seems to inch its way into every pore, every crevice of his face. Edna is pale by contrast. She has no idea how to break this news to him.

"It's Sarah," she says eventually, taking out the telegram. "She's written to say that Mair is unwell." Mair, Sarah's daughter, is 13. "She's lost a great deal of weight the past month. They can't keep her fever down, now, and so they took her to the doctor down in Swansea. She has leukaemia. They've told Sarah to expect the worst."

Will sits down heavily at the table. Mair is Sarah's only child, her beloved daughter. "Just 13," he whispers. "It's no age, Edna, is it?"

She shakes her head, tears springing to her eyes. "Go to them, Will," she says. "Go tomorrow."

"Edna, I'll be sacked."

"It's one day, Will Rees. You cannot desert Sarah. Go to them. It's a couple of hours' ride, no more. Take our Sally with you."

Sally, the golden-haired, blue-eyed child, is the sunshine of the family. All jokes and sweetness and laughter. She's the perfect antidote to this hideous situation. Willie nods, knowing Edna is right, and sets off the following morning. By nightfall, his niece Mair has died, in a bedroom still decorated with hand-drawn ducks and geese, rabbits and foxes, strewn with tiny figurines, sack-cloth dolls and modelling clay.

"There might have been a way to save her," Willie's sister sobs, much later that night. "The doctor said. He showed me the list of medicines they could use to help her. She mightn't have survived all the same, Will, but it would have given us more time."

Willie knows the terrible pain of Sarah's situation. He doesn't need to ask why Sarah didn't order the doctor right there and then to administer every drug in his leather case to Mair. He shakes his head, wondering how it can possibly have come to this. A medical man with all the tools to help, a family powerless in the face of cost.

When Willie returns home four days later, he is alone. "I've left Sally there awhile, kid," he says. Edna's mouth opens once, shocked, but she gathers herself quickly and nods. "It was the right thing to do, certainly."

Sally, our sister, ended up staying with our aunt Sarah for six years – living with a woman who, try as she might, could never shake the ghost of her child, could never quite recover from the speed of her loss, the terrible memories of it, the fact that she was still here and Mair was not.

Sally grew up far away from the rest of us, just one more life transformed by the inability of doctors to provide life-saving medicine when it was most needed. Their hands, as they so often were, remained tied, the Hippocratic oath an ideal that flew in the face of reality, that didn't take into account the stark, bare facts of life. And what facts they were.

EIGHTEEN
THE BOY WHO STAMMERED

Zoom out with me for a moment. We're dashing back in time, flying over the tops of houses, east towards London. It's 1919, and a young man with a mop of thick black hair and piercing blue eyes is standing on a piano stool reciting poetry. His words fall like a dripping tap, slowly, one by one, hanging in his mouth for a moment before he lets them go. Clara, as usual, looks nonplussed. She's 38, 16 years older than the young man, though she doesn't look it. Today she's half sitting, half reclining on a day bed, not looking at him. In fact, zoom a little closer and she appears to be examining her fingernails.

The young man has paused on the word "slay." S sounds are particularly tricky and he frowns, scrunching up his face. From her inert position Clara begins to recite the poem from the beginning, and he joins in:

> *What cometh here from west to east awending?*
> *And who are these, the marchers stern and slow?*
> *We bear the message that the rich are sending*

Aback to those who bade them wake and know.
Not one, not one, nor thousands must they slay,
But one and all if they would dusk the day.

This time, the man manages to move past "stern", over "slow", and barrels headlong into "sending", before Clara holds up a hand. "Don't rush it now, Nye. It's about speed as much as confidence. If you over-congratulate yourself you'll trip up later. Keep the rhythm." She waves her hand softly, like a conductor, as the man continues to speak, holding the piece of paper between trembling hands.

They're in London, this unlikely-seeming pair. Sometimes it still feels like a dream, what has happened to him, to Nye, a young man from Tredegar in Monmouthshire. He's one of 10. He left school at 13, having already repeated a year. Between then and six months ago he worked at the Tytryst Colliery. He spent much of his time at the Tredegar Workmen's Institute Library, devouring the writing of HG Wells and Jack London. Having joined the Independent Labour Party, he was sacked from the colliery for his activism on behalf of the South Wales Miners' Federation.

He cannot know this just now, as he stands in Clara's living room, but he will spend the next decade in and out of unemployment – refused entry to the mines for advising local people back home in Wales. He will even consider emigrating to Australia – and my story, my entire family's story, would then have been very different indeed. In just six years' time, his father – a man who spent most of his waking hours down the pits – will die of pneumoconiosis in Nye's arms.

Somehow, through it all, and unaware of the fight that is to come, here he is: on a two-year scholarship to study economics, politics and history at the Central Labour College, sponsored by his old friends at the Federation. Clara was recommended to Nye by one of his professors, a kindly man with a toupee, who scrawled her address on a piece of paper and was kind enough to call them "elocution lessons."

There's something about the idea of learning to speak with a little more refinement that irks Nye, but if he wants to make a blind bit of difference with the gifts he's been given, he needs to be able to speak well. It's not about accents, or hard vowels, he tells Clara gruffly. He wants to sound Welsh still, at the end of the day. What he needs help with is actually getting the words out. Since he was a small boy, Nye's stammer has grown steadily worse – he's been mocked for it, mimicked, kicked about the school yard. Clara says she can help him – perhaps she can.

Nye likes *Death Song*, the poem they're currently working on. It's by William Morris, whom Nye has never heard of, but who cares? It strikes something in him.

> *We asked them for a life of toilsome earning,*
> *They bade us bide their leisure for our bread;*
> *We craved to speak to tell our woeful learning;*
> *We come back speechless, bearing back our dead.*

Not one, not one, nor thousands must they slay,
But one and all if they would dusk the day.

* * *

By 1926, Nye is back in Wales, as a full-time union official. He's at the forefront of miners calling for change at the strike, walking the streets, painting notices to place above the mines' entrances. Not a penny off the pay, not a minute on the day. He meant it, just as Edna's father Tommy had meant it: just as my grandfather suffered, so too did this young man with the sharp gaze.

His election to the Monmouthshire County Council in 1928 was followed a year later by his entry to Parliament, becoming the Independent Labour Party member for Ebbw Vale. By 1945, Labour had won a landslide victory, and to his surprise – and the surprise of the country – Clement Attlee selected Nye, the youngest member of Cabinet at 47, as minister for health, housing and local authorities.

Clara hadn't just rectified Nye's speech, she'd equipped him with the ability to deliver the most cut-throat, waspish put-downs, and Nye never pulled his punches. In July 1929, Bevan claimed of then Prime Minister Neville Chamberlain, "The worst thing I can say about democracy is that it has tolerated the Right Honourable Gentleman for four and a half years." Of Winston Churchill, the man widely regarded as the victor of the Nazis, Bevan stated, "He is a man suffering from petrified adolescence." Churchill hated him – and no wonder – but although he termed Bevan the "Minister for Disease" and announced "he will be just as great a curse to this country in peace as he was a squalid nuisance in time of war," he nonetheless regarded the Welsh-born troublemaker quite highly: "He is one of the few people I would sit still and listen to." Quite a feat for the notoriously restless Churchill.

Bevan was a master of language, a first-class orator. In May 1945, while giving a speech at Blackpool, he announced: "This island is made mainly of coal and surrounded by fish. Only an organising genius could produce a shortage of coal and fish at the same time."

The National Insurance Act had provided some measure of protection up until this point. A paltry one, perhaps, but it *was* there. Workers seeking personal protection from loss of income related to unemployment or injury made monthly payments into the scheme, brought about in 1911, which their employers matched. Much like the creation of the Poor Law all those years before, the hope of the Treasury was to safeguard the public purse against destitution by requiring workers to make contributions – rainy day money, essentially.

Now, Nye had a plan. It would not be easy, but it was needed now more than ever before. A bill was passed through Parliament, one that would offer a state-wide health service governed by four basic principles: it was to be free at the point of need; available to everyone, regardless of wealth or social standing; it was to be used responsibly; and it was to be funded through taxation. It was the National Health Service.

Hospitals would be nationalised. Labour would effectively take control of their operations and fund the treatment and diagnosis of every single patient in the UK, should they require it. The service covered the work of doctors and nurses, dentists and optometrists. It allowed for free prescriptions, access to life-saving medicine. It allowed, in short, for hope, and it was a far cry from what had come before. At London hospitals such as Guy's, governors decided on which patients were "deserving" of care and admission. They were required to pay for their treatment, and provide financial surety for their own burial costs, in case they died. The poorest patients sought out support from their parish, or from local business-men – though this was not always guaranteed. Wards were often full, and admission was very much luck of the draw.

And yet not everyone was happy about Nye's plans, least of all the Conservatives and the British Medical Association. In order to appease the latter, Bevan was forced to allow consultants to continue working on a private basis, as well as providing NHS treatment, effectively – as he put it – "stuffing their mouths with gold."

Opposition continued right up until the date of the NHS's conception, but there was little the Tories could do. On 5 July 1948, Sylvia Diggory – a 13-year-old suffering from a serious liver disease – was treated for free on the NHS. She was the first patient to benefit from the service.

Aneurin, known as Nye, died on 6 July 1960, barely 12 months after his diagnosis of lung cancer. Principled to the end, he had resigned as Minister of Labour in 1951, following the introduction of prescription charges. The stocky, gimlet-eyed boy with a stammer – a blight on his teachers, a scourge on the mining magnates and a perpetual bother to his Parliamentary opponents – had come a long way in a short space of time, and he'd revolutionised the way people in this country gained access to healthcare.

We see it as a basic human right, but it wasn't always. If the stories of my ancestors show me anything, it is this. Human survival, and a decent quality of life, came at a premium. Nye Bevan changed this, but lived barely long enough to witness the societal transformations his work brought about. As his wife – the Scottish Labour MP Jennie Lee – so aptly and poignantly put it, "Nye was born old and died young."

NINETEEN
"IT'S FREE"

So here she is, my mother, in the hospital. The very idea would have seemed ludicrous just 10 years ago. She cannot believe the bustle and pace of the place, the equipment lining the corridors. Everything, it seems, is ready – there are beds, but a good many of them are empty. Jars of medicine sit labelled and unopened on pristine-looking shelves, tubes and swabs and metres of curled gauze sit in baskets. She sees the occasional patient – a man or woman not in nurse's uniform or the white doctor's coat – but the staff seem to far outweigh those they are treating. It'll take time for people to realise they can come here, that this place is open to them, whatever they do or however much they earn.

Funny, now, to think of it, with the current squeeze and speed of a modern accident and emergency department. If we're ill, we get ourselves to hospital, and we trust that we will leave treated, if not cured completely. It is a service so fundamental, so essential, and yet once we leave the emergency room, leave the waiting area and carry on with our lives, we'll spend more on a packet of crisps than we ever do on saving our own lives.

The Amman Valley village hospital takes its fair share of patients, but mostly in the winter. Many of the men admitted to the wards have suffered injuries down in the mines that have been left untreated. From November through to March, during the winter months, a fall or broken bone is far more likely to cause complications down the line. The cold is biting and there's less opportunity to take the air, more chance of getting soaked to the skin. Pneumonia, bronchitis and chest infections are rife during this time, and they force the men to seek help they cannot afford. They are rankled, often, by having to come to hospital in the first place. The doctors will treat the broken bone, the deep cut, the injury sustained down the pits, while also curing the disease brought about by the cold weather. The men leave the wards cured, but broke.

"Can't you leave the arm, doc?" asks a man brought in with suspected miner's lung in 1946. He had a bad break four months before but has told his boss he's fit to work, and now this. "Just sort the breathing. I can wait for the arm to heal, it's no bother." The doctor's stern looks, the sighs and the roll of the eyes tell the wheedling man all he needs to know about this suggestion. The smashed bones have been allowed to grow without setting properly, and were X-rays an option, they'd have revealed an arm now so twisted and misshapen it'll be a miracle if the man ever works again.

When the consultants come to visit Rhydycerrig the month prior, Edna is flabbergasted. The two men stand on the front porch, smiling in their suits, and shake my parents' hands before asking if they might come in for a moment. "Of course," my mother says, beckoning them inside.

Willie shoots Edna a confused look as the men take their seats around the dining table. The house tells a real story, by this point. Skirts and dresses hang drip-drying on the line, just visible through the window – they're almost grown now, Marilyn and Beryl, and their clothes jostle for space among the muslins, the nappies and baby suits belonging to Eddie. The children are all different ages, needing different things, and now there's one more on the way.

Edna rubs her hand over her belly as she watches the men. One of them is taking a sheaf of paper from his briefcase. He catches her touching the bump and smiles. "That's what we came to talk to you about, Mrs Rees," he says.

"The baby?" Edna is nonplussed. What can they want with the baby?

She stares at them. "My seventh child," she says eventually. "Probably my last, too."

"Bloody hope so," says my father, chuckling. Something about his manner, his easy-going attitude and the way his eyes twinkle as he speaks these words, suggests he doesn't mean it. "Don't know where we'd keep any more of 'em, to be honest with you."

"And, Mrs Rees, if I might ask," says the other man, who speaks with a clipped, southern-sounding accent, but who has a kindly smile, "Were you planning on having the baby here, in the presence of the midwife?"

"Always have done," says Edna. She tells the men the story of Eddie's birth, about the poor cow stuck in the barn door. How she heaved at it, tried to get it to move, just two weeks before she delivered her own son in the same barn.

"Have you ever had any complications, during your pregnancies?" the man with the briefcase is writing things down on a piece of paper.

"Oh, you know," says Edna.

The men both look up at her. She isn't used to speaking about things like this, my mother. Willie, sat with his feet crossed over the table, doesn't look like he's used to hearing them.

"Well," says Edna slowly. She thinks back. Has she ever been afraid, when having her children? Was there ever a moment of panic, of feeling that things might go very badly wrong, a mad thought amid the frightful contractions, the sweat and the laboured breathing? She doesn't think so, but then—"Sally, my third child, was in a bit of bother," she recalls suddenly. The two men lean forward to listen. "The nurse, the midwife I mean, said the baby was beached."

One of the men nods while the other looks baffled. "Beached?"

"Breech," says the one with the briefcase, while his colleague smacks his forehead.

"Breech?" says Willie, his brows furrowing. "What's breech?"

"It means that when labour begins, the baby is preparing to be born feet first. It can cause all sorts of complications."

Willie stares at Edna. "You never told me that," he says.

"Will, I never knew it fully myself," says Edna. She looks at him imploringly. "The midwife just kept muttering to herself, I didn't know what she meant. And what good would it have done me to know, anyway?"

"Your wife has a point, Mr Rees," says the posh man. "All that matters in that moment is listening to the instructions of the midwife. But without medical assistance it's very likely your baby would have died before she was born, in that particular case."

Willie's face has paled. "So how exactly is a breech baby born safely?"

The man with the briefcase responds quickly. "It's all about timing, with such deliveries," he says. "The midwife has to encourage the mother as much as possible to push very gently. To push and then stop. It's a most uncomfortable feeling, rather like pausing in the middle of passing water... Once the baby's feet or bottom have been delivered, it's essential that they hang, for a few moments, out of the mother's body, before the baby is turned a quarter-clockwise."

Willie looks distinctly green.

"And then, during the next round of contractions, the shoulders are eased out very carefully, followed by the head. It doesn't always work. It entirely depends on the efficiency and level of training of the midwife, to be frank. You must have had a very good one, Mrs Rees."

"Sally," says Edna, remembering. "That was her name, the midwife. That's why we call our Sarah Sally."

"Is it?" says Will, looking for the umpteenth time during this conversation as though the rug has been pulled quite spectacularly from under his feet. "You never said, kid."

"Willie, you never asked," says Edna. There's no reproach in her tone – it would be unthinkable to her to divulge the details of any of her births. None of her friends' husbands have the slightest idea about the toils and troubles their wives endure during delivery. It will be many years, still, until men are routinely accepted into maternity suites. At this stage, of course, the only ones permitted are the doctors themselves. And here they sit, smiling at my mother.

"Mrs Rees, the reason we're here today is because of your due date," says the posh English man. "Your baby is due to be born at the beginning of July, is that correct?"

"That's what I reckon," says Edna. "I mean, I've done the counting myself. It's more an estimate, if I'm honest."

"Has a midwife confirmed it, though?"

"Oh yes. She came to visit when I was three months or so gone. She agreed with me, start of July."

"And this fits perfectly. You see, Mr and Mrs Rees, from next month we'll be able to offer a very different kind of medical care to you, and to your family."

The man with the briefcase takes a series of papers from the bag and passes them over to my parents. Three letters stand out across the header in blue, coupled with a grainy black-and-white photograph of a team of doctors, besides another of a round-faced man in glasses.

"NHS?" asks Edna. "I know this man," she says, pointing to the photograph. "Seen him in the papers."

"The National Health Service commences its operations next month," says the doctor. "And this man," he taps the photograph, "was born and raised not too far away himself. He's the brainchild of the health service. It's being rolled out across the country."

"And what exactly is the service?" Willie leans forward, his elbows on his knees. "It's all very well telling us it's starting, but how much is it costing? We can't afford any more than we pay the midwife, and that's very little. We can't afford hospitals, we've never been able to. So either tell us how much it'll be now, or we can leave the discussion there, gents."

"It's free, Mr Rees," says the other doctor, softly.

* * *

Edna gave birth to Eddie, my brother, in the beudy. The cowshed was usually Rosie's domain, and on the balmy August day in question, my mother had been milking the cow – also expecting a calf herself. Rosie was relaxed, blowing great steam-clouds of air through her nose. Her eyes were half-closed. In the distance, Edna could hear Marilyn playing with Phil, and Beryl's shouts of excitement as she hid from the others.

Edna was a dab hand at delivery, by this point, and as she sat back on the milking stool, she felt a slight twinge in her abdomen. So minor it felt, and so often had she been through the motions by this point, that she ignored it. The cow continued her low, slow breaths.

Suddenly the pain gripped her and twisted. She stood quickly from the stool just as Will entered the cowshed, looking from Edna to Rosie and back again. "Something wrong, kid?" he said, uncertainly.

"It's here, Will. The baby."

In the shed, then, Edna lay down and began to push. There was nobody to help and nothing to be done. Not even time to send for "Mam Low", who lived in the Lowlands, and was known far and wide for her healing powers and trusted by the village for her remedies for all ills and deeds. Time was of the essence. Any complications, any problems, and the baby would surely die. Neither Edna nor Will had the slightest idea what to do, besides what Edna had done four times before.

At 10 and a quarter pounds, my brother – her and Willie's second and final son – was quite something to behold. He entered the world as Rosie looked on, chewing the straw that Willie used to wipe his son down with. Edna, shaking slightly on the floor of the beudy, held out her arms for him. The older children came running, Marilyn with a great pail of water, Beryl with some old rags Edna used for cleaning. Billy, or Phil as he now liked to be called, stared in open-mouthed amazement at the scene that greeted his eyes. A new baby brother.

Two weeks later, Rosie's time had come, too. My father shooed her into the beudy, but by this point she was too big to fit through the door, and quickly became stuck. The children, Will and Edna pushed and heaved as Rosie bellowed, becoming increasingly frantic. Eventually, sobbing as they've never seen him sob, Willie took the horse and rode out to find the vet.

Rosie could not be saved. The vet could not persuade her to move, and her distress was palpable. She was killed with a single bullet to the head, and her calf died along with her.

Will insisted on standing beside Rosie through the ordeal, his hands upon her flank. The vet would never charge my father for his services that day.

* * *

"So you'll agree?" says the man with the briefcase. He is beaming at my parents. He asks the same question of my father, this time in Welsh. Willie's face softens. The man speaks it well. Most likely it's his mother tongue.

"The man responsible for all this grew up not too far away," repeats the Englishman. "We'd like to honour him by ensuring the first child born under this new service – this new, entirely free service – hails from the same land he calls home."

Edna is suddenly overcome. What they're suggesting has sunken in. She stares at Willie, who looks equally taken aback.

"And you want that baby…" she says slowly, "to be mine?"

"Yes," they say together. "You'll be the first woman who needn't worry about her health costs while she's giving birth," says the first doctor. "The first woman to do something none of your family will have been able to do. You've told me so yourself."

It's true. Edna and Willie have felt something unfurl in them, as they sit with the men. They don't seem to be in any hurry, and for once the kids appear to be behaving themselves. They've been chatting for over an hour. Edna has told them everything she knows – about Tory, about her clever, brave sons and the move to Wales. About her father, perilously injured in the mines, and the death of poor Esther. Willie, who has been told less of his own family history, occasionally adds a few of his own experiences: about Hannah, and Mary, and his poor sick father dying at this moment of miner's lung, of his little niece, Mair. Now they think about it, so much of their own family history could have been changed, were such a service available sooner. Everything could have been different.

In 1947, the number of babies being born across the country is at an all-time high. The post-war boom is well and truly on. The following year, just a few months after the conversation in my parents' smallholding takes place, a baby is born to Her Royal Highness the Duchess of Edinburgh, a son she will name Charles. For the very first time in living memory, that baby will stand the same chances of surviving and thriving as one born, like Eddie was, in a barn in Cefneithin. Now you can leave a village hospital after a month's stay, having been checked and monitored, given medicine, fluids and three square meals a day, a clean bed, washing facilities – and buy a twopenny newspaper. And that newspaper will cost more than then entirety of the hospital stay put together.

PART FIVE

FRESH STARTS, NEW BEGINNINGS 1948-2019

TWENTY
WISH IT SUCCESS

Very few days go by without some mention of the NHS. Ministers pledge to increase funding while junior doctors strike against their working conditions. Misdiagnoses are widely reported, GP waiting times are bemoaned. Headlines rarely mention the lives – thousands of them – that are saved or improved each and every day as a result of this service, the envy of the world and the thing, consistently, and despite what the media would suggest, that makes most people in the UK proud to be British.

If we puzzle over the lack of fanfare for this all-encompassing, cradle-to-grave service, we need look no further than the reporting produced on the morning of its inception. The birth of the NHS received scant coverage, mostly hidden in the papers' back pages, and when it was mentioned, editorials were peppered with distrust. "Everyone, from duke to dustman, earl to errand boy," wrote the *Daily Mail*, referring to the new system of the NHS' funding-through-taxation, "must pay, even if they decline the free services or scorn the cash allowances."

The *Manchester Guardian*, which ran a story of Nye Bevan's inaugural visit to Davyhulme Park Hospital, titled its picture "The Transfer of the Hospitals". There was a sense within these lines that a nationalised, unified service risked the focused surveillance and accountability required for medical facilities. If anything, the *Guardian*'s caption suggested a lack of control, a risk, the beginning of something uncontrolled and dangerous. And it wasn't much better, over at the *Daily Express*, which merely commented: "The new National Health Scheme is launched. Wish it success."

It may well be that such an overarching change, such a huge and unique overhaul of current systems, might have prompted the distrust. Perhaps many feared the NHS was little more than a pipe dream – noble in theory but impossible to implement in practice. The notion that lives could be saved for less than the cost of a loaf of bread might have not entered national consciousness until such a feat was experienced in the flesh.

I suppose my mother, in the hours following my birth, was one of the first to realise just how momentous the change had been. For hours, she had laboured over my birth, seen to by the nurses and doctors on duty, given pain relief, had her baby delivered and wrapped up warm and handed back to her, checked over and healthy. It was such a far cry from Eddie's birth four years previously, as Rosie the cow lowed in the corner and Willie covered the infant in straw.

Leaflets were strewn across town hall corkboards, in doctors' surgeries and popped through letterboxes:

"Your new National Health Service begins on 5 July. What is it? How do you get it?"

The leaflet was brief – to the point. Just like the NHS – what it is and how it works requires little explanation. It's such a simple concept.

"It will provide you with all medical, dental and nursing care. Everyone – rich or poor, man, woman or child – can use it or any part of it. There are no charges, except for a few special items. There are no insurance qualifications. But it is not a 'charity'. You are all paying for it, mainly as taxpayers, and it will relieve your money worries in times of illness."

It's interesting, this notion of separating the service from charity. No doubt many would have abhorred the idea of seeking free treatment they could otherwise have paid for. It was evidently important to make it clear that the funds keeping the NHS afloat came from taxes.

It is incredibly important, I think, not to shy away from just how much needed to change in our healthcare services before 1948. Patients admitted to hospitals spoke of family members having to clean bathrooms themselves, of dust and grime and mixed wards, of old women being left on commodes for hours while calling for help. They were crowded, dirty places – no wonder everyone feared them.

Amman Valley Hospital lies just south of the Black Mountains, and is bordered by little streams flowing into the Amman River. Originally opened as a cottage hospital in

1936, it was gifted to the local community by a wealthy family. Most people locally were miners.

On the day of my birth it became an NHS hospital, and the maternity wing a dedicated mother-and-baby unit. The hospital is still fully operational today, but the maternity ward was closed in 1984. It stands shut up and derelict to this day, its long, empty corridors strewn with three-legged chairs, broken prams and hospital gowns. Bath tubs are encrusted with grime, while the old calling system – Lab, Nurse 3, Theatre, Ward 4, Doctor – still hangs above the doors, small white circles with orange stars in the middle, ready to light up. The walls of the delivery rooms are dotted with stick-on cartoon figures, little penguins dancing. It's an eerie, silent place. The sort that has known great drama, great happiness and jubilation, and great tragedy too. Such is the nature of maternity wards. In a way, I'm glad it has been left untouched. Its walls are witnesses to history.

Had my mother pushed when she wanted to, I'd have been born on 4 July 1948. Edna and Willie would have had to pay sixpence to the hospital for the privilege of having their child there. They were stressed enough by this point: my poor sister Sally was in isolation at Llanybydder Sanitorium at the time with scarlet fever. She wept when she was told Edna was at Amman Valley. That was how families reacted to news their loved ones were in a hospital, back then. Hospital was reserved for the most serious, most life-threatening cases.

It was the doctors' "hold on, Edna!" that stopped her. They had told her about the importance of waiting. Of course, while she gasped at the pain, willing herself to hold back, she reflected that it was bloody rich coming from a pair of men. What would they know about it?

But she held on. She waited until that long, achingly slow clock hand ticked over, and then she pushed. I came barrelling into the world at a minute past midnight, the first baby to be born on the NHS.

The doctor and Nurse Richards are both misty-eyed. They've spoken with Edna and Willie beforehand. They know what this moment means – not just for the country, but very specifically for my family.

Edna has had many hours since being admitted to Amman Valley to chat with Nurse Richards. She has told her much of the family story. Of her great-grandmother, the workhouse, the cramped and disease-filled conditions, her ancestors working in the pits, pianos being sold and children crying, empty larders. Nurse Richards has nodded sympathetically throughout. As a member of the Royal College of Nurses Union, she has seen great change in the industry throughout her long career. Nurse Richards remembers the days spent tramping through fields, just like Hannah – Will's grand-mother – once did. She remembers makeshift bandages, tourniquets made of fishing wire. She tells Edna about the war, about the days spent carrying whole families into the voluntary hospitals on stretchers. During the bombardment, there was no room to treat them, and many were laid out in the long corridors.

By and large, the day of my birth passes much like any other. It's a new system, a novel one – unrivalled in countries across Europe. Perhaps it's too soon for anyone to truly champion it. It might not work, after all. The only people who can truly advocate for its success or otherwise are those who are treated by it.

Had the newspapers come to interview Edna, as she recovered back at Rhydycerrig, they might have been able to impart some of the disbelief, the joy that this new service had already brought about. For Edna had experienced something she never thought she would: she delivered a baby safely, in the knowledge that medical help, and lots of it, was close at hand. What's more, she delivered a baby understanding that if there were complications these would be seen to immediately, without the need for her, Willie and the kids to go without for months on end to make up for it. There was, in short, a safety net.

TWENTY-ONE
THE WILDER THE BETTER

My early life was spent in part at the smallholding of Rhydcerrig and then at a new council estate called Is-Y-Lyn, or "Below the Lake." The lake in question was Llyn Llech Owain, named after Owain Glyndwr, the Welsh Braveheart, a ruler from 1415 whom many regarded as an unofficial king. It was Owain who instigated the Welsh revolt against Henry IV of England. Every day he'd go to the well at Mynydd Mawr to collect water for his horses, always careful to replace the great stone slab back over the top of the deep pit afterwards. And yet one day, so the legend goes, he forgot – water cascaded down the side of the mountain, creating the unofficial swimming pool we spent all our summers almost drowning in.

So here I am at last. The next line of the family tree. It was a happy childhood. A busy, fun-filled one – with six elder siblings, I never lacked playmates like Eddie and Margaret Maris (nicknamed Mashi) to play with. We spent hours sitting up in bed singing The Beverley Sisters: *"Sugar in the morning, sugar in the evening, sugar at supper time."* I was the loudest, the shrillest by far, but I never got the blame for the racket we made. "For goodness' sake, Will, cut her some slack..." was Edna's constant refrain: I think my father was shocked beyond belief at this wayward, cheeky child – so very different to those who'd come before me. My rebellious, outgoing spirit was becoming more evident by the year. At the bottom of the garden stood the toilet, and we'd sit at the table cutting up old newspapers to use as paper. "If you come across one with Hitler's face on it," my dad said, "save that one for me!"

Is-Y-Lyn was open and safe, with plenty of space to explore. We were wild children, allowed to roam as we liked. Money was still tight, of course, but things had eased up a little. It took some time, and a certain change in attitude, for people to start believing they didn't need to suffer in silence any longer.

Case in point: my father. I'd be about a year old, by this point.

"What's up, Will?" Edna asks, standing by the sink. She's washing muslins – a never-ending task, it seems.

"Ruddy back's playing up again," he says, grimacing and rubbing the tops of his shoulders. "It's been aching all week. Kept me up last night."

"Go into town tomorrow, then," says Edna. "Book yourself an appointment, or I can do it for you. Might as well get it looked at."

"But—" my father begins, and then he remembers. "Ah, yes..." he says quietly.

It takes some time to get used to the idea that an appointment can be made, a possible solution offered, and not a single penny spent. Over the course of my first year I receive inoculations, treatment for a rash, and cough medicine – all of it handed over to my wide-eyed mother.

On the street, people stop Edna to point and coo at the baby in the pram, at my blonde curls and sparkling blue eyes. "What's her name?" they ask, and my mother will tell them: "Aneira, my National Health baby."

She's never had access to this sort of care, this level of potential intervention with the other children, and a part of her feels guilty about it. She wishes she could have had these chances with all of them. But that is set to change, when Sally – who spent all those years with Willie's sister after the death of Mair – contracts tuberculosis.

We had the news by letter. Sally had been training as a nurse over in Chichester, Sussex, and after many months working on the wards, had contracted the disease herself. I can remember my parents discussing the matter in the kitchen, Edna wringing her hands while Willie hastily wrote back to say he and my mother were coming.

Throughout the Industrial Revolution, incidences of TB had spiked. Poverty, desperate conditions, poor hygiene and squalor provided the perfect breeding ground for the bacteria responsible for this deadly infection in the 19th century. As nutrition, socioeconomic prospects and the discovery of the antibiotic streptomycin in 1943 improved patients' chances of survival, it was widely thought that tuberculosis could be confined to the past – a horrific thing that had once claimed the lives of one in seven people across Europe.

Following the two world wars, however, TB was back as a major killer. It's different from contracting the common cold, where only a few droplets from a sneeze or cough can infiltrate the system. TB requires prolonged contact, and Sally – caring for incredibly sick patients day in, day out – was in a prime position to contract it. It was absolutely devastating to all of us, a real sign of the times, as well. I remember the introduction in schools of the BCG jab – which for a time was routinely given to children aged between 12 and 13 – and marvelling at how one small, sharp little scratch could transform a family's chances of happiness forever.

Sally was transported to a sanatorium at Llanybydder, and remained there for 18 months. Amazing, again, to think that nowadays a short stay in hospital, intravenous medicine and a course of oral antibiotics would do much the same work. The sanatoriums were a wretched business. As the infection was consumptive, and patients tended to experience a gradual "wasting away", it was thought that total bed rest, clean, fresh air and minimal exercise would help rehabilitate the body. Certainly the removal of infected patients from the home, and into one designated area responsible for control of the infection, was a step in the right direction. But it was awfully dull – there was very little to do, very little stimulus, and I imagine this must have been torture to Sally, who so loved the hustle and bustle of hospital life.

By the time Sally fell ill, she'd already met the man she was going to marry. Ian was an RAF pilot. He was posted to

Germany before he heard of Sally's illness. Maris, my mother and I would go down to Llanybydder as often as we could to visit her. I remember once we were sitting in the waiting area, when a man appeared outside the glass doors, waving at us. As Mam walked towards him he tried to pull the door, couldn't manage it, and promptly fainted! It was Ian, and while on leave from work he'd missed the only bus to the san. He had walked the entire 20 miles to reach the hospital in the blazing summer heat, and now he'd collapsed. It was a testament, to Maris and me – two little girls on a strict diet of fairy tales, magical powers and princes from faraway lands – that love really would find a way, just as my father wrote to my mother all those years before.

"Give them some space, Nye," my mother barked at me, as Maris and I jostled for space by Sally. Ian seemed to be getting all the attention today.

"Go on, Sal," said Mam eventually. "Take him outside, go for a walk – away from these two." Her eyes twinkled down at me. The moment her back was turned Maris and I sprinted off after the mooning couple, throwing ourselves into a hedge not far from the bench Sally and Ian had taken up.

"What are they doing?" said Maris, horrified, trying to cover my eyes.

"Get off! Can't you see they're kissing?" I muttered, my eyes glued to them.

"Then why," hissed Maris, furious, "Are we *watching* them?"

* * *

In 1944, one patient – following diagnosis of TB in her right lung – was advised by the doctors to stick to a plan of "absolute and utter rest of mind and body – no bath, no movement except to toilet once a day, no sitting up except propped by pillows and semi-reclining, no deep breath." She goes on to write, in her personal diary, that she's been told to "lead the life of a log, in fact. Don't try, therefore, to sew, knit, or write, except as occasional relief from reading and sleeping."

It must have been an awful time for Sally, but she was fortunate enough under our new system to be treated, all that time, for free. After her discharge, however, she was not permitted to return to nursing.

It wasn't until the 1990s, when everyone had let their guard down a little, that increased migration, the spread of HIV, lack of access to health, economic crises and drug-resistant strains of TB all mingled to welcome the infection back with open arms. It's an interesting thing, disease control. As the rising rates of tuberculosis in London has proved, once you've caught something, it's important to keep it caged.

* * *

I wanted for absolutely nothing as a child. That may seem odd, I know. There is nothing in my family's history to suggest privilege or wealth – nothing, that is, to grease the wheels, either on my father's or mother's side. But I was delighted with our lot.

There were six other girls my age on the estate; I don't think I left the village until I was around 10. Why would I? We made our own fun, given free rein to roam and wander at will. We'd spend evenings and weekends at Llyn Llech Owain, Owain's Lake, skimming stones and picking lilies of every colour to thread through our hair, pulling wimberries (English bilberries; American huckleberries) off the bushes. These small, bitter-tasting fruits would leave our hands and mouths smeared with red and purple – we looked like we'd eaten whole fountain pens.

On Tuesdays my *Bunty* comic would be delivered and I'd race home, ready to fall into the storylines and dramas of The Four Marys – bored and frustrated at their insanely posh boarding school – and Bella the Bookworm, plus The Dancing Life of Moira Kent, the ballerina whose graceful poses and pirouettes I became utterly obsessed by, and copied endlessly in all my drawings.

Edna cooked endless stews, broths, great steaming vats of porridge – once, I returned home to find her boiling a pig's head. Absolutely nothing was wasted.

Sometimes my mother enlisted the help of Mima and Millie, my aunties, who had both returned to the Valleys at the outbreak of the second world war. We loved coming down to the seaside town of Aberavon, Maris and I, and would spend hours by the water or at the fairgrounds with our cousin Linda, only returning when Mima, still in her slippers and with a cigarette clenched between pursed lips, marched us bodily back home. "What time d'you call this? Food and bed, and make it fast."

"We lost track of the time, Auntie Mima…"

"Bloody liars," she'd mutter. Her husband Bertram would return from the steel works after a 10-hour shift, give her a peck on the cheek and drag himself straight upstairs to bed.

Millie and Mima, I came to realise, were very different kettles of fish to Edna. I loved Mima she was messy and chaotic – but fun, like me, the backs of her slippers all worn down and her stockings never quite pulled up properly. Millie was round and fair – she had a beautiful face and always wore pink lipstick. My mother, in contrast, was more demure. She was deeply proud of her personal appearance, and determined that we'd never look scruffy. She'd insist on us washing our hands and faces and behind our ears before school, and would comb mine and Maris' hair into neat ponytails or plaits.

I loved school, especially English and arithmetic, and was delighted to pass the 11+ unconditionally, one of just three girls in our class of 24 to do so. My elder brother Eddie, who was working by this point, didn't give a hoot, but when I came home that evening I spotted my mother waving in the doorway and my Auntie Wena's green Morris Minor parked outside.

Rowena was a fearsome woman, one of my father's half-sisters following his father's remarriage. She was by this point the matron of Whitchurch Hospital in Cardiff, and had a real reputation. On the wards she was known privately as "the Dragon": if she asked you to jump, you'd sure as sugar be best answering "How high?" I was delighted to see her looking so proud of me that day. "Now you can go on to become a nurse, like your sisters," said my mother.

I wasn't sure about that: I was only 11, after all. And besides, I had other things to worry about that night. Firstly I had to run to the shops for Willie's cigarettes – "10 wild Woodbines," Edna told me, "the wilder the better." I ran all way the way and all the way back: time was tight. I had to be back at school that evening for the Carnival Queen competition. I was in the running, and tonight the judges were making their selection. I shimmied into the blue-and-white-striped dress Marilyn had bought for me, pulled on my mismatching sandals and dashed for the door. Just at that moment, I remember my father being led inside by Edna and Wena, his face and hands dripping with blood. "Go on now, Nye, off you run," said Wena. She was already opening the satchel she carried with her everywhere she went, taking gauze and bandages from the zipped pockets and a bottle of something green and strong-smelling. "You'll be late otherwise."

Such was life. Great success coupled with absolute terror. I understood enough about our new healthcare system to know that if my father was injured he would be cared for. But it was still awful to think about just how much higher his chances were of being injured in the first place.

There is something primal in most people's fear of the underground. Something in our reptilian brain that reacts violently against the lack of light, the closeness of the air. I shudder at the thought of all that heat, as the little wagon dropped the men lower down the shafts, at the smell of all those bodies working to capacity, shovelling and drilling and hauling all day and all night.

Meanwhile, there I was at school, brimming with pride for my academic success on the one hand, dreaming about Carnival Queens, and on the other desperately scared for my dad. For years, the scars he'd sustained from injuries down the pit were tinged blue from all the coal dust that had settled deep into his wounds as they healed.

* * *

Words cannot describe the pride I felt as my Auntie Maggie and I set off on our shopping trip to Blackwood. Compared to Cefneithin it was incredibly metropolitan – there was so much to see. We marched up the High Street and along to the General Store, where Maggie pushed the door open for me.

"In you go," she nodded. Inside the smell of leather was overpowering, but I quickly forgot all that when I heard Maggie's next words. "My niece is starting grammar school," she said. "She needs a satchel, a good one, with her initials on the front too."

In that moment I loved my Auntie Maggie more than anyone else in the world. We left with a brand new bag embossed in gold with the letters *AR*. I'd never felt such pride. As if that wasn't enough, we stopped off at the end of William Street and Maggie surprised me with tickets to the cinema. In we went, into the cool darkness, to take our seats. The air smelled of sweat and popcorn and I loved it. I was entranced. I placed the bag lovingly under my seat and sat up straight, waiting for the film to begin. This, too, was a surprise. I had no idea what we were about to see. But within a few moments a terrible tornado was blazing across the screen, a witch was cackling and a pair of feet was squashed unceremoniously underneath a house. A young girl's ruby-red shoes were glittering so brightly I laughed out loud, half-covering my eyes.

Back at home, carrying my new bag proudly into the living room, Eddie had been causing chaos. Edna had given him a severe dressing down and Willie a clip on the ear. It transpired that poor Maris had been asked to bring a reading book to school, and had happened to tell Eddie about it. Big mistake. He'd gone into her satchel and swapped the Enid Blyton for a different work of fiction, something Maris hadn't realised until she took the book out next morning to show the class. Despite having been recently removed from the UK publishers' censors list, I still wonder to this day how Eddie had procured his copy of *Lady Chatterley's Lover*.

TWENTY-TWO
IN AT THE DEEP END

"Aneira's a dreamer; she could do better." My father's face was thunderous as he read the school report. Some years had passed and I was soon to take my O Levels. My favourite subjects were Art and Biology, but I struggled with Maths and was quickly losing interest.

There were more important, more pressing concerns for me now. Along with my friends Gladys and Angie, I'd hitch rides into Swansea and Cardiff to see a hip new young singer called Tom Jones. Angie was drop-dead gorgeous, with great red corkscrew curls; Gladys was blonde and innocent-looking, which belied her wicked sense of humour and her inability to stop laughing once something set her off. She'd poke me in the ribs during assemblies, as we belted out *"For those in peril on the sea"* and there'd be a Mint Imperial stuck under her top lip. We'd cackle before the head marched up on stage and demanded to know who the culprit was. No one ever snitched on us, but they did send us to Coventry afterwards.

* * *

"Ugh, Maris, you've got flour all over the bed."

"Be quiet," she said.

Maris worked at a bakery now. We still shared a bed, she and I, and when she came home in the late afternoon she was always so exhausted – having started her shift at 4am – that she climbed straight in, in all her clothes. She smelled like loaves and yeast, like icing sugar.

All I wanted was to stare at the ceiling awhile and think about Eirwyn, or David, or Ken: ours was a mixed school and we were all, shall we say, very social. My passions for these boys changed as frequently and with as much warning as the weather in April. It was incredible to me how in an instant I'd be imagining white weddings with one of them and then, moments later, completely revolted by a bicycle helmet I saw them wearing, a tie, an expression.

"Maris, if you're going to snore the afternoon away, I'll go downstairs. But at least let me borrow that jumper." This was a bargaining tool I often employed, especially when she was sleep-deprived.

She wasn't having any of it today, though. "No, you'll only ruin it," she said.

"Ah, ok then," I trilled, prancing to the open bedroom door. "I'll have to tell Mammy about all those fags you've been smoking, in that case..."

Maris, with a groan, reached under the bed and flung the new jumper across at me. "There," she muttered. "Bloody take it!"

As our O Levels crept closer, it became apparent to me that I wasn't going to pass with as flying colours as had been predicted when I sat the 11+ all those years ago. I was happy, though. When Beryl came to visit one afternoon, Mam happened to be outside hanging the laundry. It was bedsheets day and she'd be out there for a while. Beryl had a day off: she was a general nurse at Graylingwell, where Sally, too, went to work before falling ill.

"So," she said, putting her feet up on the chair beside me. I was wearing my finest MOD clothes, my hair all backcombed and wild. "Thought about what's next?"

I shrugged. I loved Beryl as I was growing up, but honestly, I still felt resentment towards each of my sisters – and Eddie – when they left the family home. Soon, Maris too would accept an offer of marriage from her boyfriend Vivian, and I'd be alone with Edna and Willie.

For someone so used to the noise and drama of a big communal family, the gradual nest-leaving of the others made me sulky around them. And also, let's not forget my age. When Maris and I were small, and money was too tight for toys, Beryl would take Eddie's little shorts and jerseys off the clothes line when Edna wasn't looking, and dress the dog and cat up like little people. As I looked into her face that day, I saw all that love and kindness, the desire to make us laugh, and I fought my natural urge to shrug and claim indifference.

"Have you ever considered nursing?" she asked.

It might seem odd, but I hadn't. I'd never considered a career with the National Health Service, despite how intrinsically linked I was to it. I shook my head at Beryl.

"Well look Nye, you've gotta do something, eh? And it's a great job. Useful skills, no day's the same, pay's not bad. And it would get you out of the house, working with other people. I think you need that, right now…"

Beryl had never been more right. I needed some fresh air. Not long before, I'd accepted a date from an older boy, Ken, who'd just started work as an accountant. We were getting ever more serious. Just last week, in fact, he'd taken me to his offices, late at night, to show me around. I had no idea what I was doing, but the physicality of the relationship was overwhelming to me. I needed something else to focus on.

* * *

On Saturday mornings Dad and his friends, all of them miners, would meet at a corner of the estate and chat about the day ahead – they were a tight-knit, loud and boisterous bunch and they were determined to make the most of their day off. At one o'clock they'd set off for the first pub, all in their flat caps, and eventually they'd wend their way back to our local, The Farmers' Arms. The smell of the place is still, I feel, buried deep in my subconscious: hops and sweat and earth all mingled together. It was more than just casual drinking. Beer helped to swill the thick dust from their throats, the grime and soot they'd ingested all day.

Alcoholism was rife, and the Temperance Movement – trying to persuade the men out of the pub, and into the chapel – wasn't going to provide the comfort these pit workers needed. Often, on a Saturday night, Willie could be found in the Dynevor Arms. The piano would play from the moment the doors opened, right through until closing time, with all the men encouraged to take their turn. The miners were nothing if not musical. In the depths of those pits, when all light seemed to have been cast out, there was only one thing left to do.

"Go on, Elwyn," the men call, watching their friend as he makes his way to the bar. Maris and I are crouching outside, listening under the window. We are obsessed with our dad and his mates, the things they talk about, the private language they seem to share, the swearing and the belly-laughs.

"I can't tonight," Elwyn roars back over the din: "I haven't got my teeth in!" He pulls his lips back to reveal toothless gums, all crinkly and pink.

"Ah, come on now Elwyn," says Willie. Maris and I can tell it's him. She elbows me hard in the ribs, pointing towards the window. "Don't worry about a tiny old thing like that. You can have mine."

While Maris scrabbles to pull me back I poke my head up just a fraction and watch as our father takes his false teeth out, swills them in his beer and hands them to Elwyn. "There y'are, lad," he says.

Within seconds Elwyn has moved beside the piano and is singing a rendition of *Myfanwy*, most of it addressed to the pub's landlady, who shares the same name. We watch Dad nod his head and croon along, knowing that in a few short hours he'll be grumpy and cold, knocking on our bedroom door at six o'clock, when the coal is delivered.

The lorry that brings it to the estate tips the quota onto the pavement, and all the neighbours come out at once to help carry their share into the backs of the houses. Now that Eddie has left home, it's down to Maris and me to carry it in, filling buckets with a spade. We loathe it, but at least this year it's being delivered on a Sunday – the worst has been when we've had to do it after school, as our friends pass. The work is filthy and by the end we look like colliers ourselves. Edna insists we pull on old coats – Marilyn's, Willie's, Eddie's – to keep our school clothes clean. We stumble about looking like a pair of sooty scarecrows.

* * *

My parents were delighted when I told them. I was accepted as a nursing assistant once I'd finished school, with the eventual aim of being trained as a state-registered nurse. In 1964, at the tender age of 16, I passed the entrance exam, including the thousand-word essay component, and was duly fitted up for my uniform: pink, with a white cap I was forever running along the corridors pinning to my hair. I wondered whether I was really cut out for it all, and remembered Sarah Gamp from Charles Dickens' *Martin Chuzzlewit*, a gin-loving nurse who always carried an umbrella but seemed incapable of looking after her patients in any real sense. Could I do it, or was I too chaotic? We were about to find out.

I will never forget the fear of my first day on the wards. It was a mental-health unit, and there were 12 male patients to care for. A man whizzed past me making a noise like a fire engine; one of the nurses, hurrying by, called out to him, "I like your car, Dai!" to which Dai, turning round and smiling impishly at her, replied, "It's not a car, woman, it's a fucking motorbike." Talk about being thrown in at the deep end!

Within a week or two I'd met George, a trainee psychiatric doctor. George was German and I could tell, within a short space of time, that he was absolutely smitten. In the evenings, after our respective shifts were finished, he'd walk me back to the nurses' quarters. Whenever we all took tea together, the sisters and I, they'd pile their mugs onto the tray when they'd finished and I was tasked with washing and drying them all up – the prerogative of the youngest nurse. The bottoms of the cups would be awash with cigarette ends and the smell was awful.

"Hey, Maureen," one of them was saying, one chilly evening as I bustled about washing. "What about those robbers, eh? Tough judge, must have been... 30 years, some of 'em got."

Maureen shook her head. "You'd be fuming tonight, wouldn't you. All that trouble and you're caught and thrown in jail for the rest of your life."

Since leaving home I had been surrounded, all the time, by stories like these. There was constant news of the world: train robberies that come to be known as great ones, a film about The Beatles, Churchill's retirement. I learned these things from newspapers lying scattered around our quarters, from patients chatting to me as I changed their sheets or administered some tender loving care. There was so much conversation there, so much energy and activity. I enjoyed it, and fell into bed every night so much more exhausted than I'd ever been back at school.

As I was washing the cups that evening I noticed George outside the window, trying to catch my attention without being seen by the other nurses. I finished as quickly as I could and slipped outside to meet him. "Here, inside this door," I said, and pulled him into the bathrooms.

George grinned at me, seeing where we were. "Would you like to share a bath with me, Nye?"

I was flabbergasted, and didn't have a moment to object as he spun the taps and, in one fluid movement, stripped off. I quickly turned away, only catching his eye again once he'd told me it was safe to look. "Ah, you're so beautiful, sat there on the side like a mermaid…" he cooed. "Come on, join me!"

With a sharp tug on my arm he pulled me straight into the bath with him. I absolutely screamed the house down, and within moments there was a knock at the door. George, spluttering madly and laughing, stood up, not even bothering to hide himself. Outside stood the ward matron, her nostrils flaring.

"What on earth are you doing in here?" Her words were clipped and quiet. I was horrified: I'd only been here a few weeks, after all, and now I was about to be fired. Perhaps it was the fact that I was still fully clothed, even in my starched white apron, and George was so clearly the instigator in all this, that ultimately saved my job. Nonetheless we were both given a warning for misconduct the next morning. I suppose being the first NHS baby can't save you from mischief.

Things continued much as before at home, for Edna and Will, though my father was beginning to feel short of breath when walking upstairs, or lifting Marilyn's baby boy, Adrian, into his chair. I imagine my mother would have fretted terribly about this, but she was reassured, I know, that whatever came next could be handled by the health services.

Once upon a time, she'd have had no option but to nurse Will herself at home, relying on all of us for relief. When my dad was eventually taken for an examination at the hospital, he was found to have a growth on his lung. Nobody knew, just then, that he'd developed pneumoconiosis – the killer of miners.

On the wards, I was growing into my own style and manner with the patients. I was learning a great deal about the many ways in which a mind can warp or shatter completely. Each week, a local pastor would come to visit one of the most elderly patients, a woman called Mary. In those days, before any sort of widespread knowledge about dementia existed, those exhibiting symptoms were often categorised alongside mental-health patients. The lack of understanding seems criminal now, when we know just how prevalent Alzheimer's is around the world.

Mary was a feisty, devil-may-care sort of woman. Now in her seventies, she had been a sex worker all her life, and found particularly good business during the second world war. Every week the pastor, a sweet young man with a crinkly smile, would sit down beside her and take her hand. "And how are you today, Mary?" he'd ask. "Getting along all right?" The reply never varied, but you can imagine my absolute shock when I first heard her say it: "Cock and comfort, sir? Five bob a feel..." The pastor, who seemed used to this response, would nod back at Mary as though she'd just uttered words of the utmost profundity. Then he'd shake her hand very gently and make the sign of the cross above her. "God bless you, my dear."

TWENTY-THREE
MEN AND BOYS

I've always liked the analogy of crossroads: moments in life when decisions made can have incredibly long-lasting impacts. Sometimes we can see them right in front of us, choose this job, that house, this man, that day. Often, though, we barely notice the choices we make that will carry the largest consequences. Something as seemingly insignificant as a missed phone call or a day off sick can send ripples through our lives we'd never have envisaged. I suppose my family, in all their different ways, have known this for generations. Tiny moments can spread their tentacle-like consequences far and wide.

One of those moments occurred, for me, at the age of 17. I was returning to Cefneithin on a cold April evening, heading home to where my father was sick and my mother was tending to him. There was no one else waiting for the Number 8 to Carmarthen that day, and when the bus arrived there was no one else on it save the driver. I quickly realised, scrabbling around in my pocket, that I didn't have quite enough for the fare – and it was too far to walk, some

12 miles away. I struggled with the coins I did have, pooling them into my palm and mentally assessing how far I might be able to get.

"Don't worry about the fare, love," said the driver. He was a suave, handsome-looking man, his lapel was dotted with tiny badges that I later learned to be motorcycle clips. "Why don't you and those lovely legs of yours stand here and talk to me instead?"

By the end of the journey he'd asked me out, and I'd agreed. Dennis was 24; I was 17, though he didn't know this, or at least pretended not to. For months we saw each other almost every weekend, and those Monday mornings – knowing I'd be at work all week, for five whole days without him – could be torturous.

It progressed quickly, our relationship. He was dashing in a charcoal-black suit and Brylcreemed hair, and I liked spending time with him, driving through the fields and valleys. Eventually, he took me to meet his parents in their hometown of Loughor. It was a smart house, quite posh, I remember thinking. Outside the front door stood a man, completely soaked from head to foot and bellowing at Dennis as he parked.

"Look what the bloody hell she's done to me now, boy!"

Dennis turned to me, looking embarrassed. "My dad," he said simply.

Hilda, Dennis' mother, was a formidable woman who'd been employed at the local steel works for years. On this particular occasion, the first time I met her, she had just poured an entire bucket of freezing water over her husband and then whacked him with a kitchen chair.

"I think she's broken my arm and all," said Dennis' father. From inside the house, we heard Hilda's high, cross-sounding voice: "Bloody baby. You only married me for my onion gravy!"

It was one in a series of defining moments for me. I'd never seen my parents do anything like this or speak to each other in such a way. Dennis' father had served in the Welsh Regiment during the second world war; he most likely never recovered from the experience. Their house was so much grander than ours. From the outside they seemed to have it all. And yet here was a tall, handsome man clutching his arm and wringing out his shirt, spluttering through the drops of water falling from his salt-and-pepper hair.

Some weeks later, I fainted at work. This was most un-characteristic, and I can distinctly recall doing the mental maths, as my friends clustered around me, helping – thank goodness we were all nurses, eh. I knew as I stared up at the ceiling that my last, missed period was no fluke.

Dennis and I married on 24 September 1966, at St Michael's Church. My best friend Ann beside me and my handsome brother Phil walking me down the aisle. The church looks out over the River Loughor, one of the fastest-flowing tides in the world, from a pretty little hill. In the winters it would freeze over completely, and locals would skate over its sleek surface. The sunsets here are gorgeous, looking across Isambard Kingdom Brunel's famous Loughor Bridge that connects Glamorganshire and Carmarthenshire – different from anywhere else in the world, softer somehow. The last rays of the sun bathe everything they touch in a warm glow.

Dennis was late, but his green eyes flashed cheekily at me while we said our vows. I heard tittering from the congregation as we knelt before the priest. Later, Mima would tell me that a £2-19-11d sticker was still affixed to the sole of my now-husband's new shoe.

Edna had been disappointed in me. She pursed her lips when Dr Jones, having examined me, confirmed what I'd already known to be true. I think, given my start in life, there was a sense I'd be different, that I'd make different choices. Of course, getting pregnant wasn't something I'd planned, but if my parents taught me anything, it's that you cannot prepare for life – you can't prepare for what it will throw at you.

I was horrified, during the reception, when Dennis' best man called on me to make a speech. I mumbled through until, out of the corner of my eye, I saw my mother standing up. She was by far the most elegant-looking person up on our top table: her hair was so carefully arranged, her make-up (so rarely worn) neat and fresh. Her beauty was in her simplicity. It was a warm day and her periwinkle dress was long and floaty, perfect for the dancing that was to come. "I'd like," said Edna, "to say a few words on behalf of the Rees family." I had no idea what she was planning to say.

I sat down and watched her. The room had fallen silent, entranced by the power in this woman's voice – she was so small, after all – and by the very fact that a woman was speaking at all, at a wedding no less.

"My husband and I came back to Wales over 20 years ago, having lived in London for some time," she began. Nobody but Willie and I, Maris, Eddie, and the rest of my siblings would have known she was nervous. "It hasn't been easy for us, as many of you will well know. We're not a rich family. Neither of us had much growing up. We've worked hard to raise our children right. We think, on the whole, that we've done a pretty good job." There were fond chuckles from the audience, nods from some of our aunties and uncles. "Nye is our youngest child," Edna continued, "and a special one, too. Her birth represented a change for our family – a move towards something better, something equal and hard to find in today's society. I am proud of her, as proud today as I've ever been. Will you raise your glasses, please, to Aneira and Dennis."

Here, my mother twinkled at Willie, who was beaming at her. "Love will find a way."

* * *

In many respects, my life would turn out to be different to my parents', but for the first few years of my marriage it wasn't necessarily a positive difference. The wedding reception had been such a success. My mother-in-law cooking Welsh cakes at one o'clock in the morning and everyone dancing. When we went to cut the cake, I placed my hand over Dennis' and pushed down. Within moments, blood was oozing from his hand and down the icing of the multi-storey fruit cake – the knife had been positioned blade-up by mistake. In many ways, the whole day – the fun, the partying and the eventual pain – came to serve as a metaphor for our marriage, which lasted just over 40 years. It was a complicated, chaotic life full of unpredictability, and always that element of surprise.

Dennis was a party animal, committed to having a good time. If there wasn't a party, he would create one somewhere on his way home. After a short honeymoon down in London with my brother, Phil, and his wife and children, we returned to Loughor, where we lived with his parents. I had given up work by this stage, something quite normal for the times. And because I didn't feel quite at home at his parents', I spent a great deal of time in our bedroom. The boy next door would appear in the garden at weekends; he was a university graduate. We would smile and wave at each other and I just found him attractive, in the lonely mindset of my circumstances at that time. I felt he was my new best friend. At the crossroads outside stood a set of traffic lights, and I'd spend long, monotonous hours watching the lights change from green to amber to red and back again, over and over. I wished Dennis would return home a little earlier from work – surely his shift on the buses had finished hours before? I gradually came to realise that he spent a lot of time after-hours in the pub. I was dreadfully bored and unhappy, on my own with my in-laws bickering and no job – nothing like the fun, independent girl I'd been just a year beforehand.

The baby was growing. Soon enough I began to feel his kicks, feel his movements through the night as I lay on my side. On a wintry night in March I was sitting up waiting for Dennis. It was dark and my in-laws had left for the evening, out with company. Already I had begun to long for my old life. I knew that nursing would be impossible for some time now, but that I could nurse my child – and perhaps Dennis and I might move a little closer to Edna and Willie, and have our own place.

When he came in, it was one of those nights. When he wasn't drinking, my husband was wonderful. When he was, he was different – as many people are, but we were young – I only came to understand this years later. I stood up, wanting to speak to him. I couldn't understand why he'd married me, why he'd pursued me all those months if the only thing he wanted was to spend time in the pubs with his friends.

"I'm tired of this," I told him. He watched me suspiciously, stumbling slightly as he bent to untie his laces. "You're never here. It's just me, all alone, all the time. It isn't fair, Dennis. You'd always prefer to be out with your drinking buddies than with me."

"Go to bed, Nye," he muttered. "Just leave me be. I've only just got in, for Christ's sake."

"Got in from where, Dennis, because it surely isn't work!"

I was upset. I refused to go upstairs. He insisted, I resisted. The rest is a blur. My bare feet slipped off the edge of the top step, my hands squeaked against the old wooden rail, and then I was at the bottom.

The next two weeks come at me in different colours: a series of snapshots, one after the other, that never form a coherent picture. I woke up the next morning with the sheets beneath me sodden. Maris, ever the pragmatist, took me straight to hospital when I phoned her to tell her the news. After a long, traumatic labour my baby was born, weighing a healthy eight pounds, and was promptly whisked away. I never heard him cry, but the nurses – bustling around, shooting me reassuring glances – told me this was standard – he was simply shocked.

I was in hospital for days, unable to go to the toilet properly, unable to do very much at all. Dennis would arrive, occasionally on time. He seemed a very far cry from my new friend Margaret's husband. She was on the same ward as me, and we developed a close friendship that lasted many decades afterwards. I was desperate for word of my baby – I'd decided to call him Gary Anthony – but no word came. I was never told anything, despite Edna ringing up twice a day, looking for answers. After a week, a sister approached the end of my bed and explained that the baby had died.

I could barely breathe, still less understand what she was telling me. I had not seen him since the moment of his birth, and now he was gone? How had this happened?

We returned, Dennis and I, to his parents' house. It was torture. His father expressed his sorrow to me, his mother said nothing. Perhaps Hilda thought the death of the baby was my fault, somehow. Perhaps she too was just as devastated as I was, having been so keen for a little grandchild to pamper. I couldn't understand her attitude towards me, but I know now that she too had lost a child – a stillborn baby she had named Elizabeth Rose. Both of them went on to become wonderful grandparents to my children. But at the time it was extremely painful and I missed my mother more than ever. She was at home, nursing Willie, whose health had recently deteriorated to the point that he was unable to work, unable to do very much at all.

The year was 1967 and, while the NHS had now been providing free healthcare at the point of need for almost 20 years, it had a great deal of catching up to do when it came to mental care. There were few provisions in place, few support services that might have been able to help me. It's incredible, now, to think of the access young people have when help is needed. There wasn't much sense, back then, of attempting to help someone readjust after a shock such as I'd suffered. My baby was there one moment, and gone the next, and I was left with so much confusion surrounding mine and Dennis' relationship. A few weeks after we lost Gary, I was doing some shopping in Loughor. The only person I really knew to talk to was a woman called Dulcie, who worked in the pharmacy.

"Ah, Nye, how are you?" she said, opening the door for me. It was still bitterly cold, despite the occasional glimmerings of springtime sun.

"I'm ok, just fine, thanks," I lied.

"And the baby? Is the baby at home, with Mrs Thomas?" Mrs Thomas, my mother-in-law, who'd barely been able to look me in the eye since we returned from the hospital. "What did you have in the end, Nye, a boy or a girl?"

"A boy," I said tonelessly. She stared at me. "He died, Dulcie."

It was a horrific episode of my life, and one I try not to return to if I can help it. One thing it did teach me, however, on a personal level, was the delicacy of childbirth. Even with a fully functional NHS my delivery was nowhere near smooth, and my baby did not survive. The service, as with all else, is only as good as the tools it is given, only as good as the technology available to it. Just as my ancestors made do with what they had, so too did we nurses, throughout the 1960s and – once I returned to work – the 1980s and 1990s. There is always the potential for things to go wrong, with childbirth. There are a plethora of potential complications, and just one of these can represent the balancing act between life and death. Had he lived, my son Gary would have been 53 this year.

TWENTY-FOUR
RAINY DAYS

On a warm summer's day just after my 19th birthday, there was a knock at the door of my in-laws' house. Phil and Eddie stood outside, both out of breath. They'd obviously run part of the way to Loughor from our parents' house. Phil was a strapping young man by this stage, lean and neat from his years spent with the Welsh Guards. Eddie was like a Russian doll of our elder brother, a little stockier but virtually a carbon copy. They told me Willie was very unwell, and that I must come immediately. We set off, jogging over the roads until we reached Eddie's car.

I wasn't sure what to think. Our dad had been ill for so long, but he always pulled through – he was stronger than he looked. Inside his room back at my parents', I noticed his stained fingertips, still yellow from the Wild Woodbines he'd tap on the clean hearth, sending my mum into a frenzy. Mam was so happy to see us all, when we arrived. She was deeply distressed, I could tell – and this was my first inkling that the summons may, for the first time, signal something much more serious than I'd anticipated. He looked awful: his face a peculiar, dark colour, his skin so clammy and thin.

The doctor had already been to visit, before we arrived. "Give him anything he asks for, Edna," he'd said, and left her a bottle of medication. "I'll be back tomorrow." In the meantime, Willie had asked that the clock, with its loud, resonant tick, be removed from beside his bed. I helped Mam as best I could, that day. We sat together in the kitchen, sipping lukewarm tea. My aunt Maggie, a sister-tutor herself in Gloucester by this point, and my sister Sally were tending to Dad. We were silent for some time before Mam sighed.

"We were just kids when we met, Nye," she said sadly. "Nothing more than children. I don't know a world without him in it."

I didn't know what to say to this. As the youngest child, and with money so tight, I'd barely seen my father growing up. Marilyn, Beryl and Sally had much closer relationships with him, by contrast. Phil was his golden boy, and even Maris seemed to remember more of their childhood games, more of the person behind the flat cap, than I ever could.

I remember him pottering around in the glasshouse at Rhydycerrig, tending to long stalks of ripe tomatoes in the summer, and spraying the leaves of budding chrysanthemums in the winter. On the shelves sat an old dried-milk tin full of threepenny pieces – "I'm saving it for a rainy day, chuck," he'd say, his cigarette hanging loosely from a corner of his mouth. He'd throw a coin to me and clap if I caught it. "Good on you, girl. Go and bury it in the garden, now, and see if a money tree grows in its place."

My father spent a lifetime swilling coal dust from his mouth, washing it from behind his ears, his neck, under his arms and between his toes. When he'd return from his Saturday jaunts at the local pubs, he'd toss all his loose change onto the rug and tell us to share it out as pocket money. How we scowled at him on Sunday mornings when, groggy and clutching his head, he'd demand it all back again.

My mother had given him the medicine he'd asked for, just as the doctor said, about an hour ago. Suddenly, we heard a cry from Maggie in the next room. "Edna," she yelled. "Edna, Nye, come now. He's... he's going."

Everything seemed to be happening in slow motion: my mother folding herself over my father's chest, cradling his head as he took his final breaths, Maggie standing to one side, placing the stoppers back onto bottles I didn't recognise, my brother Phil with his head in his hands at the bottom of the bed.

Phil would spend the night before our father's funeral in the parlour, where the coffin stood. We were grateful but unsurprised, the next day, by the sheer numbers of people who came to pay their final respects to Willie Rees.

It was a sweltering day, and the sun poured through the stained-glass windows of the village chapel as we sang *Calon Lan*. For centuries, Welsh mourners had stood around the graves of loved ones and sung *Cwm Rhondda* or, in English, *Guide me, O Thou Great Redeemer*. Two days later, we received the death certificate with the word we'd known, all along, would appear – our father, Edna's husband, died of pneumoconiosis at the age of 60. Just another young man, taken too young, his lungs as black as the pits he'd spent so many years toiling within. 'The Price of Coal'.

* * *

I returned, after the funeral, to my parents-in-law's house. This was not an easy decision to make. I would come to learn, very quickly, that my marriage was not destined to be the same as my parents'.

One by one my next two children were born: Kevin in 1969 and Lindsey in 1974, precious babies whose births were just as traumatic as Gary's, but who nonetheless survived and thrived. I required transfusions after Lindsey's birth and, just as the service had brought me into the world, so it saved me time and again through difficult pregnancies and messy, complicated births. Dennis was, and this I do know, a good, generous, loving father to them, at any rate. He was a workaholic, but he did his best.

I was euphoric at the prospect of having a little girl – there was nothing so wonderful – and I was excited to be bringing her home for Dennis and Kevin to see. However, not long after her birth I was told she was shocked, too cold – the nurses wrapped her in tin foil. Having had such a terrible experience with Gary, I was wracked with fear – at any moment, would they whisk my child away from me, never to be seen again? I couldn't know for sure, but was too weak to do anything but moan and beg for the nurses to hand her over. When they eventually did, having stabilised her, I couldn't believe the miracle I held in my arms. I knew, even then, that she would be mine and Dennis' last child, that I would not be going through the trauma of childbirth again.

The contraceptive pill was approved for release in 1960, and became widely available on the NHS from 1961 – though only for married women. It changed the lives of millions, and is regarded, quite rightly, as one of the most significant advances of the 20th century. By 1967, any woman, regardless of her marital status, could pick up a prescription, and thus alleviate centuries' worth of worry in one fell swoop.

It was a startling realisation, in that moment, as I thought back to all my father's old stories, as he worked in the green-house with an old tie holding his trousers up, and cigratette ash in the turn-ups. The way he looked like a Lord on Saturday nights, recounting the grandmother wandering over the moors to deliver the babies of her village, the complications at Mary's births, her death when he was just two. On Edna's side, I thought of Tory, of the band of brothers, of all the hardship they'd endured – and I tried, oh so hard, to bring myself back to the present moment, to appreciate how lucky I was to be here, in a clean bed with fresh sheets, being helped by nurses with years of training and in a ward scrubbed immaculately clean. I could choose not to have any more children in a way none of my ancestors had been able to.

I never lost sight of this fact, but I was not to know that five brutal years of depression awaited me, following the birth of Lindsey. It was as though all the fight, all the survival instinct and the pressure, the organisation required to care for and raise children, had finally exhausted me. I remember it now as a cloud, black and opaque, which descended and hovered over my head every morning – I could see nothing through it and neither, on the worst days, did I want to.

Sally, my angel sister, kept me going through those dark years. Some days she'd let herself into the house – once Dennis had left for work – dress my boy, come into my bedroom, lift Lindsey from her cot and make everyone breakfast. "Please, Nye," she'd say, "can't you try to get up?"

Nobody, least of all the healthcare worker who came to see me in the first months after Lindsey's birth, picked up on my condition. Again, this is no failing on the part of the NHS – there was no provision for mental health, save in the most chronic, debilitating and obvious cases, and even less understanding of it.

As much as the time into which I was born benefited me – indeed I was the first person to benefit – I was also a victim of the time I was born into, when it came to being depressed. The 1970s were not an ideal decade in which to need help of that kind.

The problem continued, and began to manifest in other, even more terrifying ways. I was frightened of Lindsey, frightened of her vulnerability. Going outside to hang up the washing I'd be gripped by fear – a dread of being somehow struck down, eaten alive, attacked and therefore unable to care for my daughter or my son.

One evening, as I was bathing Lindsey, I was struck very forcibly by an immense pain, just under my ribs. Terrified, I asked Dennis to call the doctor. By the time he arrived, I was convinced I was having a heart attack. I'd been so unwell, so stressed and overtired, and now I couldn't believe I was about to lose my life as a consequence. "It's a little far south to be a heart attack, Mrs Thomas," said the doctor. He injected me with morphine for the pain and proceeded to examine me, ultimately diagnosing me with gallstones, for which I'd need an operation in hospital. It was just six weeks after Lyndsey's birth. I had no idea how they'd manage at home without me. But within a few days of being at hospital, it became evident to the staff that I wasn't coping, gallstones or no gallstones.

I am forever grateful to whoever recognised this. They quite literally saved my life, both physically and mentally. They put a comprehensive plan in place for my discharge, complete with a health visitor, who'd come to check on my progress for as long as was required, and a home help. Glenys ended up staying with us for two years. During that time, I was prone to days spent unable to move, I was so immobilised by the depth of my despair. I'd stare out of the window, refuse to go outside or talk to anyone. A psychiatrist was sent over to assess me: I cannot remember our conversation, but I was prescribed Valium – a wonder-drug indeed, and one of the things that kept me alive, I've no doubt. I was desperate to be a mother again, desperate to feel that rush of maternal drive and energy, but it took time.

Once again the National Health Service had identified a problem that would have otherwise killed me and, for no charge at all, guided me through it.

* * *

There was a great deal about Dennis that charmed me, and a great deal – an equal part – that did not. Lying in bed one night, the children all asleep, I was woken by the sound of the telephone. Dennis had been away working in Germany for a few years, by this point. He was whispering down the line.

"Nye, you've got to help me," he said.

"Hello?" I was half asleep. "What's going on?"

"I've been arrested," he said urgently. I started, almost dropping the phone. "I need you to come and help get me out of here."

Dennis was in Stuttgart police station, it transpired, for driving down the autobahn the wrong way. There was no way I could come to his aid – we barely had enough money for the school lunches that week. How on earth was I to afford the passage over to Germany? Knowing this, and knowing too that he must at least try and get home for Christmas, Dennis broke free of this one-man police station and ran back to his lodgings. Grabbing his passport, he somehow found his way to Ostend, where he was helped onto the ferry by a lorry driver who agreed to smuggle him aboard.

The way he told it, he arrived in London, walked to Paddington Station – where a homeless man bought him a cup of tea – and was just in time to hear the tannoy announce the train to Swansea in five minutes' time. "Cheers, lad," he called over his shoulder as he boarded the train, hiding in the restrooms every time the ticket inspector came along.

He made it back to the house, all the way from Stuttgart, without a penny in his pocket. I suppose one could never accuse him of a lack of resourcefulness. I grew to expect the unexpected with Dennis. There was hilarity by the bucket-load, but it was a nervous laughter.

Dennis may have been a party animal, but he left the party prematurely in 2007. We released his ashes to the four winds during the last of the TT races on the Isle of Man. He had ridden his BSA motorbike in the Mad Sunday many years previously. He lived his life in the fast lane so, fittingly, he was in death.

TWENTY-FIVE
TENDER LOVING CARE

Our lives went on. The children grew. I'd been prescribed Valium and, along with the help put in place by the occupational therapy teams at the hospital, I got better. It was a slow process, but gradually – by the time Lindsey started primary school at the age of five – I was able to walk her down to the gates in the morning and collect her in the afternoon: a huge step.

As they always do, things improved. You can't stay at rock-bottom forever – there will be highs and lows and the low points might feel insurmountable at the time, but they aren't a life sentence. After a time, and with help from my mother-in-law, who helped with the children, I went back to work.

When Lindsey had been at school for a year, she was sat on the rug playing with her dolls when she looked up at me and sighed.

"I wish I had a sister."

I stared at her.

"You'd like that?"

I was aware that Lindsey was an anomaly in our house, Kevin and her father older and often out. I felt a knot in the pit of my stomach – not long after Lindsey's birth, after I'd returned from the hospital, I'd elected to undergo sterilisation. At the time, I was terrified of the prospect of more children and the looming spectre of the depression's return if I did fall pregnant again.

Nonetheless, now I wanted to at least try, to see if this might be a possibility. I booked an appointment with my doctor, who referred me to the hospital.

I was seen by an eminent gynaecologist, Mr. Bowen Simpkins, who had performed the procedure in the first place and who was kind enough to reassure me as we had our initial consultations. He seemed to understand how I was feeling. Ultimately, the operation couldn't be reversed: my fallopian tubes had been tied, something that would be impossible to change without putting me in life-threatening danger. Nonetheless, and though I was sad for Lindsey, I felt that perhaps it was for the best. Dennis and I already had two children, and money was tight enough – even before I factored in my own mental health.

When I think back to that time now, though, knowing everything I do about my ancestors, it amazes me that such a procedure is available at all. It would have transformed the lives of the women in both Edna and Willie's families. It would have proved instrumental to the working-class women of the valleys. What the NHS provided was choice: the choice to have a child, not to have one, to take active steps to ensure your own body and your own mind would be affected by such a fundamental thing as childbirth and delivery.

* * *

There had been some drastic changes since my early days of training, back when I first met Dennis at the age of 17. It was, in many ways, fascinating to return to the work after a hiatus. At the mental-health facility I'd worked at before having my children, there was very little family involvement. People would be brought in for any number of perceived problems and left there, some never to be contacted by their loved ones again.

My duties were to wake the patients up in the morning, help them to wash and dress, and occasionally to drive them to various appointments at local hospitals. What I remember most intensely was the noise of the place, of people shouting, crying and screaming, of heads being banged repeatedly against walls. That, and the amount of sex between patients – mostly the men and women were kept apart, but we'd quite often find couples in the grounds together, and we'd be obliged to report it.

One man I remember particularly was Kenneth. He'd been brought to his first psychiatric unit when he was just 14, and he missed his mother so much. He carried a picture of her with him at all times, and would frequently kiss it. The early days of care-in-the-community, following the criticisms of psychiatric facilities throughout the 1960s and 1970s, meant that we were now tasked with supporting people like Kenneth back into everyday life once they left hospital. We began taking him to a day centre, where one day he found his way into the boss' office. Ignoring his wallet and any item of monetary value, he instead cut out a picture of the boss' wife's face from a framed photo on the desk, as it reminded him of his mother.

Care in the community was a wonderful thing – scary I think, at first, for many people who didn't understand very much about mental health. But it achieved a great deal. For the most part it enabled a sense of normality, of independence. Mental disquiet could be managed, we came to realise, but seldom cured. This represented a contrast with other types of physical illness, where the treatment was to bring about a recovery – or was intended to. We intervened when necessary, but on the whole our process was meant to provide care for these people, teaching them life skills and ensuring they were able to take a measure of care for themselves.

The country was, at this time, being called "the sick man of Europe" because of our economic downturn and rising industrial action. In some ways, the intention of care in the community practice was good – in others, it was simply because the pot of gold was empty. It's a double-edged sword. But there's no doubt the closure of the old lunatic asylums, where lives were written off as quickly as possible, was progress.

In many ways the attitudes towards people with mental-health problems and elderly people was much the same when I first entered the NHS. I've worked at a nursing home, an elderly-care facility in Gorseinon, and – later – at a women's centre. People who suffered from chronic mental illnesses, and those who were elderly, were often lumped into the same sad categories. It was easier to pretend these problems simply didn't exist.

Things changed from 1959, when the Mental Health Act integrated mental wellbeing into general healthcare provisions within standard hospitals and doctors' surgeries. At the time of my birth, over 145,000 patients were being treated in 100 psychiatric hospitals around the country. By the 1960s and 70s, a wave of new psychotropic drugs, and increased discussion about the prevalence of mental health, was beginning to transform the care on offer. On top of this came a series of scandals centred on long-stay hospitals, all of which helped raise the public's support for deinstitutionalisation, for enabling people to leave and attempt to live independently.

There was much to be gained by allowing people who'd previously been institutionalised back into the community, but for some there was also a lot of trauma that hadn't been addressed. It takes a certain amount of mettle to work in these spheres, to see these things every day, but luckily I've always been a dreamer – able to detach myself from even the most horrific cases.

I'd help them with their benefits, see that they attended their counselling appointments, teach them how to cook. I worked a lot of overtime, but there was so much empathy, so much time for bonding.

There were, and still remain, vast changes necessary to adequately protect the most vulnerable in our society. We are getting better at discussing mental health, but there's still so much stigma and embarrassment. It's the invisible illness – and yet one in four of us will suffer some form of mental disquiet within our lifetimes.

I remember many of the people I eventually came to care for through my support work. Some I will never forget. Many of them had been through mental health facilities since their teens. There were also those in elderly care provision and supported housing for women who had long histories of battling with mental health issues. Their problems often arose as a result of domestic abuse and alcohol and substance abuse. Sometimes a combination of both, and many of them had been subject to the criminal justice system, very often including imprisonment.

One woman was often detained although she had never actually committed a crime. The idea of committing a terrible, violent act was only in her mind, but nevertheless her thoughts and fears had to be taken seriously.

My role as a support worker was to provide the help and care they needed, with the aim of enabling them to live satisfying, independent and social livers. They had to develop the living skills needed to live in the community and to gain the confidence they had lost along the way.

Sadly, not every case worked out for the best. Some minds were too broken to reach, no matter how long we tried. And some could lead you a merry dance! Manipulation could be the name of the game, testing your intelligence and ability to think on your feet. Often having the rug pulled from under my feet when things went unexpectedly wrong – I learned so much – and life was never dull, that's for sure!

* * *

It doesn't surprise me, and it may not surprise you, to learn that Lindsey's career took her straight into the NHS. She works as a frontline paramedic, and is first on the scene when things go amiss. Her job takes her into the very murkiest corners of the human experience. It takes a great deal of courage to do what she does, day after day.

Lindsey has seen a lot in her time. She tells me about her day, sometimes, and I marvel at her cool-headedness. Among the young, particularly, she has noticed a vast increase in the numbers of young people needing help for alcohol- and drug-related emergencies. Happy hours have a lot to answer for, and she's picking up the pieces afterwards. She worked as a paramedic technician for her first two years, and has since spent 15 years as a paramedic.

Her first shifts were on Saturdays and Wednesdays, busy student nights. What's changed is that not *every* evening shift, all 12 hours of it, is now a student night. She takes frequent refresher courses in everything from ambulance driving – with one practice lasting 24 hours – to intra-osseous cannulisations, intubations, thrombolysis and subcutaneous infusions. As a paramedic, her role is not to diagnose but to treat whatever is presented.

Five years ago, I was at home one morning when the phone rang. It was Lindsey's eldest son, one of my beautiful grandsons, Sam: he was only 22.

"Mam's had an accident," he said breathlessly. "We're going to the hospital."

I couldn't get much more information from him: after all, he knew about as much as me. I drove faster and more furiously than I've ever driven to the hospital, where a consultant informed us Lindsey had suffered a subarachnoid brain haemorrhage. There was a strong chance, we were told, that she would not wake up if surgery was unsuccessful.

People often comment that in moments of high stress, in times of strife or bad news or bone-crushing disappointment, at times when it seems all hope is lost, that the most bizarre, most inappropriate images can come flying into the mind. I felt numb as the consultant gave us this grim prognosis. I couldn't believe what he was telling me. Even so, I recalled the stories my mother told us, the ones about Tommy and the mines, about amputations at the kitchen table, about the lack of anaesthetics. I knew that, however awful this situation might seem, it could be a lot worse. Everything that Lindsey would endure in the hospital would be carried out with painkilling medication, with expert knowledge, with a team and with consultants, nurses, machines to monitor her through the night. It made me realise, as I sat in the chairs of the waiting room and beside her bed, just how much uncertainty, how much terrible fear my mother and her family must have grown up with.

But just as the villagers around Tory, around Hannah and Mary and Esther, and all those who'd come before us had rallied, so my own friends and relatives, as well as Lindsey's amazing colleagues, came to our aid. Some things don't change, and for that I'm eternally grateful.

One afternoon I was returning to the ward, some weeks since Lindsey's haemorrhage. She was in a coma, and it was proving exceptionally hard on her two sons and daughter, all so young and vulnerable. I'd been staying at the house, doing my best to communicate what little I could understand to the children, and trying to keep calm in those lonely moments of the night. Lindsey's brother, always so protective of her, was near-desperate for answers. How had this happened? Why had she suffered such a major bleed? Would she need help after she woke up and, if so, what kind?

I had no answers.

Again, a lesson learned. We can do our very best with the technology available to us and yet, time after time, the body will surprise. Every time one solution is found, a problem solved and a means of moving forward discovered, another raises its head. The human body, so remarkable in some ways, so incredible and fine-tuned, so instinctive and self-protective, is also a many-headed Hydra when it comes to unknowns. There are so many.

I was trying my best, but I felt helpless, powerless to reassure them that everything would be ok when this so patently wasn't true. I walked down the corridor – as I had walked many times before when my son Kevin had also suffered a brain haemorrhage ten years previously – and a man held the door open for me. His smile was gentle but tired; he looked as though he was doing everything on autopilot. His long white tunic was spotless, his hair clean and neatly brushed off his forehead. "Morning," he said, nodding at the coffee cup in my hand. "Long night?" I nodded mutely. I didn't have the energy to have more conversations about what was happening, about what might happen. "I've been at the prayer room," he said, gesturing down the hallway. "It's so peaceful. Soundproofed, I'll bet. Couldn't hear a thing."

I looked back behind us and saw two other men emerging from the prayer room. One was holding a frayed but beautifully patterned mat in his arms.

I noticed, then, that the man was holding a plant. A long-stemmed, sprawling thing, so colourful and natural-looking in this spotlessly clean, sterile environment. He saw me looking and grinned. "It's all the way from Jerusalem, this," he said. "Where the sun always shines." He broke off a stalk and handed it to me before nodding and moving away up the ward. I clutched it like it was the most precious thing in the world – it's funny how, in times of horror, we cling to such things, how we ascribe meaning and attempt to claw back some control. I wanted to bargain, to make a deal with God, to make a pact. I would do anything, I thought then, anything to help this plant live – to make these small leaves survive somehow.

Heading back into the section of beds where Lindsey lay, I watched her for a moment before touching her hand gently with the stalk. The sun always shone, he'd said. I put the cutting in a jar of water, folded my elbows on the bed and went to sleep.

"Nanny, nanny, wake up!"

I came to. It was mid-morning, I'd guess, by the light streaming into the room. My granddaughter Caitlin and middle grandson Joe were shaking my shoulder. Caitlin had sounded, in the past few days, so much younger than her 11 years, so much like the little girl she'd been such a short time ago. Now her voice was clear, distinct, newly adult.

"She's awake, Nanny! Mammy's awake!"

I scrambled to my feet, looking down at Lindsey. My girl, my child, so pale but now her eyes, blazing green, were open. She was alive. She was smiling.

"Hello, mam," she said weakly.

The doctors and my grandsons arrived, crowding round the bed. The consultant was making fast notes, allowing the nurses to begin the monitoring of Lindsey's temperature, heart rate and blood pressure that would continue for weeks to come. "Well done," said the doctor, coming round to Lindsey's side and touching her arm. "You came through. You're stronger than you think, Lindsey."

"All that time I was asleep," Lindsey would later tell me, "I could feel Daddy's rough hands in mine."

I felt shivers throughout my body, as her father had passed away 7 years previously. In my mind I was saying, "Thank you, thank you, thank you, Dennis, for bringing my girl back."

Once again, a life saved. She has, since then, made a full – and remarkable – recovery.

* * *

Maris, Beryl, Sally and I were staying with Edna intermittently during the early part of the nineties. She had so loved meeting little Caitlin, Lindsey's only daughter and final child. There was something intensely poignant about seeing the two of them together: the eldest member of the family holding the youngest.

By 2004, Mam was 95 years old. She'd been told by her doctors that she had the lungs of a miner – she did quit smoking, but not until her 70s, and was suffering from emphysema. I can remember helping her to bed, settling myself back into the easy chair and hearing her cry out from the bedroom. Was she in pain, I thought, or did she need something? But no: "Nye, darling, pour yourself a Bailey's, love – you're not driving, after all." Jolly to the end of her life, she had been making her own ginger beer, Baileys, and elderberry, rhubarb, sloe and parsnip wines at home, and here she was now – despite being so ill – always thinking of others before herself.

"I might as well have seen a vet," she'd chuckle, after consultations with the doctor. "There's nothing for it – just old, aren't I?" She was suffering, true, but she was fortunate enough at this stage in her life, having lived throughout almost all of the 20th century, to be dying from old age. Mightn't we all live to say the same in our final days?

From the beginning of her life, before either world war ripped the country apart, Edna's lot had been a hard one. There was no reason, no guarantee that she would survive, let alone thrive. Her parents were poor, poorer still after 1926, and after each successive child. She'd borne the death of her own dear mother when Esther was just 44. Willie, the love of her life, would never live long enough to retire with her, to spend some time together without the spectre of work, of the pits, hanging over them. She'd raised seven children, and helped raise 21 grandchildren and 60 great-grandchildren. She'd been the first person to directly benefit from the creation of our National Health Service, and its inception had added a further 60 years to a life that could have been cut short well before. Maris, my beloved sister, has been saved not once, not twice, but three times – she's beaten cancer time and time again. She, too, has dedicated her life to the National Health Service, retiring from her work as a mental-health nurse after 45 years.

On 1 February 2004, she and I went back to her cottage for a few hours' sleep, leaving our sisters behind to spend the night with Mam. Children and grandchildren had filled the house all day; we knew there wasn't long to go now.

At half past three in the morning, we were woken by the telephone ringing. Mam had gone, and I felt my world crumbling around me. It was the single worst experience of my life, losing her. She had taught and continues to teach me so much; I owe her my life in more ways than one. I never knew such depths of pain and grief could exist, before little Edna May left us for the last time.

And yet I couldn't help reflecting – on that last drive back to her house – that it wasn't the sort of terrible, pitiful news she was so used to receiving via telegram, through snail mail or via word-of-mouth in the village. This was expected and, though no less painful, at least the timing was right. As we say, timing is everything.

My thoughts went back to my wedding day. When my mother and I were alone she told me she loved me, then said, "Please be careful, my darling, as I've always worried about you more than my other children." She then relayed how, shortly before my birth, she had been standing in a field when she saw a vision of a man with a bloodied face.

"He" never appeared to her again, but this warning stayed with me all my life. It has often puzzled me. Flashes of that conversation would come to the fore very often.

I waited 50 years to get my answer. It came to me through a chance meeting with a very beautiful Indian lady on the steps of the Vatican in the city of Rome. Her name was Nigissi. She asked me what I thought of the wondrous art in the Sistine Chapel. I told her it was breathtaking, as we are all looking for answers. She said, "What is your question, my dear?" I told her the story of the vision my mother had on our farm, and she put her hand on my arm and said, "Look no further, you know who that was, it was the Lord." I cried and thought, could it be? Did she see Jesus Christ as He cried tears of blood in the Garden of Gethsemane the night before His crucifixion? Well, I do believe that both of my children have been saved and that He has saved a wretch like me, over and over.

TWENTY-SIX
ONE FAMILY'S STORY, A COUNTRY'S PRIDE

In the run-up to 5 July 2018, I was given many opportunities to reflect on this, my family's story. The invitations flooded through my letterbox – something I hadn't anticipated, and which made me feel so deeply honoured. On one occasion I was asked to address an assembled congregation, which included Prince Charles, at Llandaff Cathedral with a 100-word speech. It was daunting, of course, but I got through it, and afterwards found myself chatting to the future king, born just a few months after me in 1948.

"Congratulations," he smiled, "Your mother truly did make history that night."

"Well," I remember laughing, "I might well have been born just before midnight, but I expect the attending doctor would have pushed me back in – just to make sure a Welsh baby was born first!" His belly laugh rang throughout the room.

One of the events was a banquet held for the Great British Menu. It took place in the great hall at St Bart's Hospital in London. There couldn't have been a more appropriate setting. Despite being founded in 1123, it's still the largest teaching hospital in the world, and specialises in stem-cell transplantation, fertility services, cardiac issues and cancer management. There's even a nine-storey extension allowing for the most up-to-date diagnostic and treatment facilities. Every day, patients enter and leave here treated, cured, made to feel their lives matter. They will wander down the streets of Clerkenwell, perhaps nipping into the supermarket for a banana or a loaf of bread. In doing so, they'll spend more money on the food they buy than any of the treatment received at hospital.

I think of my family, on this night in particular. I think about the fact that my great-great grandparents would have shaken their heads and lamented the standards inaccessible to them – the private doctors, the care, the tests and diagnostics, the attempts to save them, and all because some pockets were deeper than others.

As technology advances and machines can do so much more, accidents down mines or in the factory lines will diminish. But were these industries booming today as they boomed during Tory's lifetime, during Hannah and Mary's lives, there would be safety nets. To me, what seems so tragic now is the total lack of provision that was available to those who needed it the most. To the men down the mines, the men who never knew whether today would be their last day, whether they'd be maimed or crushed or otherwise debilitated, the NHS would have represented a freedom and hope they could never have dreamed of. And to the women, as well. The ones who'd never been told the most basic facts about their own bodies, what to expect and how to prevent pregnancies, what giving birth would entail. So many lives – of both mothers and children – lost without the safety net of money.

I myself have been rushed to hospital more times than I can count, in recent years. To the doctors' surprise, I'm allergic to any opioid painkillers. And yet, here I am nonetheless. They find a way. 100 years ago there's little doubt that given my many experiences, and the class into which I was born, I would not have thrived.

When men returned from war broken, diseased and exhausted, there was nothing to help protect them – and no work available for a man with one leg, a missing thumb, deafness caused by the blast of canons across the trenches. We are lucky to live in peacetime, now: how much more would a health service be needed if another war were to descend upon us? It's a sobering thought, imagining the truckloads of men returning – coming home to a lesser existence, a smaller life, less security than when they'd left.

I pondered all this as I looked around the hall at St Bart's. In the doorway stood a smartly dressed older woman, very graceful in her movements, the kind of person who suited whatever age she happened to be. I went over and introduced myself. She beamed at me – a wide smile that crinkled the corners of her eyes. "I'm Ethel," she said. Ethel Armstrong was here in her capacity as an MBE – an award she'd been given for decades of service to the NHS. "I've worked within the service, in one way or another, all my life," she said. "I'm 88, would you believe! It's a lot of years."

I couldn't believe it, but at the same time, it made perfect sense. She was exactly the sort of spritely, energetic person any patient would want helping them: she exuded warmth, kindness, a sense of calm.

We chatted and laughed and have remained friends since that day. She told me about the beginnings of her career, just half a crown in her pocket, her shoes shined and ready for action.

Ethel was born in Durham in 1930. She was hard-working and talented at school, but was advised by her headteacher to leave at the age of 17 and find a job. There were no grants for working-class women to study dentistry or medicine, back in 1947. Ethel's introduction to the National Health Service mirrored my own. She worked in the mental-health ward of a large hospital in Newcastle, cutting her teeth in arguably one of the most challenging environments for any experienced nurse, let alone a teenager in her first professional job. On 5 July 1948, Ethel then joined the radiography team, and was appointed a Junior Radiologist just three years later. She moved up to Senior Radiologist and then Deputy Superintendent, and worked within this method of diagnosis until the end of her career. Ultimately, she worked within the NHS for 70 years. After her retirement from radiography and nursing, Ethel volunteered for two charities that provide support to both current and past NHS employees. It's a lifetime of service, a lifetime of dedication to this ideal that has and continues to save lives each and every day.

We sat at the tables dotted around the great hall, which is over 900 years old. It was here when nations as we now know them remained undiscovered, it was here before the great plagues that wiped out the citizens of this city, before the Great Fire, before the signing of Magna Carta, before so many thousands of battles and wars and skirmishes, and it stood firm while disease and illness wreaked havoc around its walls. As I looked around, and as the four chefs emerged with their dishes, I said a silent prayer that our unique system of social welfare – of working for the many, not the few – would continue and thrive for as long as Bart's itself had stood.

Each of the chefs was asked to describe their dish, why they'd chosen it, and to explain their own personal reasons for showing gratitude to the NHS. The dessert was prepared by Chris Harrod, a Welsh chef. Before this was served, I'd been asked to read a poem. I was nervous, of course, and felt the gravitas of the moment weighing upon me. I had so much to thank Nye Bevan for: Nye, who'd implemented the service that helped give me life and supported it, time and time again. The service that saved my life and the lives of my children. That enabled opportunities and chances families like mine had never enjoyed before, and would never enjoy otherwise. From my very first breath, and no doubt to my very last, the NHS is central to who I am.

As we know, illness does not discriminate. It hits the wealthy as much as the poor, the king and the pauper alike. There is no monopoly on when or how sickness strikes, there is no quota for how often we might be struck down with something that could do us serious harm. There are factors, of course: age, profession, genetics, stress levels, geographic location, diet, use of alcohol and drugs, tobacco, salt and sugar intake and levels of exercise. But a man who's never smoked a cigarette in his life might contract lung cancer tomorrow, and a woman who's avoided all sugar since the 1980s could have found herself with a diabetes diagnosis yesterday.

We can do everything in our power to keep ourselves healthy, and yet the unthinkable happens. We are not robots, not infallible. Our bodies may fail us – and when they do, our sickness does not give a fig as to how carefully we've maintained them, how much we have earned or how wealthy our ancestors were. It doesn't care if our forefathers lived in castles or shacks, if they owned estates or worked the land around them.

Today, we hear reports that the infectious bacteria that give rise to tuberculosis – the dreaded ailment that my sister Sally suffered, all those years ago – is on the rise once more. The moment we think we've conquered something, it rears its head once more. There is no room for complacency where illness is concerned. And as our population ages, as we tackle the problems associated with this, and as our understanding of vicious mental health problems deepens, the service Nye

Bevan worked so hard to build will become increasingly difficult to manage.

And yet it is so vital that we try.

I stood up, cleared my throat and started to read.

"These are the Hands," I said, "is a poem by Michael Rosen. It captures all that the National Health Service does for us, and all it will – we hope – continue to do."

These are the hands
That touch us first
Feel your head
Find the pulse
And make your bed.

These are the hands
That tap your back
Test the skin
Hold your arm
Wheel the bin
Change the bulb
Fix the drip
Pour the jug
Replace your hip.

These are the hands
That fill the bath
Mop the floor

Flick the switch
Soothe the sore
Burn the swabs
Give us a jab
Throw out sharps
Design the lab.

And these are the hands
That stop the leaks
Empty the pan
Wipe the pipes
Carry the can
Clamp the veins
Make the cast
Log the dose
And touch us last.

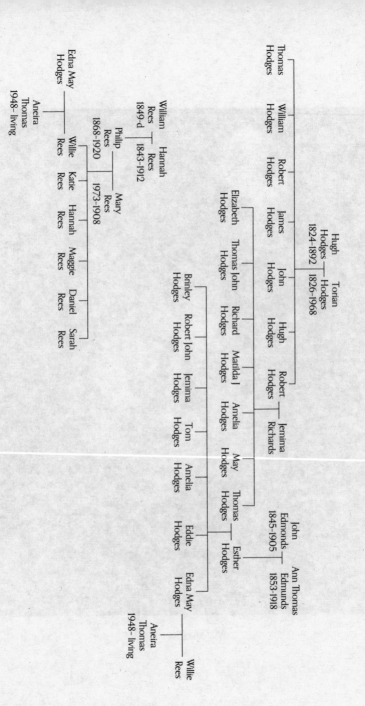

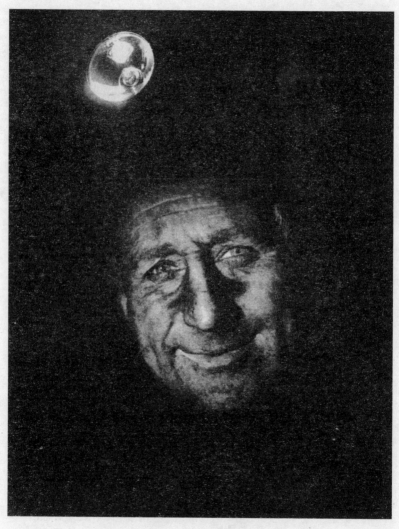

My brother, Eddie

ACKNOWLEDGEMENTS

With thanks to the Royal College of Nursing, the Royal College of Obstetricians and Gynaecologists, the Florence Nightingale Museum, The Old Operating Theatre Museum, the Royal London Hospital Barts Health Trust, The Worshipful Society of Apothecaries of London, the BBC WW2 People's War Archives, Trevor Chalkley, Ceri Thompson and Big Pit National Coal Museum, Polly Powell, Lindsey Jenkins and Caitlin, and the A&E team at St George's Hospital in Tooting.

Thank you to Nye Bevan for your vision and creation of our NHS.

I'd like to thank everyone who encouraged me to write this book, which has taken me decades of dithering.

Thanks to my teacher Mr Wynford Nicholas who described me as a dreamer, but here I am still dreaming, and I've written a book, sir...

Also my loyal and pushy friend Susan Maybank, and the late Vic, the late unforgettable Clive and Brenda, Dai Double Glazing for his encouragement (nagging) me to get the book underway. To Chris and Margaret, my special friends and confidantes.

My lovely brothers and sisters. Before Mam passed away she told them all, "You must look after Nye, she's the baby of the family." They certainly have every step of the way, but they reckon I take advantage of them all.

My many supportive cousins and friends: even their friends have played a part on my stage. Thanks a million. To my own beloved children, I admire them for how they live their lives and I owe them.

My special divisive grandchildren, for their unique personas that give me such a fulfilling life to live, fun and joy to be around.

My lovely supportive long-standing neighbours, the Johnsons, the elegant Brace sisters, never forget.

Firm friends at the local Boating Club and the Loughor Inshore Rescue Service, and the supportive communities of Loughor, Gorseinon and Swansea City, which has been described as an "Ugly Lovely Town" by the late poet Dylan Thomas – but it's our ugly lovely town for sure.

The late Aeronwy Thomas, daughter of Dylan; Dawn and Adriana for their kindness, wonderful drunken nights of fun and poetry and friendship.

To my mysterious sister Maris for her love and her many invitations to her fascinating world of art, culture and travel.

To our sister by another mother, Lady Jean Bobbett of Godney – a special person.

Dean, Beth and Rosie for having a part in parenting my grandchildren.

To the late Auntie Mabel, and Sister Beryl (Zilla) King, two inspirational nurses: thanks for the memories.

And all my nieces and nephews for putting up with my talking about myself (it's all about me!!)

Thank you Katie Taylor, for giving time and good advice in the typing of my handwritten manuscripts, and my loyal friend Diane.

Thanks, too, the teams of varying NHS Campaigners, also the unforgettable Mr NHS himself, the late Mr. David Bailey.

All Health Professionals and non-medical health workers that make a difference to how we live our lives, and the phenomenal 'Front Line First on Scene Paramedics'. I have my favourites, they know who they are, I love and thank you all from the bottom of my heart.

UNISON and Unite for their tireless support for the NHS workforce. Also great thanks to the wonderful Nurses Charitable Trusts Organisations, especially The Edith Cavell Trust, The Junius Charity, the Sandra Charity..

Thank you Dennis my late husband, for letting me on that bus when I didn't have enough fare, our two worlds collided when you took me on that long long journey long long ago, not on a Gold Wing motorbike around the world as you promised...

My thanks to my lovely mate and journalist friend Martin Bagot, who believed in my story and guided me. Thank you to Hedley, Mr Dave Ubee Esqand and the formidable Mrs. Patricia McGladdery for your combined unshakable and unwavering faith in my ability to achieve the impossible.

Thank you to everyone at Mirror Books, especially my editor Jo Sollis, and to Zoe Apostolides for helping to bring my story to life.

Finally, my own mother, Edna May, for holding her breath for one more minute and pushing me out at that historical moment, making me the Poster Girl of the NHS. Thanks Mam. It's been fun.

Forgive me if I have forgotten anyone, but you are in here and in my heart...

The great war was not long over
*   when the good lord sent the Welsh people*
*   two precious gifts from heaven.*
One was a baby girl who was named Aneira.
And the other, the iconic Nye Bevan.
Both came from working class families,
*   with no sign of affluence or wealth.*
But thankfully Aneira brought us her beauty and charisma.
And of course Nye Bevan, The National Health.

By Kenny Griffiths
(Nye's very dear friend)